SCIENCE VISUAL RESOURCES

WEATHER AND CLIMATE

An Illustrated Guide to Science

The Diagram Group

CHELSEA HOUSE
PUBLISHERS
An imprint of Infobase Publishing

Weather and Climate: An Illustrated Guide to Science

Copyright © 2006 The Diagram Group

Editorial:	Michael Allaby, Martyn Bramwell, Jamie Stokes
Design:	Anthony Atherton, bounford.com, Richard Hummerstone, Lee Lawrence, Phil Richardson
Illustration:	Peter Wilkinson
Picture research:	Neil McKenna
Indexer:	Martin Hargreaves

Chelsea House
An imprint of Infobase Publishing
132 West 31st Street
New York NY 10001

For Library of Congress Cataloging-in-Publication data,
please contact the publisher.

ISBN 0-8160-6169-6

Chelsea House books are available at special discounts when purchased in bulk quantities for businesses, associations, institutions, or sales promotions. Please call our Special Sales Department in New York at 212/967-8800 or 800/322-8755.

You can find Chelsea House on the World Wide Web at
http://www.chelseahouse.com

Printed in China

CP Diagram 10 9 8 7 6 5 4 3 2 1

This book is printed on acid-free paper.

Introduction

Weather and Climate is one of eight volumes in the **Science Visual Resources** set. It contains nine sections, a comprehensive glossary, a Web site guide, and an index.

Weather and Climate is a learning tool for students and teachers. Full-color diagrams, graphs, charts, and maps on every page illustrate the essential elements of the subject, while parallel text provides key definitions and step-by-step explanations.

The atmospheric engine outlines the overall structure of Earth's atmosphere, its composition, and the global processes that drive its patterns of circulation.

Components of weather looks in detail at all the major weather phenomena, from winds to fog, rainfall, and snow.

Weather systems provides an overview of the formation, movement, and interaction of large air masses and shows how these determine the local weather.

Extremes of weather looks at the range of weather phenomena across the globe, giving examples of the regions that experience extremes. Simultaneously energetic and destructive weather phenomena such as tornadoes and hurricanes are also covered in this section.

Meteorology concerns the science of observing, recording, and predicting weather and climate.

Climates and seasons provides an overview of the major climate types and describes the crucial factors that determine climate at a particular location.

World climate data gives the average monthly temperatures, rainfall, and sunshine data of 83 representative cities across the world.

U.S. climate data gives the average monthly temperatures, wind speed, precipitation, and sunshine data of 35 U.S. cities.

Human impact on climate examines the evidence that human activity is changing Earth's climate. It also outlines the likely outcome of such changes.

Contents

1 THE ATMOSPHERIC ENGINE

2 COMPONENTS OF WEATHER

3 WEATHER SYSTEMS

4 EXTREMES OF WEATHER

5 METEOROLOGY

6 CLIMATES AND SEASONS

7 WORLD CLIMATE DATA

8 U.S. CLIMATE DATA

9 HUMAN IMPACT ON CLIMATE

APPENDIXES

Atmospheric structure

Key words

atmosphere	troposphere
equator	
ionosphere	
mesopause	
mesosphere	
pole	
stratopause	
stratosphere	
tropopause	

Atmospheric layers

- Earth's atmosphere can be divided into layers according to variations in air temperature. These temperature changes correspond to differing chemical and physical properties of the atmosphere.
- The troposphere is the layer closest to Earth's surface. It contains about 80 percent of the gas in the atmosphere.

- The troposphere is up to twice as thick at the equator as it is at the poles.
- The thermosphere is the highest layer of the atmosphere. Temperatures can be as high as 2,200 °F (1,200 °C) because of intense and direct solar heating, but heat energy is low because the gases are extremely diffuse.

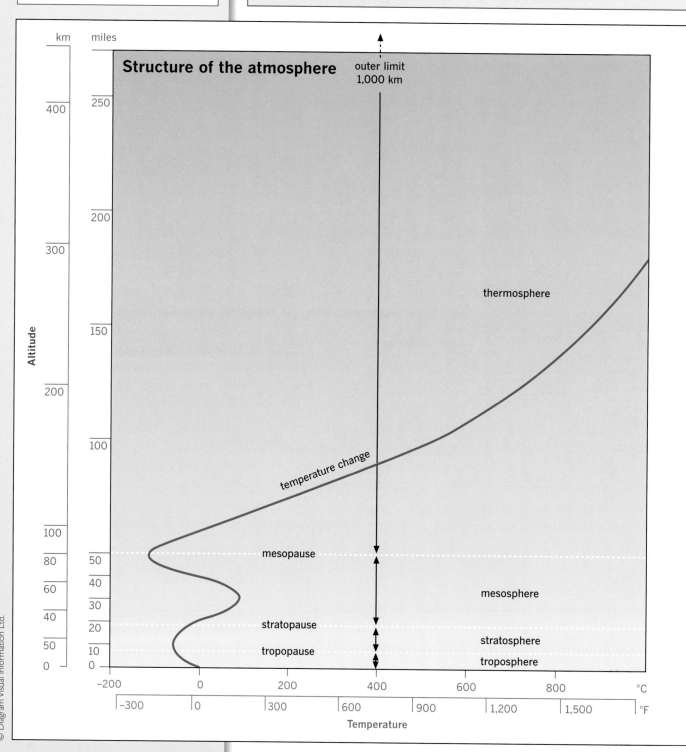

Structure of the atmosphere

Temperature change with height and latitude

Temperature variation

- Earth's atmosphere can be divided into four layers, each with distinct temperature characteristics.
- The *troposphere* extends from the surface of Earth to an altitude of between five and ten miles (8–16 km). The troposphere is thicker near the equator because greater solar heating in that area causes the air to expand.
- Air temperature in the troposphere drops with altitude at a rate of about 3.5°F per 1,000 feet (6.5°C per 1,000 m). This is known as the *environmental lapse rate*.
- The *stratosphere* extends from the tropopause to an altitude of about 30 miles (50 km). In the lowest six miles (9 km) of the stratosphere air temperature remains constant. Through the rest of the stratosphere temperature increases with altitude. This warming is due to

concentrations of ozone gas that absorb ultraviolet radiation from the Sun and radiate heat. This band of the atmosphere is also known as the *ozone layer*.
- The *mesosphere* extends from the stratopause to an altitude of about 50 miles (80 km). Temperature falls with altitude throughout the mesosphere to a minimum of about –130°F (–90°C).
- The *thermosphere* refers to all elements of the atmosphere above an altitude of about 50 miles (80 km). There is no definable upper limit to this layer. It becomes increasingly diffuse until it is indistinguishable from interplanetary space.
- Due to the intense solar radiation at this level, air molecules can have temperatures of 2,200°F (1,200°C) but heat energy is very low because the gas is very diffuse.

Key words

atmosphere	solar radiation
environmental	stratopause
lapse rate	stratosphere
mesosphere	thermosphere
ozone	tropical
ozone layer	tropopause
polar	troposphere

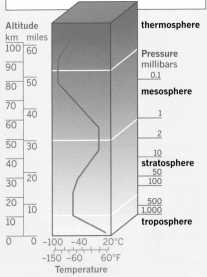

Temperature in the atmosphere

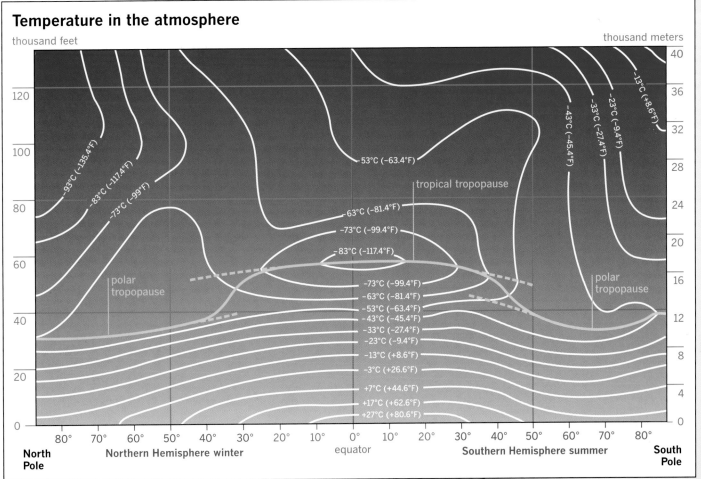

© Diagram Visual Information Ltd.

© Diagram Visual Information Ltd.

Key words

atmosphere	third atmosphere
first atmosphere	
ozone	
second	
atmosphere	

Composition of the atmosphere

Major components

These figures are for an idealized sample of air with no water vapor content.

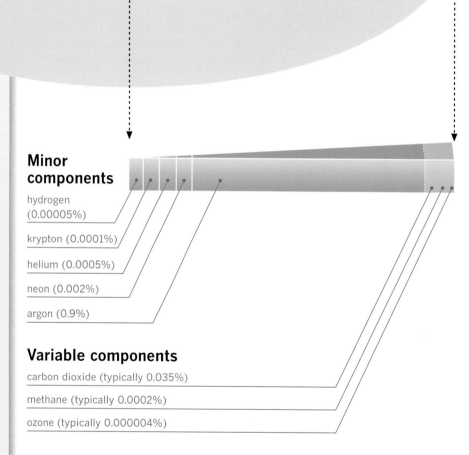

oxygen (20.9%)

nitrogen (78.1%)

Minor components

hydrogen (0.00005%)

krypton (0.0001%)

helium (0.0005%)

neon (0.002%)

argon (0.9%)

Variable components

carbon dioxide (typically 0.035%)

methane (typically 0.0002%)

ozone (typically 0.000004%)

The third atmosphere

● The atmosphere that surrounds Earth today is sometimes referred to as the *third atmosphere*.

● The *first atmosphere* was the mainly helium and hydrogen atmosphere that surrounded Earth when it first formed.

● The *second atmosphere* was the layer of carbon dioxide and water vapor that was pumped from Earth's interior by a multitude of volcanoes. During this era Earth's atmosphere may have been up to 100 times denser than it is today.

● The third atmosphere is thought to have developed as Earth cooled and volcanic activity became less frequent. Water vapor condensed in the atmosphere and fell as rain for millions of years. Up to 50 percent of the carbon dioxide in the atmosphere was dissolved in this rain and locked into the oceans that it formed.

● From about three billion years ago, cyanobacteria in the oceans began to convert some of this carbon dioxide into oxygen.

● Nitrogen and oxygen make up about 99 percent of the atmosphere today. The remaining one percent is composed of a variety of gases some of which—such as water vapor— are present in variable quantities.

Earth–atmosphere heat budget

Key words

atmosphere
latent heat
longwave
shortwave
solar radiation
troposphere

upper atmosphere
UV radiation

Heat

- The vast majority of heat energy on Earth originates as shortwave radiation from the Sun (*solar radiation*).
- Solar radiation is either absorbed or reflected by elements of the atmosphere and Earth's surface.
- Physical laws dictate that the amounts of energy flowing into and out of the system must be equal.

- This balance is known as the "Earth–atmosphere heat budget."
- The Sun's shortwave radiation is eventually returned to space as longwave radiation. The transition from short to long wave occurs because the energy is absorbed, becomes heat energy, and is then radiated.

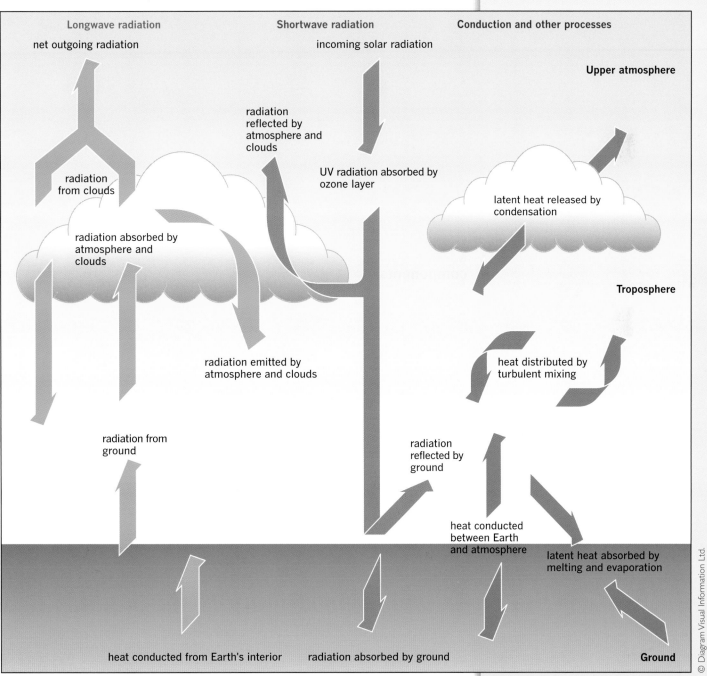

Longwave radiation

net outgoing radiation

Shortwave radiation

incoming solar radiation

Conduction and other processes

Upper atmosphere

radiation reflected by atmosphere and clouds

radiation from clouds

UV radiation absorbed by ozone layer

latent heat released by condensation

radiation absorbed by atmosphere and clouds

Troposphere

radiation emitted by atmosphere and clouds

heat distributed by turbulent mixing

radiation from ground

radiation reflected by ground

heat conducted between Earth and atmosphere

latent heat absorbed by melting and evaporation

heat conducted from Earth's interior

radiation absorbed by ground

Ground

Key words

absorption	solar radiation
atmosphere	
reflection	
scattering	
shortwave	

Effects

- Solar radiation reaching the top of Earth's atmosphere is subject to three atmospheric processes before it reaches the surface. These processes are *scattering*, *absorption*, and *reflection*.
- *Scattering* refers to the diffusion of shortwave solar radiation by particles in the atmosphere. Particles scatter radiation in all directions, which means that a significant proportion is redirected back into space.
- The scattering of radiation does not change its wavelength.
- The presence of large numbers of particles in the atmosphere with a size of about 0.5 microns results in the preferential scattering of the shorter elements of solar radiation. This is why Earth's sky appears blue.
- *Absorption* refers to the phenomenon by which some particles and gas molecules in the atmosphere retain solar radiation in the form of heat energy.
- Energy absorbed in this way is radiated in all directions as longwave radiation. A significant proportion of this longwave radiation is lost to space.
- *Reflection* refers to the redirection of solar radiation by atmospheric particles along a path at 180° to its incoming path. All reflected solar radiation is lost to space.
- Most reflection in the atmosphere occurs when solar radiation encounters particles of water and ice in clouds. Clouds can reflect between 40 and 90 percent of the solar radiation that strikes them.
- Direct *solar radiation* is the solar radiation that reaches the surface unmodified by any of these effects.
- Diffuse solar radiation is the solar radiation that reaches the surface after being modified by any of these effects.
- Some of the radiation that reaches the surface is reflected.

Scattering, absorption, and reflection

Effects of the atmosphere on solar radiation

incoming solar radiation (100%)

top of atmosphere

reflected by clouds (27%)

scattered back into space (6%)

scattered radiation absorbed by atmosphere (14%)

reflected by ground (2%)

direct radiation absorbed by ground (34%)

scattered radiation absorbed by ground (17%)

Earth's surface

The water cycle

Water transfer

- The *water cycle* refers to the continual transfer of water between the atmosphere, the land, and the Ocean. It is also known as the *hydrologic cycle*.
- The water cycle describes the behavior of water in the *hydrosphere*. The hydrosphere is the collective term for all the water on Earth in any form.
- There are four processes that drive the water cycle: *evaporation*, *precipitation*, *infiltration*, and *runoff*.
- *Evaporation* refers mainly to the transfer of water from oceans and lakes to the atmosphere as a result of solar heating. It also includes the transpiration of water from plants (*evapotranspiration*).
- *Precipitation* refers to the transfer of water from the atmosphere to the ocean or the land. It occurs as a result of the condensation of water vapor.
- *Infiltration* refers to the transfer of water from the surface to beneath the surface. It occurs because water permeates rock.
- *Runoff* refers to the transfer of surface water to the oceans, usually via rivers.

Key words

atmosphere
evaporation
evapo-
  transpiration
groundwater
hydrologic cycle
hydrosphere

infiltration
precipitation
runoff
water cycle
water table

Key processes in the water cycle

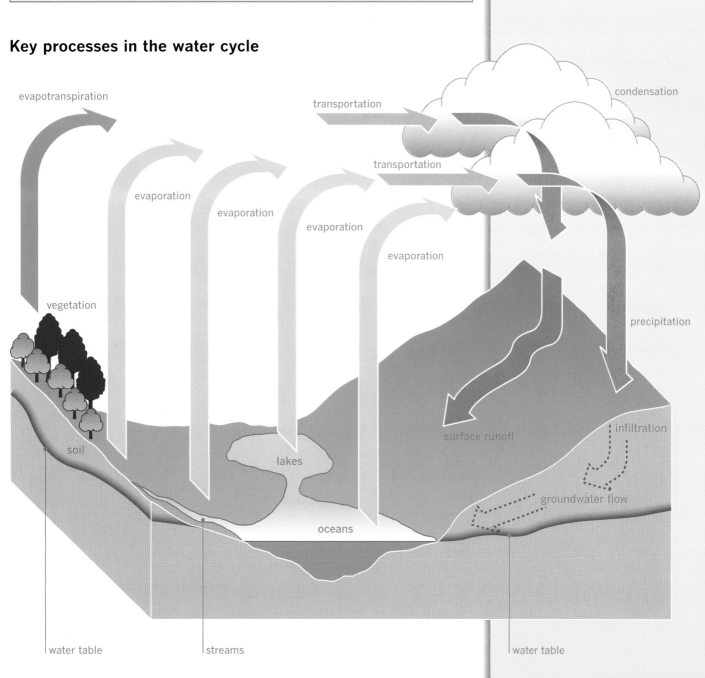

evapotranspiration

transportation

condensation

evaporation

transportation

evaporation

evaporation

evaporation

vegetation

precipitation

soil

surface runoff

infiltration

lakes

groundwater flow

oceans

water table

streams

water table

The carbon cycle

Key words

atmosphere
biogeochemical
  cycle
carbon cycle
hydrosphere

lithosphere
photosynthesis
pole

Role of carbon

- Carbon is a necessary constituent of all life on Earth. The *carbon cycle* refers to the continual transfer of carbon between the atmosphere, lithosphere, and hydrosphere.
- The carbon cycle is a *biogeochemical cycle*, which means that it involves biological, geological, and chemical processes.
- Carbon is present in the atmosphere primarily in the form of carbon dioxide. It is transferred from the atmosphere by photosynthesis, and at the surface of the oceans where it is dissolved in seawater. More carbon is dissolved in seawater at the poles because colder water is able to dissolve more carbon dioxide.
- Carbon is transferred into the atmosphere via the respiration of plants and animals, by the decay of animal and plant matter, by the combustion of organic matter, through the chemical breakdown of limestone by water, by the eruption of volcanoes, and at the surface of warm oceans where dissolved carbon dioxide is released.
- Carbon enters the lithosphere when organic matter becomes sediment, which is eventually converted into rock.

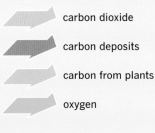

carbon dioxide

carbon deposits

carbon from plants

oxygen

Key processes in the carbon cycle

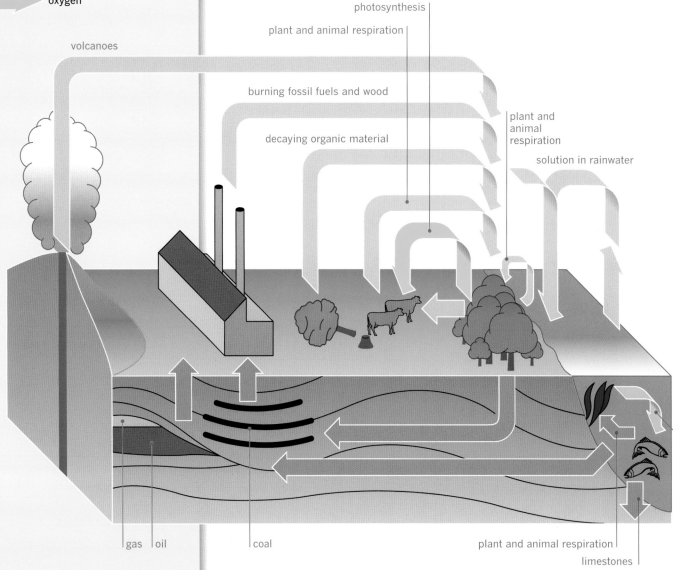

photosynthesis

plant and animal respiration

volcanoes

burning fossil fuels and wood

decaying organic material

plant and animal respiration

solution in rainwater

gas oil

coal

plant and animal respiration

limestones

photosynthesis

Insolation

Insolation

Key words

atmosphere	langley
insolation	solar radiation

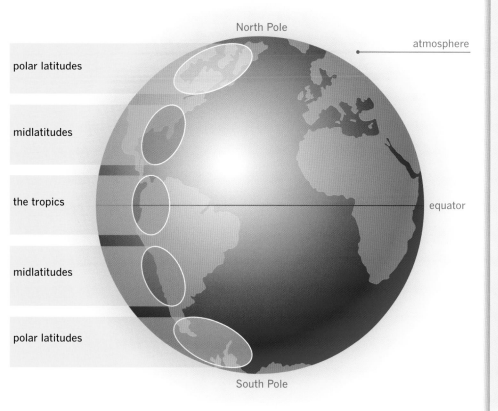

North Pole

polar latitudes

midlatitudes

the tropics

midlatitudes

polar latitudes

South Pole

atmosphere

equator

Insolation

- *Insolation* is the amount of direct or scattered (diffused) solar radiation that reaches Earth's atmosphere (atmospheric *insolation*) or Earth's surface (surface insolation).
- Atmospheric insolation is always greater than surface insolation.
- Atmospheric insolation varies across latitude according to the orientation of Earth to the Sun.
- Surface insolation varies across latitude according to the levels of atmospheric insolation and the effects of the atmosphere on solar radiation before it reaches the surface.
- Surface insolation is less where solar radiation must pass through a greater thickness of atmosphere.
- Surface insolation at all latitudes is greatest over oceans and deserts where there is little or no cloud cover.

Seasonal variation in insolation

Incoming radiation (langleys)

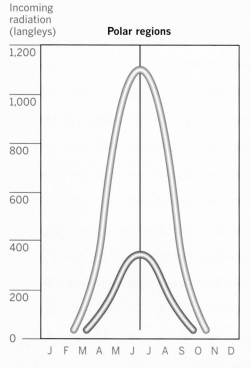

Polar regions

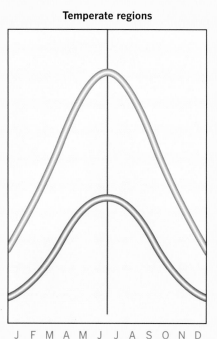

Temperate regions

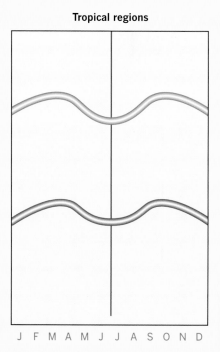

Tropical regions

—— Northern Hemisphere summer solstice	amount of radiation reaching the edge of the atmosphere
	amount of radiation reaching Earth's surface

Key words

Coriolis effect	latitude
equator	polar cell
Ferrel cell	polar front
Hadley cell	pole
insolation	three-cell model

Simple model

- A simplified model of air circulation on Earth can be arrived at by assuming that Earth is not rotating on its axis and that the surface is composed of a uniform material.
- In this simplified model, the greatest insolation is at the equator. Warm air rises at the equator and flows toward the poles at high altitude. At the poles it cools, sinks, and flows back toward the equator at low altitude.
- There is one heat convection cell in each hemisphere.

Three-cell model

- A more accurate model of air circulation can be arrived at by taking account of Earth's rotation.
- The *Coriolis effect*, which is a consequence of Earth's rotation, results in three principal heat convection cells in each hemisphere. These are the *Hadley cell*, *Ferrel cell*, and *Polar cell*.
- Air rises at the equator and moves toward the poles. The Coriolis effect deflects this north or south movement so that, by about latitude 30°, the air is moving east or west instead. This creates an accumulation of air at these latitudes, some of which sinks back to the surface and is drawn toward the equator, completing the Hadley cell. The rest of this air flows toward the poles at low altitude.
- At about 60°, warm air traveling toward the poles meets cold air traveling away from the poles. The interaction of these air masses creates the polar front. The warm air is uplifted and some is diverted back into the Ferrel cell.
- The rest of the uplifted warm air travels on toward the poles where it is cooled, sinks to the surface, and moves toward the equator, completing the polar cell.

Atmospheric circulation

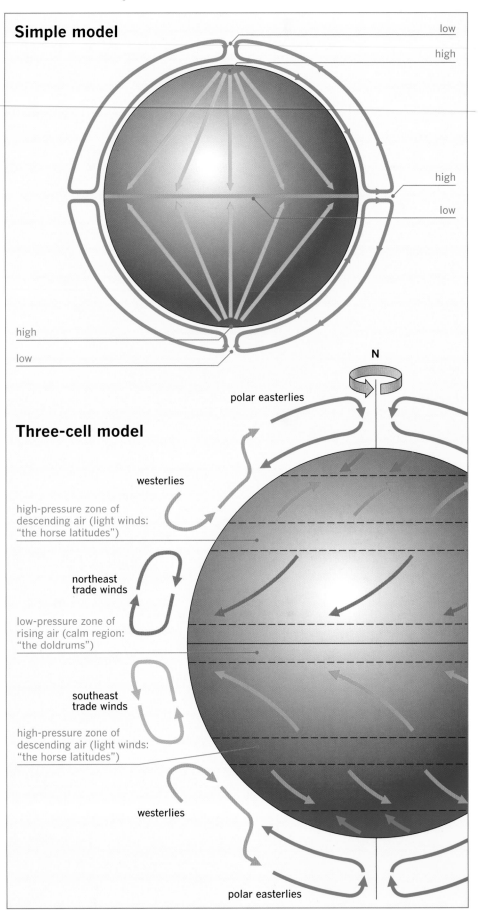

Simple model

Three-cell model

Ocean circulation

Surface currents

- Ocean currents are the horizontal movement of seawater at or near the ocean's surface.
- They are driven primarily by winds at the ocean surface. Friction between moving air and the surface of the water causes water to move in the same direction as the wind.
- Major ocean currents reflect the overall global transportation of energy from the tropics to the poles.
- Ocean currents are more constrained than patterns of global air circulation because the continental landmasses obstruct their flow.

- Landmasses produce ocean current gyres.
- A *gyre* is a largely closed ocean circulation system that transports seawater around an ocean basin.
- Each ocean basin has a major gyre at about 30° latitude. These are driven by the atmospheric flows produced by the subtropical high pressure systems.
- In the Northern Hemisphere, smaller gyres develop at about 50° latitude. These are driven by polar low pressure systems.
- Gyres do not develop at similar latitudes in the Southern Hemisphere because there are no landmasses to constrain current flow.

Key words

gyre	polar
latitude	pole
ocean basin	subtropical
ocean current	tropics

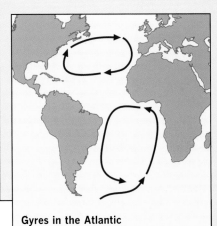

Gyres in the Atlantic

Principal ocean currents

← warm currents
← cold currents

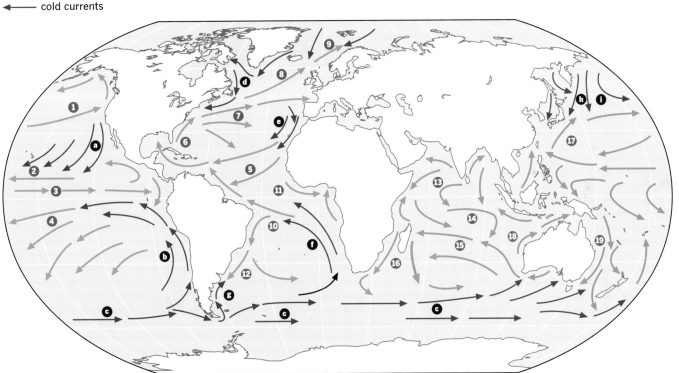

Principal warm currents
1. North Pacific Current
2. Pacific North Equatorial Current
3. Pacific Equatorial Countercurrent
4. Pacific South Equatorial Current
5. Atlantic North Equatorial Current
6. Florida Current
7. Gulf Stream
8. North Atlantic Current
9. Norway Current
10. Atlantic South Equatorial Current
11. Guinea Current
12. Brazil Current
13. Indian North Equatorial Current
14. Indian Equatorial Countercurrent
15. Indian South Equatorial Current
16. Agulhas Current
17. Kuroshio Current
18. West Australia Current
19. East Australia Current

Principal cold currents
a. California Current
b. Peru Current
c. West Wind Drift
d. Labrador Current
e. Canaries Current
f. Benguela Current
g. Falkland Current
h. Oyashio Current
i. Aleutian Current

The magnetosphere

Key words

atmosphere	magnetosphere
aurora	solar wind
aurora australis	Van Allen belt
aurora borealis	
magnetopause	

Magnetosphere

- The *magnetosphere* is the region around Earth in which Earth's magnetic field is dominant.
- It contains magnetically trapped plasma. The Van Allen radiation belts are two layers of intensely charged particles within the magnetosphere.
- The pressure of the solar wind distorts Earth's magnetosphere such that it is flattened on the side facing the Sun but extrudes on the opposite side.

Undisturbed field

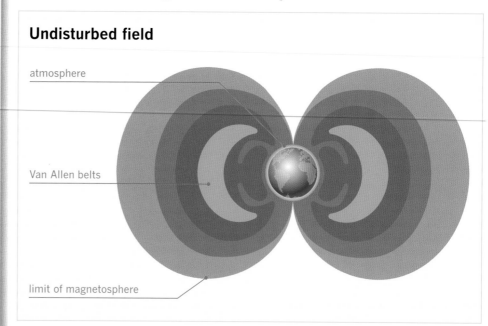

atmosphere

Van Allen belts

limit of magnetosphere

Effect of the solar wind

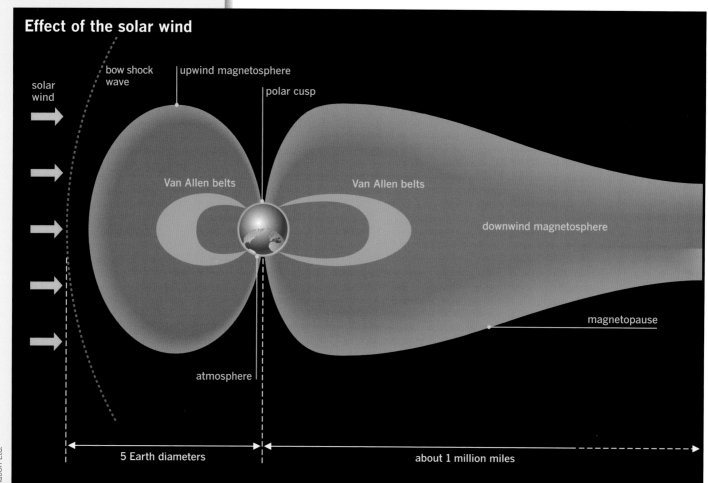

solar wind

bow shock wave

upwind magnetosphere

polar cusp

Van Allen belts

Van Allen belts

downwind magnetosphere

magnetopause

atmosphere

5 Earth diameters

about 1 million miles

Within the magnetosphere, two doughnut-shaped belts of concentrated radiation surround our planet. These so-called Van Allen belts contain lethal quantities of high-speed charged particles. When some of these particles hit molecules in the atmosphere near Earth's magnetic poles, polar night skies glow with colored "curtains" called the *aurora borealis* (Northern Hemisphere) or *aurora australis* (Southern Hemisphere).

The Coriolis effect

Stationary world
Winds blowing in various directions
on an imaginary nonrotating globe.

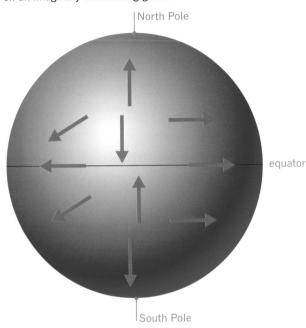

North Pole

equator

South Pole

Spinning world
The same winds,
showing the deflections
caused by the Coriolis effect.

North Pole

equator

South Pole

Resultant winds
Winds blow from areas of high pressure
to areas of low pressure, but the Coriolis effect
deflects them and produces the angled paths of
Earth's dominant wind systems.

North Pole

60°
low
40°
high
30°

5°
low   0°   equator
5°

30°
high
40°
low
60°

South Pole

  winds

Key words

Coriolis effect
equator
ocean current
pole

Coriolis effect
- The *Coriolis effect* refers to the
  deflection of the path of objects
  moving across Earth's surface caused
  by Earth's rotation.
- It is because of the Coriolis effect that
  winds and ocean currents circulate in
  a clockwise direction in the Northern
  Hemisphere and a counterclockwise
  direction in the Southern Hemisphere.

Coriolis effect model
- An imaginary projectile launched
  from the North Pole toward a
  point on the equator
  provides a good example
  of why the Coriolis
  effect exists.
  - As the projectile
    travels south, Earth
    is rotating from
    west to east
    underneath it.
  - Tracing the ground
    track of the projectile
    as it heads toward the
    equator would produce a
    line on Earth's surface that
    curves to the right (with
    reference to the direction of travel).
- When the projectile arrives at the
  equator, it will hit a point to the west
  of the original target point. This is
  because the target point has moved
  with Earth's rotation to the east while
  the projectile was in flight.
- Winds and currents experience the
  same deflection as the imagined
  projectile.
- The Coriolis effect only occurs along
  paths that have a north–south
  component. It does not affect paths
  that are precisely east–west.

Local winds

Key words

land breeze
mountain breeze
sea breeze
valley breeze

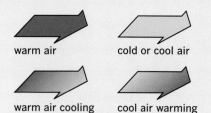

warm air cold or cool air

warm air cooling cool air warming

Land and sea breezes

- Land and sea breezes occur because of the different heating and cooling characteristics of the land and the sea.
- Land heats up and cools down more quickly than the sea.
- In areas where the land and the sea are adjacent, these differing characteristics create pressure gradients.
- During the day, pressure is lower over the land, driving an airflow from sea to land. During the night, pressure is lower over the sea, driving an airflow from land to sea.

Mountain and valley breezes

- Mountain and valley breezes occur in areas that contain large variations in topographical relief.
- During the day, air at the bottom of a valley is heated and begins to rise up the mountain sides as a valley breeze.
- During the night, air on the high slopes of mountains rapidly loses heat and begins to sink into the valley as a mountain breeze.

Land and sea breezes

Sea breeze: day

Land breeze: night

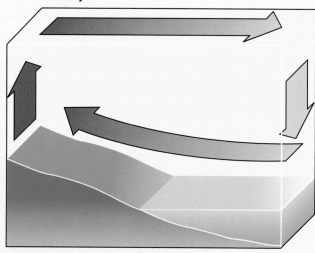

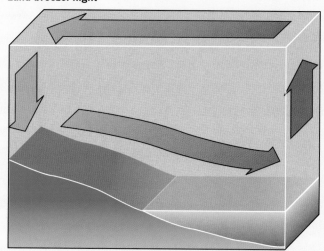

Valley and mountain breezes

Valley breeze: day

Mountain breeze: night

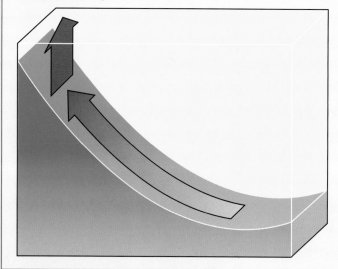

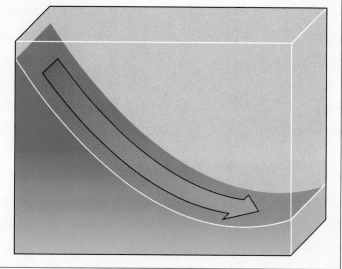

Beaufort wind scale

Wind speed

- Meteorologists measure wind speed using precise instruments. When instruments are not available, wind speed can be estimated from the effects it has on the environment.
- The Beaufort wind scale was devised by Admiral Beaufort (British Navy) in the 19th century to allow sailors to estimate wind speed from conditions at sea.

- The scale has since been modified for use on land.
- Hurricanes are sometimes given Beaufort numbers of 13, 14, 15, or 16. These correspond to Saffir-Simpson Hurricane Scale numbers 2 through 5. A Saffir-Simpson Hurricane Scale number 1 is equivalent to Beaufort 12.

Key words

Beaufort wind scale
hurricane
Saffir-Simpson scale

Beaufort number		Description	Characteristics	Range: mph	Range: kmph
0		Calm	No wind; smoke rises vertically.	less than 1	less than 1
1		Light air	Smoke drifts with air; weather vanes do not move.	1–3	1–5
2		Light breeze	Wind felt on face; leaves rustle; weather vanes move.	4–7	6–11
3		Gentle breeze	Leaves and twigs move; light flags are extended.	8–12	12–19
4		Moderate breeze	Small branches sway; dust and loose paper is blown about.	13–18	20–28
5		Fresh breeze	Small trees sway; waves break on lakes.	19–24	29–38
6		Strong breeze	Large branches sway; umbrellas difficult to use.	25–31	39–49
7		Moderate gale	Whole trees sway; difficult to walk against the wind.	32–38	50–61
8		Fresh gale	Twigs break off trees; very difficult to walk against the wind.	39–46	62–74
9		Strong gale	Chimneys, roof slates, and roof shingles are blown off buildings.	47–54	75–88
10		Whole gale	Trees uprooted; extensive damage to buildings.	55–63	89–102
11		Storm	Widespread damage.	64–73	103–117
12–17		Hurricane	Extreme destruction.	more than 74	more than 118

The world's named winds

Key words

monsoon
ocean current

Named winds

- Certain winds regularly occur in specific regions. These are often the result of geographical features such as mountain ranges and ocean currents combined with seasonal variations in temperature.
- Many of these winds are so regular and predictable that they are named by the people inhabiting the area.
- Among the best known are the "Chinook" in the midwest of North America, the "Sirocco" of the Mediterranean, and the "Shamal" of the Middle East.
- The "Chinook" and winds occur where dry air descends from the slopes of mountains. As it descends, the air is compressed by the mass of cold air above it, which causes it to become warmer.
- Chinook winds have been known to raise winter temperatures in the midwest of the United States from −4°F (−20°C) to 50°F (10°C) or more for short periods of time.
- The "Sirocco" occurs during the autumn and spring when hot dry air over North Africa is drawn toward the southern coasts of Europe by low-pressure centers over the Mediterranean.
- Sirocco winds can exceed 60 miles per hour (100 kmph) and carry large amounts of dust from the Sahara desert.
- The "Shamal" occurs most often during the summer months in the Persian Gulf area. It is part of the air circulation pattern of the Asian monsoon.

Locations of named winds

Named winds

1	Berg Wind	8	Chinook	15	Leste	22	Pampero	29	Southerly Burster
2	Bise	9	Gibli	16	Levanter	23	Papagayo	30	Terral
3	Bohorok	10	Haboob	17	Leveche	24	Purga	31	Tramontana
4	Bora	11	Harmattan	18	Mistral	25	Santa Anna	32	Virazon
5	Brickfielder	12	Karaburan	19	Nor'wester	26	Seistan	33	Willy-willy
6	Buran	13	Khamsin	20	Norte	27	Shamal	34	Zonda
7	Chili	14	Koembang	21	Norther	28	Sirocco		

The windchill effect

Key words

windchill

Chart of equivalent windchill temperatures

Air temperature (°F)	Wind speed (mph)							
	5	10	15	20	25	30	35	40
50	48	40	36	32	30	28	27	26
40	37	28	22	18	16	13	11	10
30	27	16	9	4	0	−2	−4	−6
20	16	4	−5	−10	−15	−18	−20	−21
10	6	−9	−18	−25	−29	−33	−35	−37
0	−5	−21	−36	−39	−44	−48	−49	−53
−10	−15	−33	−45	−53	−59	−63	−67	−69
−20	−26	−46	−58	−67	−74	−79	−82	−85
−30	−36	−58	−72	−82	−88	−94	−98	−100
−40	−47	−70	−85	−96	−104	−109	−113	−116
−50	−57	−83	−99	−110	−118	−125	−129	−132
−60	−68	−95	−112	−124	−133	−140	−145	−148

Wind speeds greater than 40 miles per hour (64 kmph) have little additional effect.

Windchill effect

Normal skin temperature 91.4°F (33°C)

Air temperature

Wind speed

Windchill

- *Windchill* refers to the apparent temperature felt on exposed skin due to the combined effects of wind speed and actual air temperature.
- Except at air temperatures above about 68°F (20°C) the presence of wind creates a lower apparent temperature.
- Above 68°F (20°C) the chilling effect of wind is considered negligible. This is because wind increases the rate at which moisture evaporates from the skin carrying heat away from the body.
- The chilling effect of wind becomes more significant at lower air temperatures.
- Windchill is most significant where low temperatures combine with high wind speeds to create conditions that can be life-threatening.

© Diagram Visual Information Ltd.

© Diagram Visual Information Ltd.

Key words

air mass	Rossby wave
Coriolis effect	stratosphere
jet stream	subtropical jet
planetary wave	stream
polar front	troposphere
polar jet stream	

Jet streams

- A *jet stream* is a narrow band of strong wind in the upper troposphere or lower stratosphere. It is typically thousands of miles long and hundreds of miles wide, but only a few miles deep.

- A *polar jet stream* is often present at the polar front. It is a result of the deflection of upper-air winds by the Coriolis effect. These winds are driven by pressure gradients that result from the interaction of cool polar air masses and warm tropical air masses.

- Winds at the core of a polar jet stream may reach 185 miles per hour (300 kmph). Wind speeds are generally greater in winter than in summer.

- A *subtropical jet stream* may be present above the subtropical high pressure zone where the Hadley and Ferrel cells meet. Subtropical jet stream wind speeds are generally less than those of a polar jet stream.

Jet streams

Polar jet streams and the formation of midlatitude cyclones

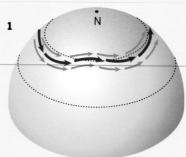

1 A polar jet stream forms at the polar front where cold polar air meets warm tropical air.

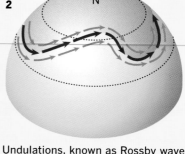

2 Undulations, known as Rossby waves, form in the polar jet stream. These waves (also known as planetary waves) form as a result of Earth's curvature and rotation.

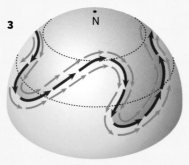

3 As the Rossby waves become more pronounced, bulges of cool polar air are carried across lower latitudes.

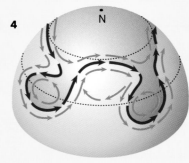

4 These bulges of cool air become the low-pressure zones that drive the formation of midlatitude cyclones.

cold air	→ jet axis
warm air	→ wind

subtropical jet stream

polar front jet stream

Location of jet streams in the atmosphere

polar front jet stream   polar cell

ferrel cell

subtropical jet stream

hadley cell

North Pole

60°N

30°N

altitude 12.4 miles 6.2 miles
          (20 km)   (10 km)

equator

Average temperatures: January and July

below −30°F (−34°C)

−30°F to 30°F (−34°C to −1°C)

30°F to 50°F (−1°C to 10°C)

50°F to 70°F (10°C to 21°C)

70°F to 90°F (21°C to −32°C)

more than 90°F (32°C)

Average temperatures
- Temperatures are highest in July for the Northern Hemisphere and in January for the Southern Hemisphere.

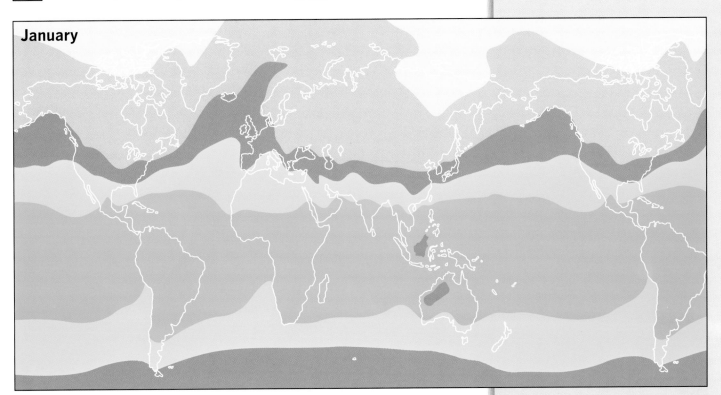

January

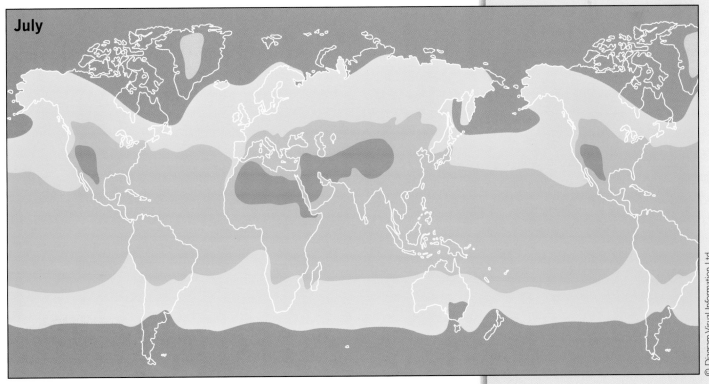

July

Average temperatures: USA: January and April

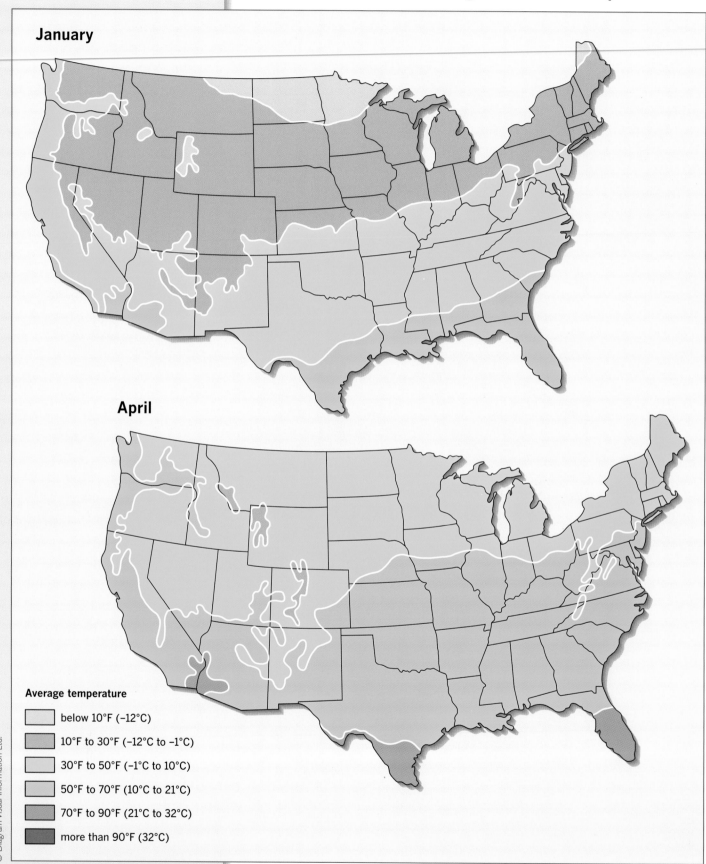

January

April

Average temperature

- below 10°F (−12°C)
- 10°F to 30°F (−12°C to −1°C)
- 30°F to 50°F (−1°C to 10°C)
- 50°F to 70°F (10°C to 21°C)
- 70°F to 90°F (21°C to 32°C)
- more than 90°F (32°C)

Average temperatures: USA: July and October

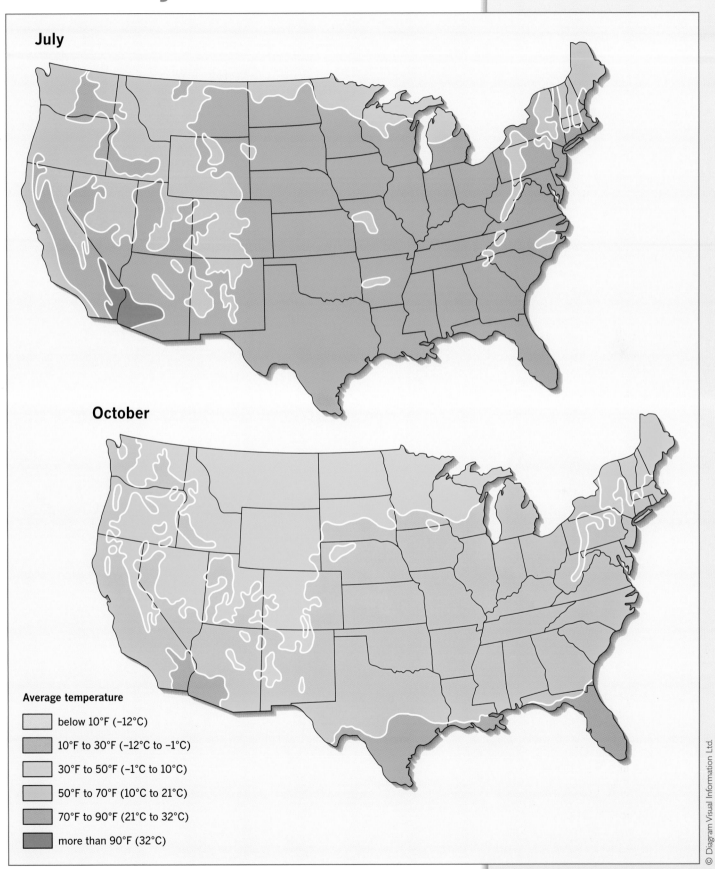

July

October

Average temperature

- below 10°F (−12°C)
- 10°F to 30°F (−12°C to −1°C)
- 30°F to 50°F (−1°C to 10°C)
- 50°F to 70°F (10°C to 21°C)
- 70°F to 90°F (21°C to 32°C)
- more than 90°F (32°C)

Solar radiation: December

© Diagram Visual Information Ltd.

Key words

atmosphere
langley
ozone layer
solar radiation
total solar
 irradiance (TSI)

Solar radiation

- *Solar radiation* refers to the total electromagnetic energy radiated by the Sun.
- About 50 percent of the electromagnetic radiation emitted by the Sun has wavelengths within the visible spectrum. Most of the other 50 percent is infrared with a small proportion ultraviolet.
- The amount of energy that reaches the top of Earth's atmosphere from the Sun is known as *total solar irradiance (TSI)*. Measurements of TSI can only be made from Earth's orbit. The currently accepted value is about 1,368 watts per square meter.

Solar radiation

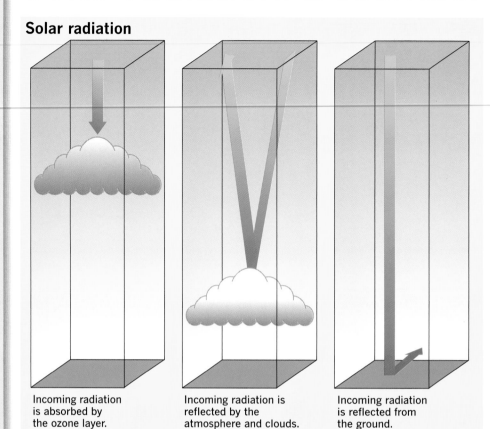

Incoming radiation is absorbed by the ozone layer.

Incoming radiation is reflected by the atmosphere and clouds.

Incoming radiation is reflected from the ground.

Global solar radiation: December

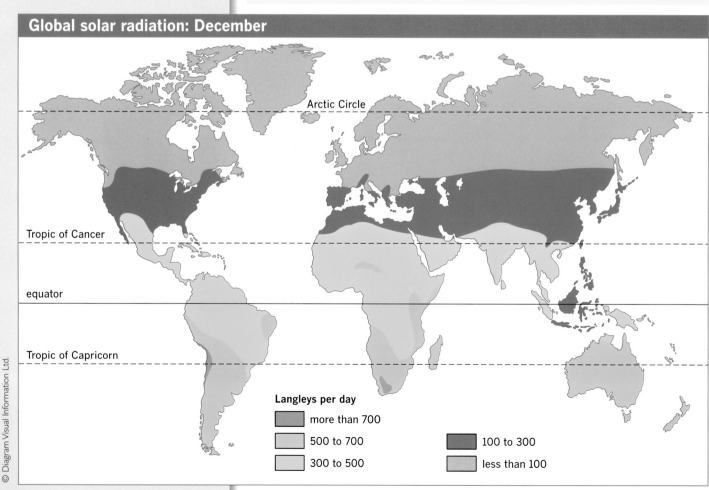

Arctic Circle

Tropic of Cancer

equator

Tropic of Capricorn

Langleys per day

- more than 700
- 500 to 700
- 300 to 500
- 100 to 300
- less than 100

Solar radiation: June

Heat transference systems

Latent heat is released by condensation.

Heat is distributed by turbulent mixing.

Heat is conducted from the ground.

Key words

atmosphere
insolation
langley
latent heat
solar radiation

total solar
irradiance (TSI)

Insolation

- *Insolation* refers to the total amount of solar radiation received on Earth's surface. It is measured in langleys per day. One *langley* is equal to one gram calorie per square centimeter.
- Total insolation is less than the total solar radiation that arrives at the top of the atmosphere (total solar irradiance). This is because a significant proportion of solar radiation is reflected by the atmosphere or by moisture in the atmosphere.

Global solar radiation: June

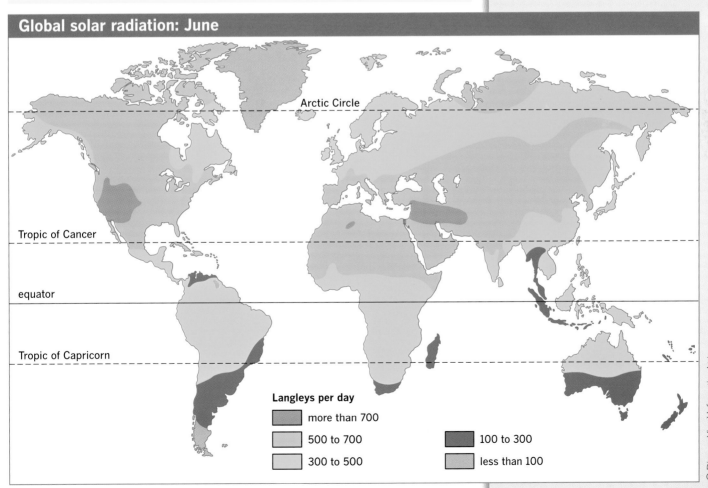

Arctic Circle

Tropic of Cancer

equator

Tropic of Capricorn

Langleys per day

more than 700

500 to 700

300 to 500

100 to 300

less than 100

Solar radiation: USA: January and July

Key words

langley
solar radiation

Langleys per day

- The langley is a unit of energy per unit area often used to measure solar radiation. It is equal to one gram calorie per square centimeter.
- In winter the low angle of the Sun, short day length, and frequent cloud cover limit the amount of solar radiation in the northern states to about 150 langleys per day.
- In summer, with long days, clear skies, and the Sun high in the sky, these states receive up to 600 langleys per day.

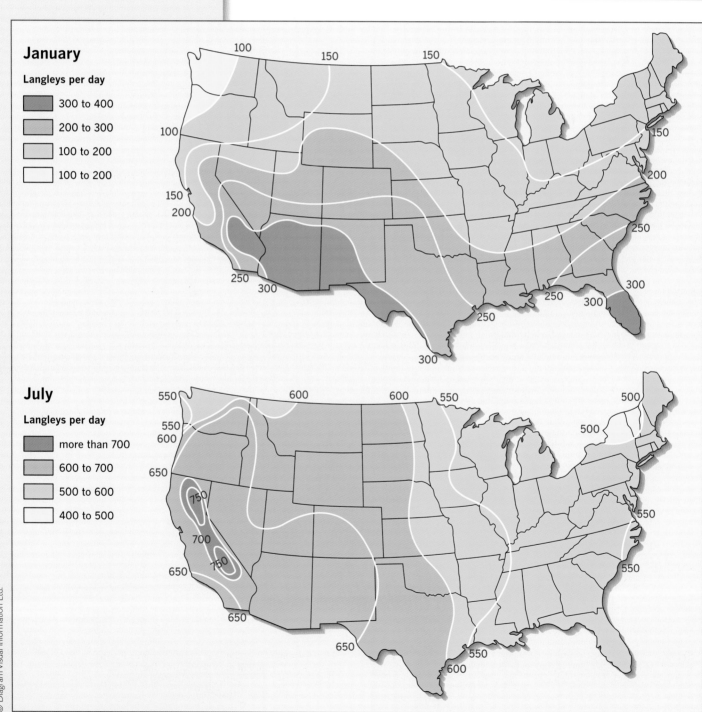

January

Langleys per day

- 300 to 400
- 200 to 300
- 100 to 200
- 100 to 200

July

Langleys per day

- more than 700
- 600 to 700
- 500 to 600
- 400 to 500

Average and extreme temperatures: cities

Capital city temperatures and ranges

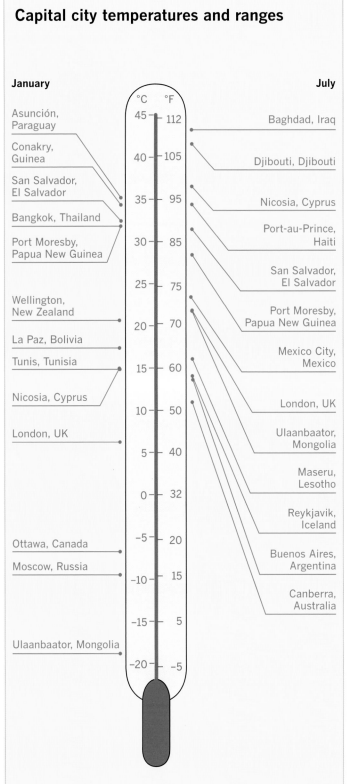

January

Asunción, Paraguay
Conakry, Guinea
San Salvador, El Salvador
Bangkok, Thailand
Port Moresby, Papua New Guinea
Wellington, New Zealand
La Paz, Bolivia
Tunis, Tunisia
Nicosia, Cyprus
London, UK
Ottawa, Canada
Moscow, Russia
Ulaanbaator, Mongolia

July

Baghdad, Iraq
Djibouti, Djibouti
Nicosia, Cyprus
Port-au-Prince, Haiti
San Salvador, El Salvador
Port Moresby, Papua New Guinea
Mexico City, Mexico
London, UK
Ulaanbaator, Mongolia
Maseru, Lesotho
Reykjavik, Iceland
Buenos Aires, Argentina
Canberra, Australia

Shown on the diagram are the average daily maximum temperatures for the hottest and coldest capital cities around the world in January and July. London, UK, is included as a temperate comparison.

Temperature ranges

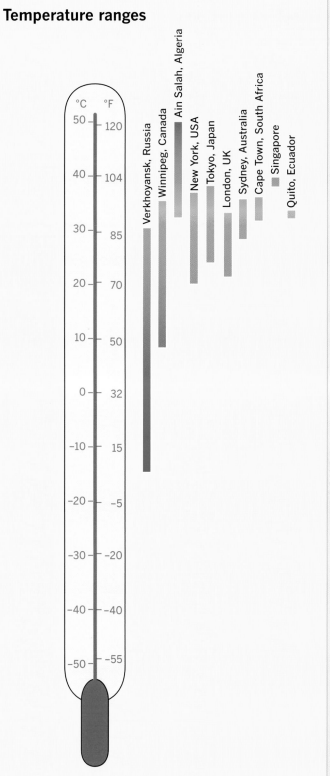

Verkhoyansk, Russia
Winnipeg, Canada
Ain Salah, Algeria
New York, USA
Tokyo, Japan
London, UK
Sydney, Australia
Cape Town, South Africa
Singapore
Quito, Ecuador

The diagram shows the temperature ranges in cities around the world. The top of each bar shows the average highest daily temperature for the hottest month. The lower end shows the same for the coldest month.

Key words

*annual
temperature
range*

Global average annual temperature range

Temperature range

- The *annual temperature range* is the difference between the average temperatures on the coldest night and warmest day of the year. The range is very small in the tropics, but very large near the poles.

- At the equator, latitude 0°, there are 12 hours of daylight on every day of the year. At the poles, latitude 90°, there are up to 24 hours of daylight in summer, but in winter the Sun may be above the horizon for no more than a few hours. The variation in hours of daylight means that the difference between daytime and nighttime temperatures at the equator is greater than the seasonal difference, while in high latitudes there is a large seasonal difference.

- The effect of latitude shows clearly even within North America: San Antonio, Texas, latitude 29.45° N, has an annual temperature range of about 36°F (20°C), while Winnipeg, Manitoba, latitude 49.92° N, has a range of about 63°F (35°C). At San Antonio the hours of daylight range from 10 hours 14 mins to 14 hours 4 mins, and at Winnipeg from 8 hours 5 mins to 16 hours 21 mins.

Examples of annual temperature range

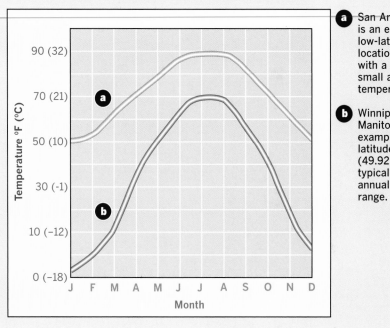

a San Antonio, Texas, is an example of a low-latitude location (29.45˚N) with a typically small annual temperature range.

b Winnipeg, Manitoba, is an example of a high-latitude location (49.92˚N) with a typically large annual temperature range.

Temperature ranges

Temperature ranges (°F)

- 0 to 10
- 10 to 30
- 30 to 50
- 50 to 70
- 70 to 90
- 90 to 110

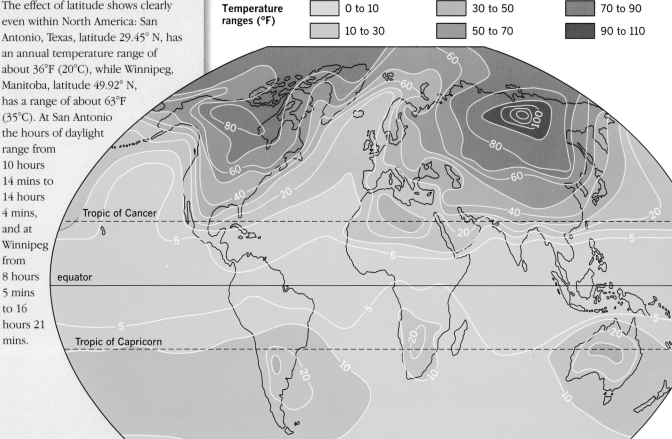

Types of cloud

Cloud types

- All clouds belong to one of two categories: *stratus* clouds or *cumulus* clouds.
- Stratus clouds are characterized by horizontal layering and a flat uniform base.
- *Cumulus* clouds are formed from dense rounded elements.
- Clouds are further categorized according to the altitude at which they form.
- Cloud altitude is measured from the base of a cloud, not the top.
- The three altitude classes are high, medium, and low.

Cloud types

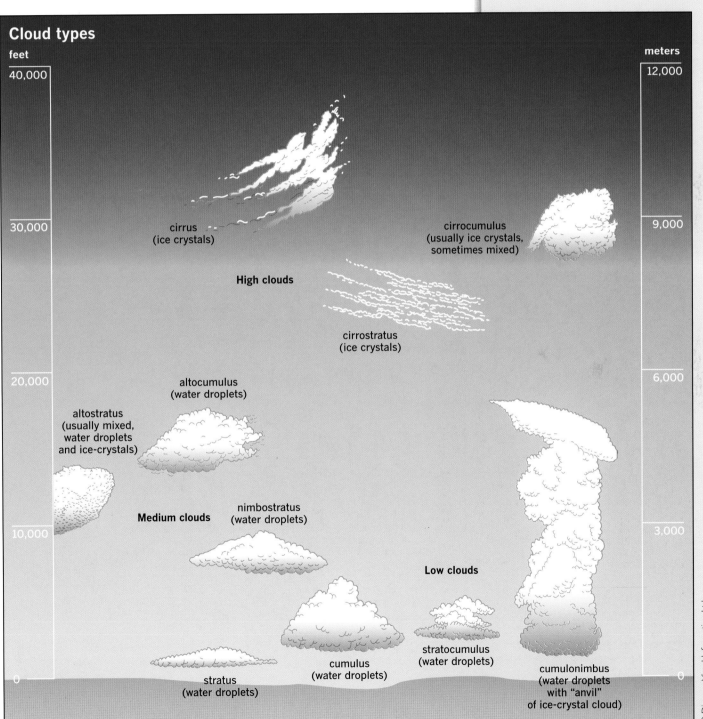

feet

40,000

30,000

cirrus
(ice crystals)

cirrocumulus
(usually ice crystals,
sometimes mixed)

High clouds

cirrostratus
(ice crystals)

20,000

altocumulus
(water droplets)

altostratus
(usually mixed,
water droplets
and ice-crystals)

Medium clouds

nimbostratus
(water droplets)

10,000

Low clouds

stratocumulus
(water droplets)

stratus
(water droplets)

cumulus
(water droplets)

cumulonimbus
(water droplets
with "anvil"
of ice-crystal cloud)

0

meters

12,000

9,000

6,000

3,000

0

© Diagram Visual Information Ltd.

Key words	
atmosphere	convection cloud
cloud	dew point
condensation	front
nucleus (CCN)	frontal cloud
condensation	precipitation
level	

Clouds

- A cloud is a collection of water droplets or ice crystals suspended in the atmosphere.
- Clouds form when water vapor is forced to condense. This occurs when the air carrying the water vapor cools to its *dew point* temperature. Cooling occurs when warm air is forced to rise. As it rises, air expands and therefore becomes cooler. The altitude at which this process cools air to its dew point temperature is known as the *condensation level*.
- If the dew point temperature is below the freezing point of water, ice crystals rather than water droplets form.
- Below the dew point temperature, water vapor will condense onto any solid surface. Tiny particles suspended in the atmosphere known as *cloud condensation nuclei* (CCNs) provide the necessary surfaces for water vapor to form water droplets.
- CCNs are about 0.000008 inches (0.0002 mm) in diameter. The water droplets that form around them to produce clouds are about 0.0008 inches (0.02 mm) in diameter.
- CCNs are usually particles of clay, sea salt, or carbon particles created by combustion. They may also be sulfates emitted by plankton activity in the oceans.
- The distribution and source of CCNs is not well understood: the frequency with which the conditions for cloud formation occur cannot therefore be accurately predicted.
- Water droplets remain suspended because the air around them is rising with enough energy to prevent the droplets falling to the ground. The air continues to rise because it is heated by the thermal energy released when water vapor condenses to a liquid. When water droplets become too massive, they fall as precipitation.

Cloud formation: convection and frontal

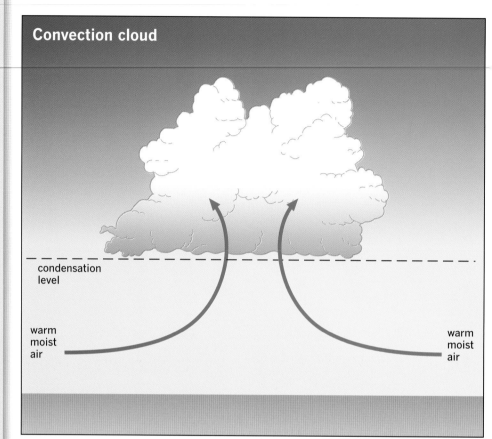

Convection cloud

condensation level

warm moist air

warm moist air

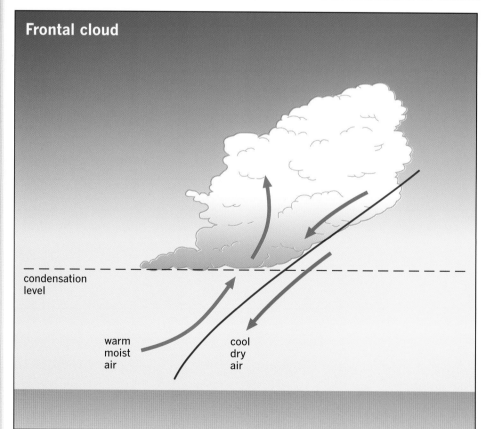

Frontal cloud

condensation level

warm moist air

cool dry air

Cloud formation: orographic and turbulence

Key words

atmosphere
condensation
  level
convection cloud
dew point

front
frontal cloud
orographic cloud
turbulence cloud

Cloud formation

- Clouds generally form when warm air bearing water vapor is forced to rise and cool. There are several mechanisms that produce this.
- *Convection cloud* forms when air near Earth's surface is heated. Air is heated by the direct rays of the Sun and by radiation from the areas of Earth's surface that have been heated by the Sun.
- As the air is heated, it expands. If it expands to the point where it is less dense than the air above it, it will rise into the atmosphere.
- As the heated air rises it cools. At a certain altitude (condensation level) it will reach its dew point temperature, and any water vapor it contains will begin to condense.
- *Frontal cloud* forms when air is forced to rise because it meets with cooler, denser air.
- At a weather front a warmer air mass may be forced to move over the top of a cooler air mass. As the warmer air mass rises it may cool to its dew point temperature, forcing water vapor to condense and clouds to form.
- *Orographic cloud* forms when an air mass is forced to rise by the topography of Earth's surface.
- As an air mass crosses an area of raised topography, such as a mountain range, a proportion of that air mass is forced up into the atmosphere.
- At a higher altitude, that air cools and its temperature may fall below its dew point, causing clouds to form.
- *Turbulence cloud* forms when an air mass passes over a topographically uneven surface.
- Turbulent eddies form, especially if the air mass is moving quickly, which carry some air to greater altitudes and some to lower altitudes.
- Clouds may form where air is carried sufficiently high by these eddies.

Orographic cloud

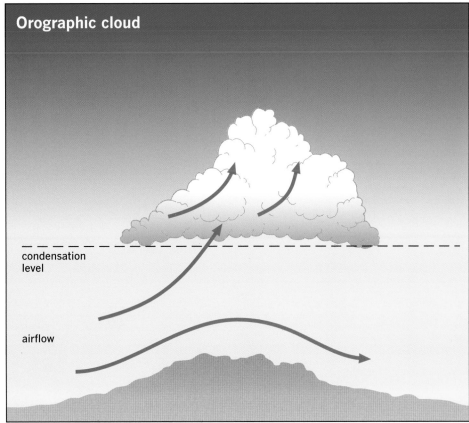

condensation
level

airflow

Turbulence cloud

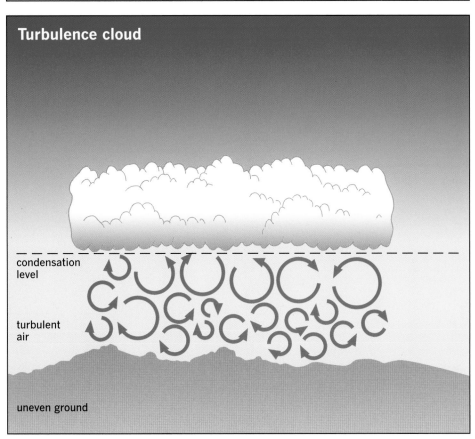

condensation
level

turbulent
air

uneven ground

Average number of cloudy days: USA

© Diagram Visual Information Ltd.

Key words

air mass	maritime polar
front	(mP)
frontal lifting	orographic lifting

Cloudiest places

- The coastal regions of Washington and Oregon are the cloudiest places in the United States.
- The climate of these regions is dominated by maritime polar (mP) air masses that originate over the North Pacific.
- These air masses always contain a lot of moisture evaporated from the ocean.
- They are subject to orographic and frontal lifting along the coastal region.

The ten cloudiest cities in the United States

Average annual number of days with cloud   Location

240	Astoria, Oregon
240	Quillayote, Washington
229	Olympia, Washington
227	Seattle, Washington
223	Portland, Oregon
213	Kailspell, Montana
212	Binghamton, New York
211	Beckley, West Virginia
211	Elkins, West Virginia
209	Eugene, Oregon

Average number of cloudy days in the USA

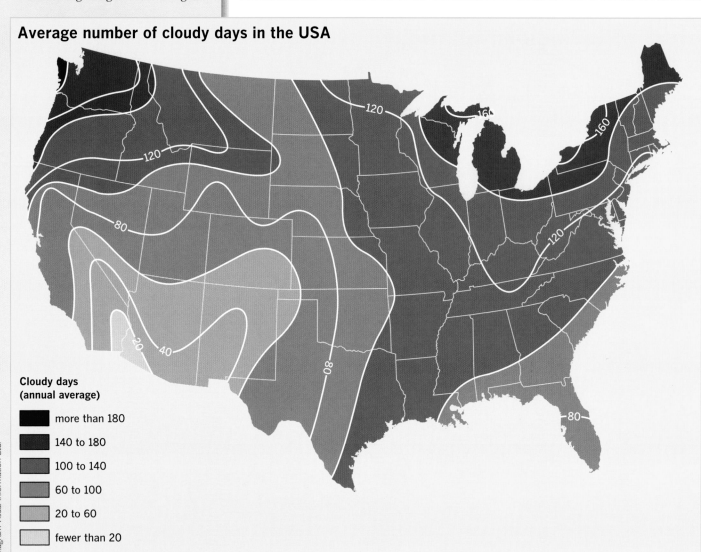

**Cloudy days
(annual average)**

- more than 180
- 140 to 180
- 100 to 140
- 60 to 100
- 20 to 60
- fewer than 20

Formation of fog

Normal atmospheric conditions

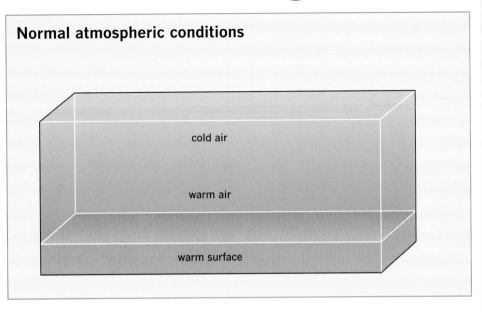

Radiation fog

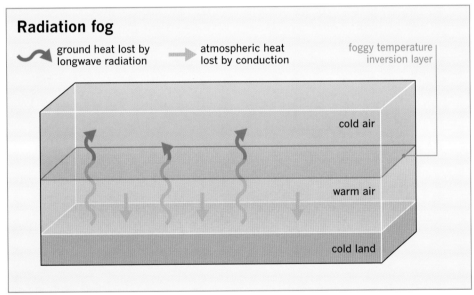

Advection fog

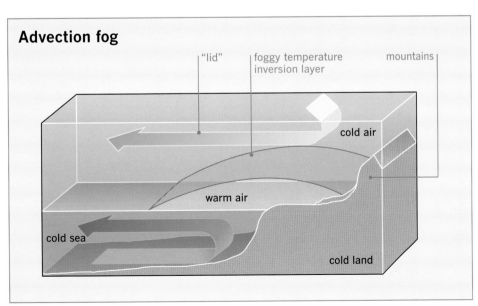

Key words

advection fog
cloud base
condensation
  nucleus
evaporation fog
fog
freezing fog

frontal fog
ground fog
ice fog
precipitation fog
radiation fog
steam fog
upslope fog

Fog

- *Fog* is cloud with a cloud base at or very close to the ground.
- It occurs when moisture carried in the air cools and condenses.
- Different types of fog are caused by evaporation and condensation.
- As is the case with clouds, particles suspended in the atmosphere known as *condensation nuclei* must be present to give the water vapor surfaces to condense onto.

Fog types

- *Radiation fog* or *ground fog* forms as Earth's surface cools overnight. Its heat is radiated into the atmosphere.
- *Upslope fog* is formed when air is forced up topographical slopes. At higher altitudes, pressure is less. The air cools as it expands and fog is produced.
- *Advection fog* is generated by winds that are warmer or cooler than Earth's surface.
- *Evaporation fog* or *steam fog* is formed when cold air moves across warm land or sea surfaces. Moisture evaporates into the cold air.
- *Precipitation fog* or *frontal fog* forms where precipitation falls into a warm dry area. The precipitation evaporates before or shortly after reaching the ground.
- *Ice fog* is a type of fog in which the water droplets suspended in the air freeze into very small ice crystals that remain suspended.
- *Freezing fog* is a type of fog in which the water droplets suspended in the air freeze onto very cold surface features creating deposits of ice known as rime ice.

© Diagram Visual Information Ltd.

Fog in the USA

Fog frequency

- The coastal regions of Washington, Oregon, and northern California are the foggiest areas of the United States.
- Fog and cloud readily form along this coast because of the interaction of warm air masses originating over the land and moist air masses originating over the Pacific.

The ten foggiest places in the western United States
Average annual number of days with heavy fog

Days	Location
252	Stampede Pass, Washington
160	Sexton Summit, Oregon
89	Olympia, Washington
87	Santa Maria, California
79	Sandberg, California
68	Blue Canyon, California
61	Barrow, Alaska
60	Eugene, Oregon
58	St Paul Island, Alaska
53	Quillayute, Washington

Average number of days with thick fog in the USA

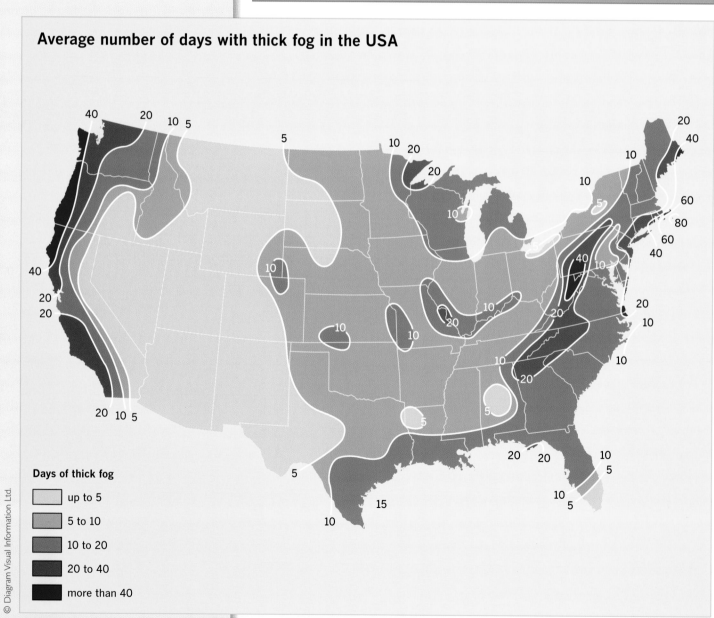

Days of thick fog

- up to 5
- 5 to 10
- 10 to 20
- 20 to 40
- more than 40

Fog and smog

Key words

condensation
 nucleus
fog
mist
photochemical
 smog

smog
sulfurous smog

Fog and visibility: altitude

The maximum range of horizontal visibility for an aircraft pilot flying over a ground layer of fog, mist, or heat haze increases as the plane gains height and decreases as it descends.

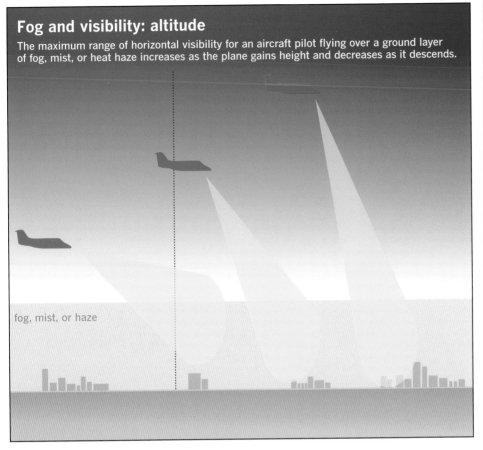

fog, mist, or haze

Fog and visibility: landing

Looking down through the fog, the airfield is clearly visible. From low altitude the line of sight passes through a much greater thickness of fog and the airfield is obscured.

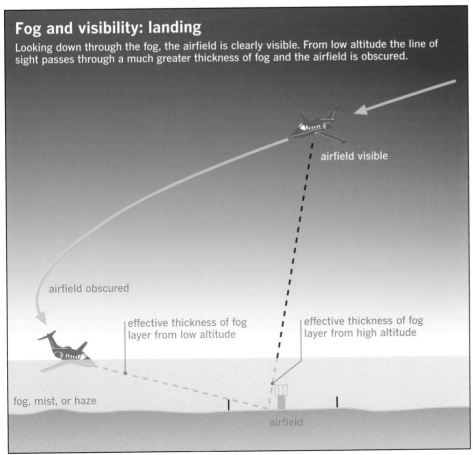

airfield visible

airfield obscured

effective thickness of fog layer from low altitude

effective thickness of fog layer from high altitude

fog, mist, or haze

airfield

Fog and visibility

- Fog can be defined as a collection of water droplets suspended in the atmosphere near Earth's surface that affects visibility.
- International convention dictates that a collection of water droplets of this kind is referred to as fog when it reduces visibility to below 0.6 miles (1 km). Otherwise it is referred to as *mist*.
- Water droplets reduce visibility because they reflect and refract light. The effect of fog or mist on visibility can depend on the point of view of an observer.
- An observer located above a layer of fog, such as an aircraft pilot, may be able to see the runway below him clearly because the layer of water droplets lying between him and the ground is relatively thin. As the same pilot descends into the fog layer he may no longer be able to see the runway because the thickness of intervening fog is much greater.

Fog and smog

- *Smog* is a term originally coined to describe a mixture of natural fog and air pollution. It is currently also used to describe urban air pollution with or without natural fog.
- *Photochemical smog* contains concentrations of nitrogen oxides and hydrocarbons emitted mainly by internal combustion engines.
- *Sulfurous smog* contains concentrations of sulfur oxides produced by the burning of fossil fuels.
- Both forms of smog can encourage the formation of natural fog because they increase the number of available condensation nuclei in the air.

Humidity

© Diagram Visual Information Ltd.

Key words

absolute humidity
dew point
frost point
humidity
relative humidity
saturation point

Humidity

- *Humidity* is a general term for the quantity of water vapor in the atmosphere.
- Humidity is expressed as *absolute humidity* or *relative humidity*.
- *Absolute humidity* is the mass of water vapor in a given volume of gas (usually air).
- *Relative humidity* is the ratio of water vapor in a given volume of gas (usually air) and the maximum amount of water vapor that volume of gas at the same temperature could contain before reaching *saturation point*.
- Saturation point is the point at which water vapor will begin to condense out of the air.
- *Dew point* is the temperature at which the moisture in a given volume of air will begin to condense. When the dew point temperature is below freezing point it is sometimes referred to as the *frost point*.
- The dew point or saturation point for a volume of air can be expressed as 100 percent relative humidity.
- Generally, the higher the air temperature, the greater the mass of water it can contain without reaching saturation.

Absolute humidity

Water (g/m³)

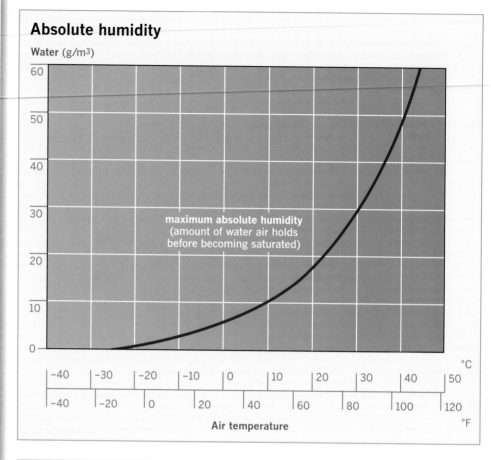

maximum absolute humidity
(amount of water air holds
before becoming saturated)

Air temperature

Relative humidity on a spring day in Washington, D.C.

Relative humidity (%)

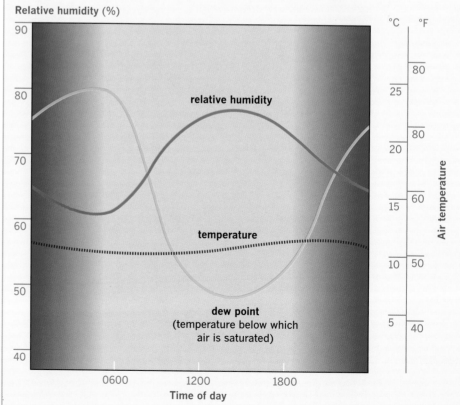

relative humidity

temperature

dew point
(temperature below which
air is saturated)

Air temperature

Time of day

Rain, snow, and sleet

Raindrop growth by collision and coalescence

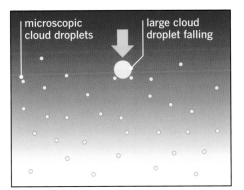

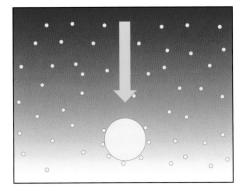

Formation of a snowflake

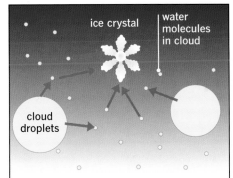

Sleet formation

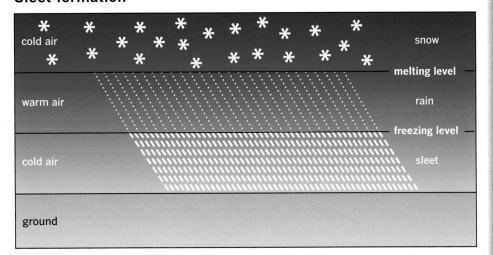

Rain

- All clouds are composed of water droplets that have condensed in a saturated atmosphere, but not all clouds produce rain.
- *Cloud condensation nuclei* (CCNs) are microscopic particles in the atmosphere that allow water vapor to condense into water droplets.
- For rain to occur, water droplets must become sufficiently massive for them to overcome updrafts.
- In turbulent air, water droplets grow in size and mass by colliding and coalescing with other water droplets. The cloud must contain water droplets of varying sizes for this to occur. Massive droplets absorb smaller droplets during downdrafts.

Snow and sleet

- Snow occurs when water vapor in a saturated atmosphere below freezing point deposits as ice on microscopic particles in the atmosphere known as *deposition nuclei*.
- This deposition produces microscopic six-sided ice crystals.
- Water vapor continues to condense onto the ice crystals, particularly at the six corners of the crystal. This produces the characteristic star shape of a snowflake.
- A snowflake grows rapidly until it has enough mass to overcome updrafts and then starts falling.
- Sleet consists of frozen or partially-frozen droplets of water rather than the distinctively-shaped ice crystals of the snowflake.
- Sleet forms when snow melts and then refreezes before it reaches the ground, or when rain freezes before it reaches the ground.

Key words

air mass	midlatitude
convective rain	orographic rain
cyclonic rain	precipitation
dew point	rain shadow
equatorial	windward
leeward	

Types of rainfall

Rain types

- Rain is the most common and widespread form of precipitation.
- When air containing water vapor reaches its dew point temperature, droplets of water form. If these droplets become heavy enough, they fall as rain.
- Air containing water vapor reaches its dew point when it is cooled. There are three principal atmospheric mechanisms that can cause air to be cooled in this way. In each case, warm moist air is forced to rise and cools as it encounters lower pressure.

Cyclonic rain

- *Cyclonic rain* occurs where a relatively warm air mass is forced to rise over a cooler air mass.
- In midlatitudes interacting air masses tend to have greater temperature differences than in equatorial regions.

Convective rain

- *Convective rain* occurs when warm, moist air rises rapidly and almost vertically. The Sun's heat and turbulence caused by small ground obstacles drives this movement.
- If the air reaches a sufficient height, it is cooled below its dew point and heavy localized showers occur.

Orographic rain

- *Orographic rain* occurs when warm moist air is forced to rise over large topographical features such as mountains.
- The rising air is cooled as pressure drops and rain is produced.
- Orographic rain occurs on the windward side of slopes and tends to be prolonged and have little seasonal variation. Rain shadows are common on the leeward side of such slopes.

Cyclonic rain

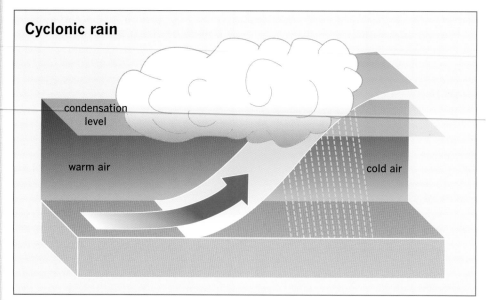

condensation level

warm air

cold air

Convective rain

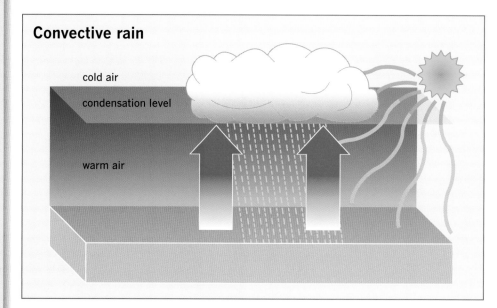

cold air

condensation level

warm air

Orographic rain

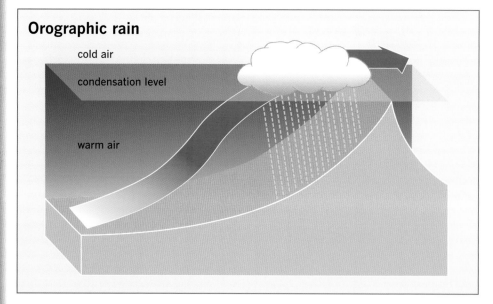

cold air

condensation level

warm air

Global average annual rainfall

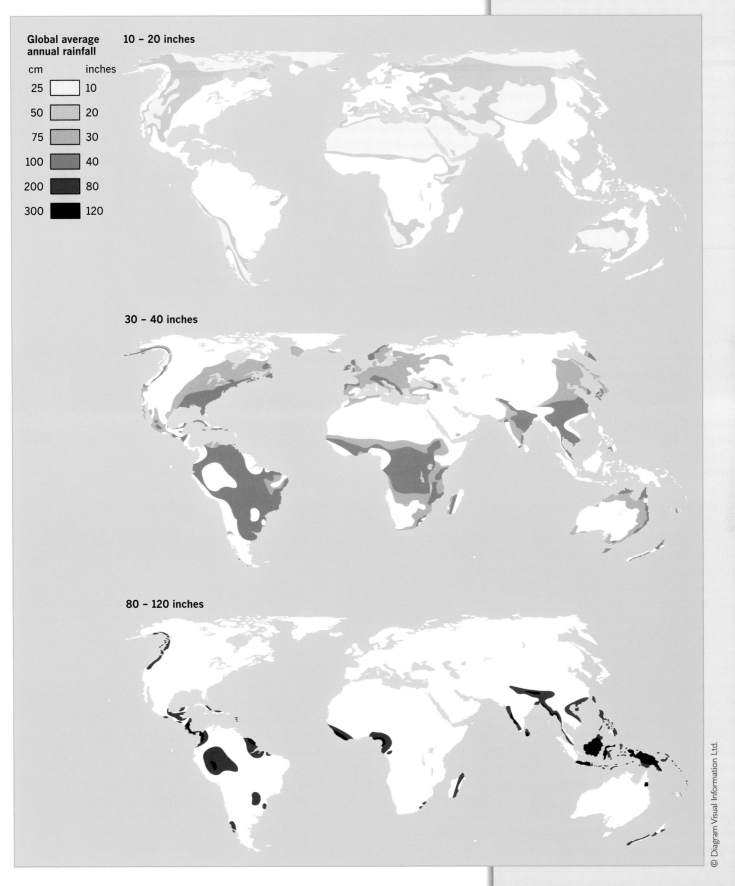

Global average annual rainfall

cm		inches
25		10
50		20
75		30
100		40
200		80
300		120

10 – 20 inches

30 – 40 inches

80 – 120 inches

© Diagram Visual Information Ltd.

Key words

leeward
orographic lifting
rainshadow

Rainshadows

- A *rainshadow* is an area that receives less rainfall than surrounding areas. Rainshadows occur on the leeward sides of mountains. Much of the water vapor in the air is precipitated due to orographic lifting before the air reaches the rainshadow area.
- Rainfall on the west coast of the United States is dominated by two rainshadows. One occurs in the inland valleys of California, Oregon, and Washington. The second lies to the west of the Sierra Nevada and Cascade ranges.

Average annual precipitation: USA

Average annual rainfall across the United States

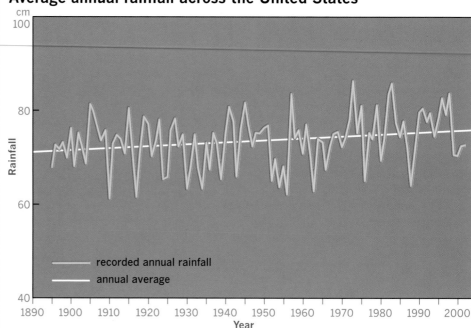

Average annual precipitation

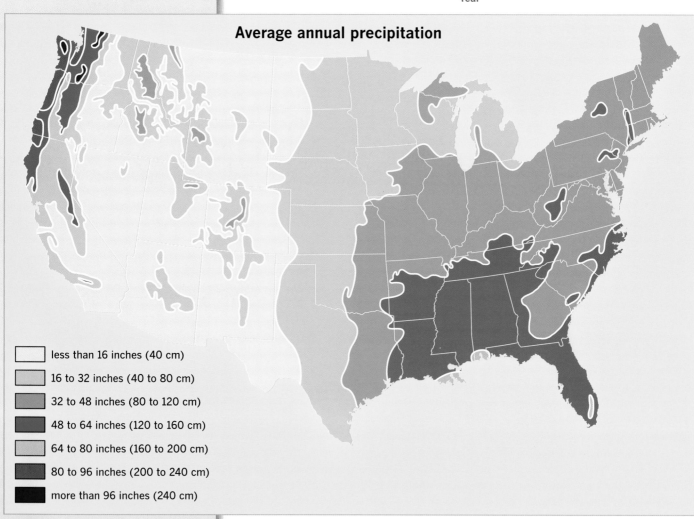

- less than 16 inches (40 cm)
- 16 to 32 inches (40 to 80 cm)
- 32 to 48 inches (80 to 120 cm)
- 48 to 64 inches (120 to 160 cm)
- 64 to 80 inches (160 to 200 cm)
- 80 to 96 inches (200 to 240 cm)
- more than 96 inches (240 cm)

Average monthly rainfall: USA: January and July

U.S. rainfall

- The coastal regions of Washington, Oregon, and northern California receive the highest average annual rainfall.
- The high rainfall along the northern Pacific coast in winter is due to maritime polar (mP) air masses that are comparatively warmer and moister than the air masses over land. They produce frequent and heavy precipitation along the coast.
- Maritime tropical (mT) air masses bring warm, moisture-laden air to the southern states throughout the year, but penetrate farther inland during the summer months.

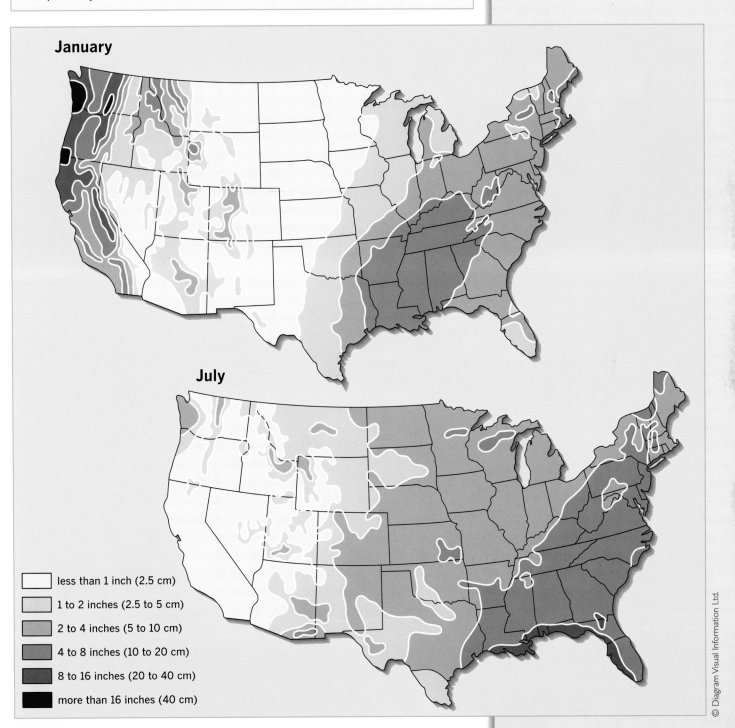

January

July

- less than 1 inch (2.5 cm)
- 1 to 2 inches (2.5 to 5 cm)
- 2 to 4 inches (5 to 10 cm)
- 4 to 8 inches (10 to 20 cm)
- 8 to 16 inches (20 to 40 cm)
- more than 16 inches (40 cm)

The world's wettest and driest places

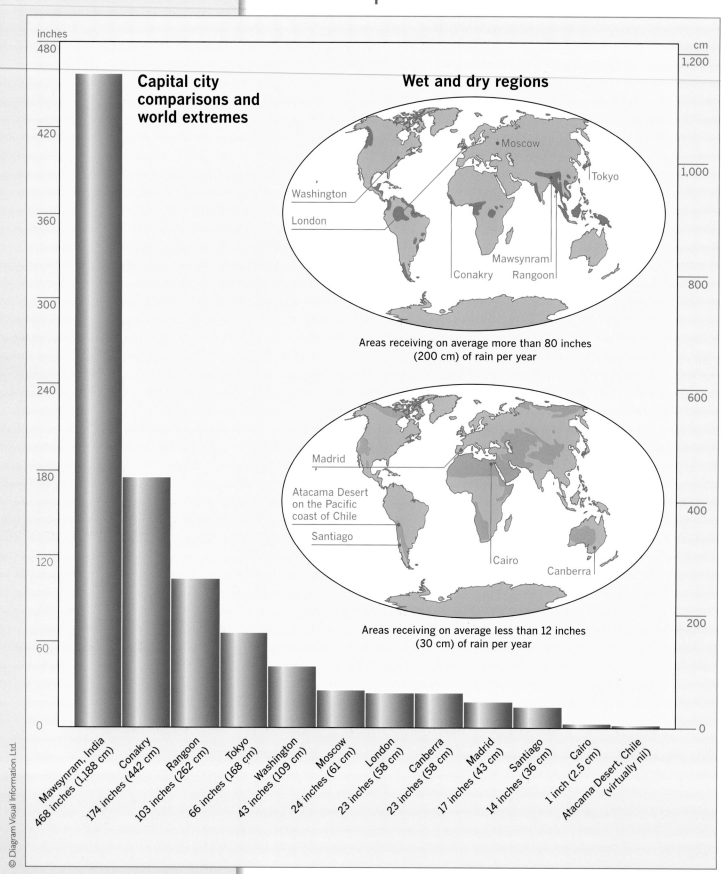

inches

480

420

360

300

240

180

120

60

0

cm

1,200

1,000

800

600

400

200

0

Capital city comparisons and world extremes

Wet and dry regions

Moscow

Tokyo

Washington

London

Mawsynram

Conakry   Rangoon

Areas receiving on average more than 80 inches (200 cm) of rain per year

Madrid

Atacama Desert on the Pacific coast of Chile

Santiago

Cairo

Canberra

Areas receiving on average less than 12 inches (30 cm) of rain per year

Mawsynram, India
468 inches (1,188 cm)

Conakry
174 inches (442 cm)

Rangoon
103 inches (262 cm)

Tokyo
66 inches (168 cm)

Washington
43 inches (109 cm)

Moscow
24 inches (61 cm)

London
23 inches (58 cm)

Canberra
23 inches (58 cm)

Madrid
17 inches (43 cm)

Santiago
14 inches (36 cm)

Cairo
1 inch (2.5 cm)

Atacama Desert, Chile
(virtually nil)

Rainfall variability

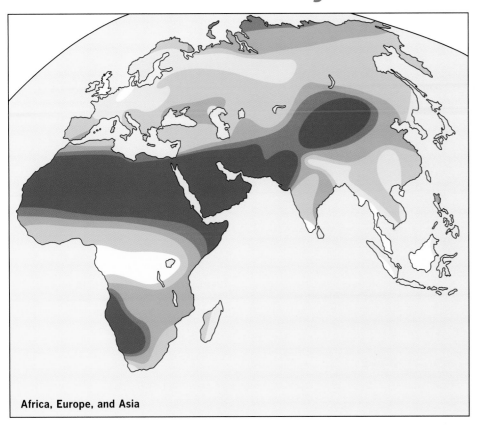

Africa, Europe, and Asia

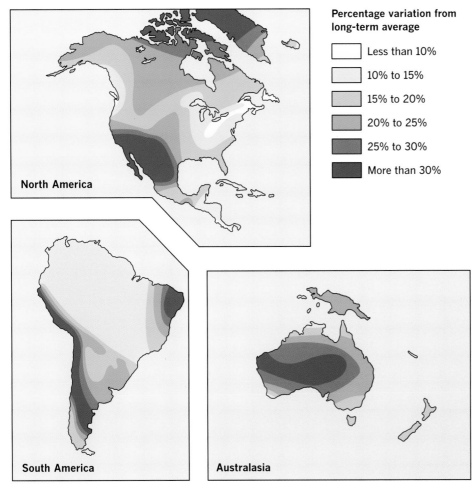

North America

Percentage variation from long-term average

☐	Less than 10%
☐	10% to 15%
☐	15% to 20%
☐	20% to 25%
☐	25% to 30%
☐	More than 30%

South America

Australasia

Key words

dry season
equatorial
latitude
rain day

Seasonal and daily distribution

- Annual rainfall figures do not reveal the marked seasonal variation in rainfall that can occur in some locations.
- For example, Los Angeles receives about 15 inches (38 cm) of rain annually, but about 60 percent of that occurs during the three winter months and almost none during the three summer months.
- Furthermore, even during the months of highest rainfall, rain only falls on about six days of each month. These are sometimes referred to as *rain days*.

Geographical distribution

- There are very large differences in rainfall variation across Earth.
- In equatorial latitudes, rainfall tends to be abundant and fairly consistent throughout the year. In other words there is little seasonal variation in rainfall, just as there is little seasonal variation in temperature.
- Between latitudes 10° and 20°, overall rainfall decreases and there is a dry season over the winter months. This effect tends to be more pronounced on the west side of a continent than the east.
- Between latitudes 30° and 40° rainfall tends to be greater in the winter rather than the summer months. Again, this is more pronounced on the west side of a continent than the east.
- For latitudes greater than 40° there is usually no dry season. However, rainfall is not seasonally constant. The western edges of continents in this region are usually wet throughout the year with a maximum in the winter. The interiors of these continents often have their maximum rainfall in the summer.

COMPONENTS OF WEATHER

Rainbows

Key words

antisolar point
primary rainbow
rainbow
secondary
  rainbow

Rainbows

- A rainbow is an optical phenomenon produced by the reflection and refraction of sunlight by water droplets in the atmosphere.
- Rainbows are seen when the Sun is behind the observer, and rain (or mist, or spray) lies in front of the observer.
- The rainbow appears as an arc because the Earth-bound observer is on the center line of the optical system. Airline passengers occasionally see a rainbow in its full glory—as a complete circle.
- A secondary bow is often seen outside the primary, with the sequence of colors reversed.

Water droplets

A ray of light striking a water droplet may be refracted and internally reflected in one of two ways depending on its angle of incidence. This is why two bows are sometimes visible.

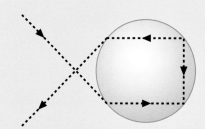

Refraction and internal reflection of ray producing a 42° primary rainbow

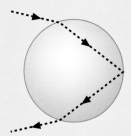

Refraction and internal reflection of ray producing a 51° secondary rainbow

Primary and secondary rainbows

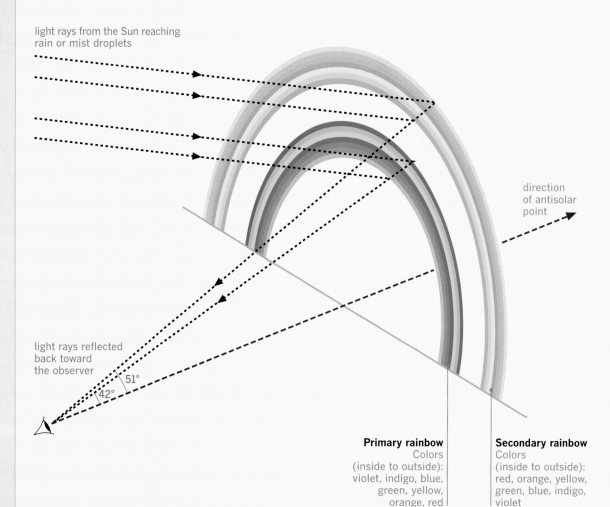

light rays from the Sun reaching rain or mist droplets

direction of antisolar point

light rays reflected back toward the observer

51°
42°

Primary rainbow
Colors
(inside to outside):
violet, indigo, blue,
green, yellow,
orange, red

Secondary rainbow
Colors
(inside to outside):
red, orange, yellow,
green, blue, indigo,
violet

Haloes, sun dogs, and arcs

Cloud crystals

- Haloes, sun dogs, and arcs are optical phenomena produced by the reflection and refraction of sunlight by ice crystals in the atmosphere.
- These crystals are commonly plate-shaped or columnar. Both types are six-sided.
- Plate crystals tend to drift through the air with their large faces horizontal to the ground. Columnar crystals tend to drift with their long axis vertical to the ground. These orientations influence the way in which light is reflected and refracted through the crystals.
- The size of ice crystals is also significant: larger crystals tend to have cleaner faces and angles and produce sharper images.

Key words

22° halo	*lower tangent arc*
arc	*parhelion*
circumzenithal	*parhelic circle*
arc	*sun dog*
halo	*upper tangent arc*

Optical effects produced by ice crystals

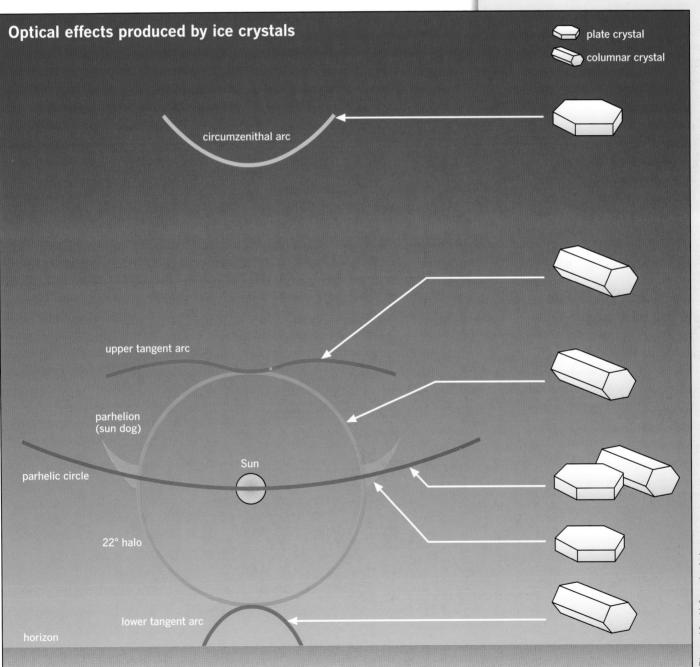

plate crystal

columnar crystal

circumzenithal arc

upper tangent arc

parhelion (sun dog)

parhelic circle

Sun

22° halo

lower tangent arc

horizon

Mirages

Key words

inferior mirage
mirage
superior mirage

Inferior and superior

- A mirage is an optical phenomenon caused by the refraction of light through layers of air with different densities.
- Mirages commonly occur where air temperature changes rapidly with increasing altitude. Cooler air has a higher density than warmer air.
- Rapid decreases in air temperature occur with increasing altitude over surfaces such as roads or landscapes with little vegetation that are directly heated by the Sun.
- Rapid increases in temperature occur with increasing altitude over cold seas or expanses of ice.
- An *inferior mirage* is a mirage in which the image produced appears below the object that is its source.
- Inferior mirages occur where air temperature rapidly decreases with height.
- A *superior mirage* is a mirage in which the image produced appears above the object that is its source.
- Superior mirages occur where air temperature rapidly increases with height.

Inferior mirage

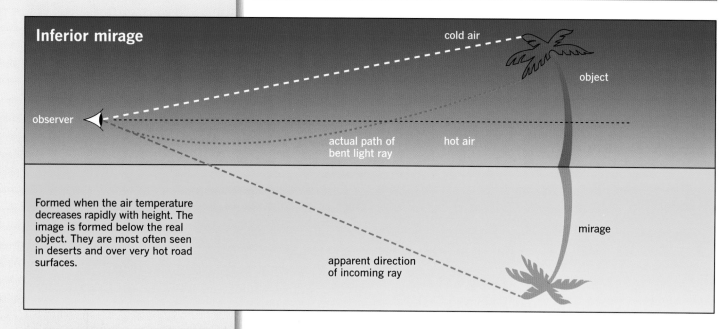

Formed when the air temperature decreases rapidly with height. The image is formed below the real object. They are most often seen in deserts and over very hot road surfaces.

Superior mirage

Formed when the air temperature increases rapidly with height. The image is formed above the real object. They are most often seen over water and in mountain regions.

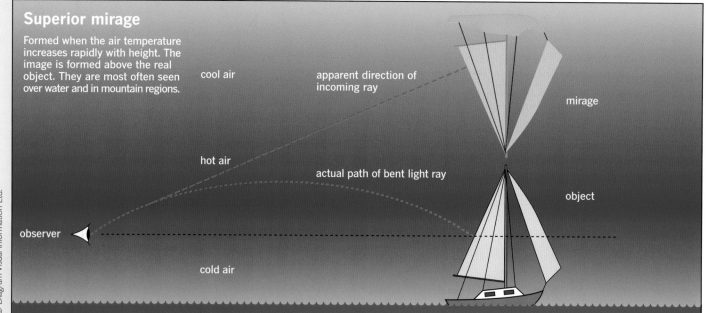

Lightning strike

Exchanges of lightning

a

b

c

Key words

leader stroke   thunderstorm
lightning
positive streamer
return stroke
thunder

Lightning formation

● Lightning is an electrostatic discharge most often produced during a thunderstorm. It may be a discharge between a cloud and Earth's surface (**a**), between two parts of the same cloud (**b**), or between two separate clouds (**c**).

● Lightning only occurs between two locations with opposite electrical charges. The movement of water and ice particles in a thunderstorm cloud is thought to result in regions of positive and negative charge.

Lightning strike

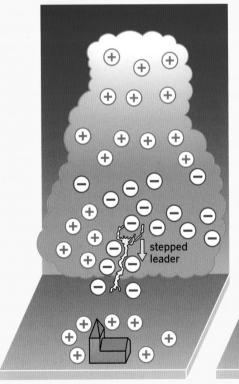

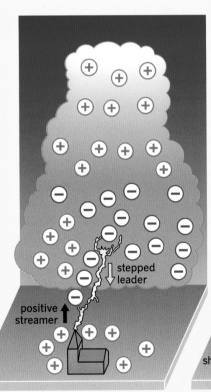

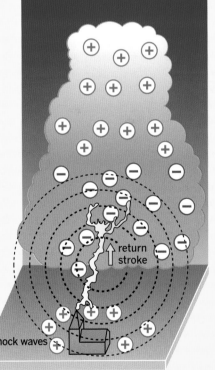

1 Stepped leader
A path of ionization air known as a *stepped leader* extends downward from the cloud toward the ground. Stepped leaders often have a branching structure.

2 Positive streamer
As a stepped leader approaches the ground *positive streamers* reach upwards from the points of tall buildings, trees, and other objects that protrude into the air.

3 Return stroke
When a stepped leader connects with a positive streamer an ionized path between cloud and ground is established. At this point a very luminous *return stroke* occurs as current flows along the path. Sudden heating of the air causes shock waves to form, which are heard as thunder.

Thunderstorms

Key words

anvil	precipitation
cirrus	squall
cumulonimbus	stratosphere
cumulus	thunderhead
dew point	thunderstorm
downdraft	
midlatitude	
cyclone	

Thunderstorm formation

- Thunderstorms are formed by the same forces that drive the formation of all cloud and precipitation. In the case of a thunderstorm, however, these forces are more intense or prolonged.
- Cumulus clouds form as moist rising air reaches its dew point temperature. If more warm air continues to be added, very large cumulonimbus clouds form that may reach altitudes of 12 miles (20 km). The top of the cumulonimbus cloud may take on a characteristic anvil shape as high winds in the stratosphere spread its ice crystals horizontally.
- When the upward flowing warm air reaches its maximum altitude it begins to sink and creates downdrafts within the cloud. These downdrafts encourage precipitation to form as water droplets collide and coalesce.
- When the upward flow of moist air slows so that downdrafts dominate, a thunderstorm enters its dissipating stage and heavy precipitation is released.
- The most common cause of thunderstorm formation is direct solar heating of moist landmasses.
- More intense thunderstorms can form in association with midlatitude cyclones.

 positive charge

 negative charge

⬅ winds

A thunderstorm

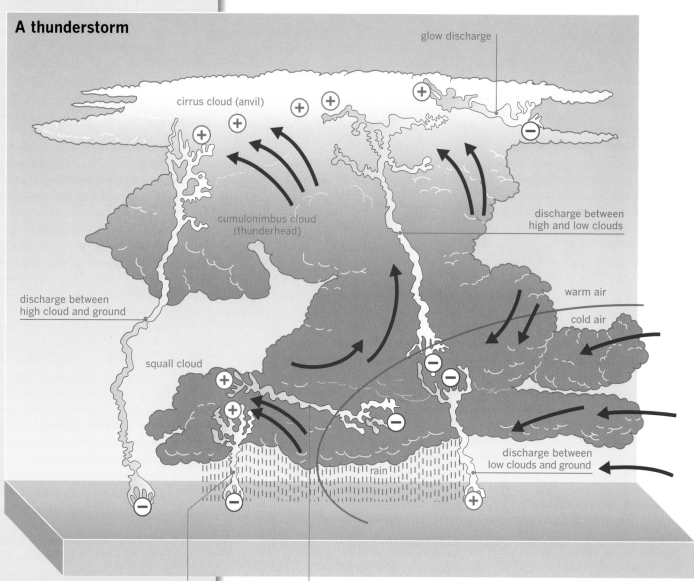

glow discharge

cirrus cloud (anvil)

cumulonimbus cloud (thunderhead)

discharge between high and low clouds

discharge between high cloud and ground

warm air

cold air

squall cloud

discharge between low clouds and ground

rain

discharge between squall cloud and ground

discharge between front and back of storm cloud

Annual number of days with thunderstorms: USA

Key words

air mass	thunderstorm
leeward	
maritime tropical	
(mT)	

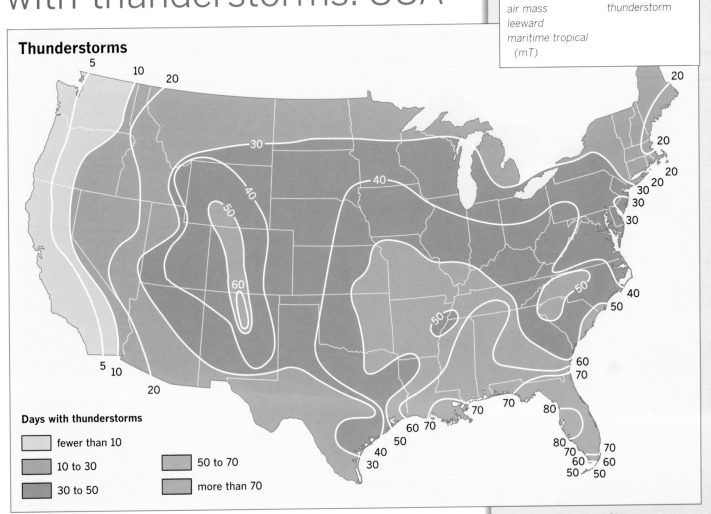

Thunderstorms

Days with thunderstorms

- fewer than 10
- 10 to 30
- 30 to 50
- 50 to 70
- more than 70

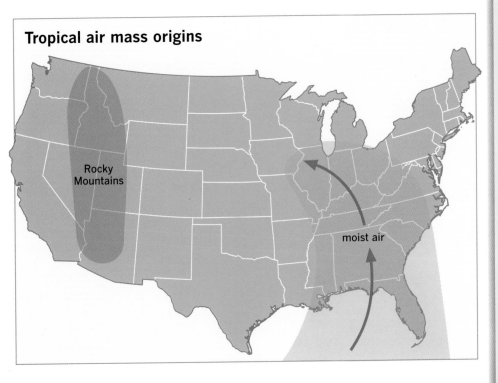

Tropical air mass origins

Rocky Mountains

moist air

Thunderstorm frequency

- Thunderstorms are most frequent in the southeast and in parts of Colorado, Arizona, and New Mexico.
- This distribution indicates that factors other than intense solar heating are necessary for their formation since these are not the only areas to experience intense solar heating.
- Moisture is also necessary and is provided in large quantities by maritime tropical (mT) air masses that form over the Gulf of Mexico.
- The pocket of high thunderstorm frequency that stretches across Colorado and New Mexico is a result of the orographic lifting of maritime tropical air by the eastern slopes of the Rocky Mountains.

Key words

atmosphere
atmospheric
 pressure
millibar
sea level

Global atmospheric pressure: January

Average global atmospheric pressure at sea level (January)

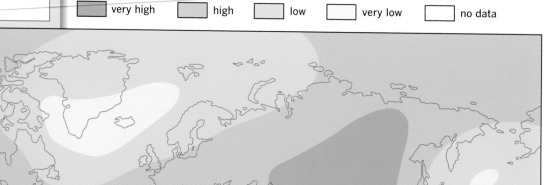

very high ▪ high ▪ low ▪ very low ▪ no data

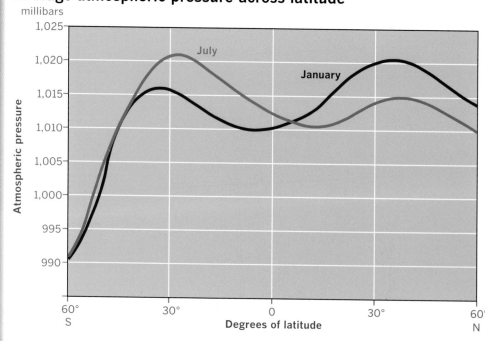

Atmospheric pressure

- Atmospheric pressure is a result of Earth's gravity acting on the mass of air in the atmosphere.
- Atmospheric pressure is expressed in *millibars*. A millibar is a force equal to 1,000 dynes per square centimeter.
- A column of air with a cross-sectional area of one square inch (6.5 cm²) stretching from sea level to the top of the atmosphere weighs about 14.7 pounds (6.7 kg). This can be expressed as an average atmospheric pressure at sea level of about 1,013 millibars.
- The density and pressure of gases in the atmosphere decreases exponentially as altitude above Earth's surface increases.

Average atmospheric pressure across latitude

Global atmospheric pressure: July

Average global atmospheric pressure at sea level (July)

Key words

atmospheric
 pressure
insolation
monsoon
sea level

subpolar
subtropical

| | very high | | high | | low | | very low | | no data |

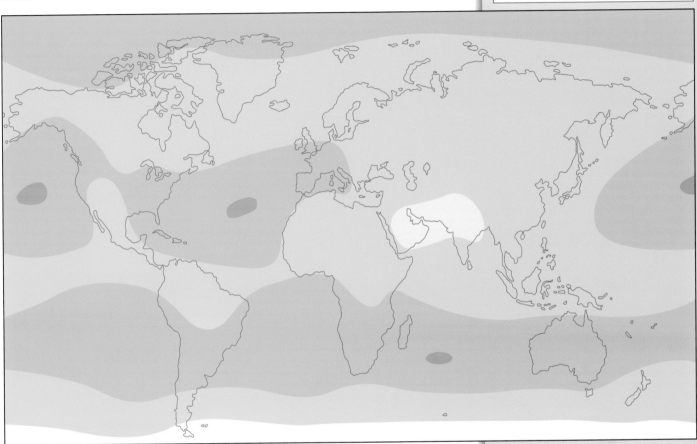

Patterns of pressure variation

- Pressure belts and cells tend to migrate northwards in July and southwards in January. This corresponds to similar patterns of seasonal migration exhibited by insolation and surface temperatures.
- Atmospheric pressure is generally higher in the hemisphere experiencing winter than in that experiencing summer.
- Subtropical high-pressure cells are most developed over the eastern margins of the oceans.
- The Southern Hemisphere subpolar low-pressure system is deep throughout the year and forms a continuous trough around Antarctica. The Northern Hemisphere subpolar low-pressure system is less deep and consists of individual cells that become shallower in the summer.

- Between December and February high-pressure zones develop over central Asia ("Siberian high"), off the coast of California ("Hawaiian high"), over central North America ("Canadian high"), over southern Europe and north Africa ("Azores high"), and over the subtropical oceans of the Southern Hemisphere.
- Between June and August major high-pressure zones in the Northern Hemisphere weaken or dissipate. The Hawaiian high and Azores high intensify and expand northwards. High-pressure zones form over Australia and central Antarctica ("South Polar high"). Low-pressure zones responsible for the Asian monsoon also develop.

Pressure variation

- No part of Earth's surface exhibits constant atmospheric pressure. Atmospheric phenomena produce localized high- and low-pressure zones that are constantly shifting. Large-scale, global variations in atmospheric pressure at sea level are also evident.
- Differences in atmospheric pressure produce "pressure gradients" between different regions.
- Air always flows down a pressure gradient. In other words, from a high-pressure zone to a low-pressure zone.
- These global patterns of atmospheric pressure variation are thought to be the driving force behind prevailing global wind systems.

Key words

air mass	frontal weather
continental antarctic (AA)	maritime polar (mP)
continental arctic (A)	maritime tropical (mT)
continental polar (cP)	source region
continental tropical (cT)	

Air masses

- An *air mass* is a large body of air with relatively consistent temperature and humidity.
- Air masses typically cover thousands of square miles and form predictably over particular geographical regions.
- Frontal weather systems form where air masses with differing characteristics interact. The general form and location of these frontal systems is also predictable from year to year.

Source region types

- An air mass is classified according to its *source region*. A source region is the geographical area in which an air mass originates.
- The temperature and moisture characteristics of a source region determine the original temperature and humidity of an air mass.
- A source region's temperature characteristic may be *equatorial*, *tropical*, *polar*, *arctic*, or *antarctic*.
- A source region's moisture characteristic may be either *continental* or *maritime*.
- Combining these two characteristics gives six possible source regions: maritime polar (mP); continental polar (cP); maritime tropical (mT); continental tropical (cT); continental arctic (A); and continental antarctic (AA). Arctic and antarctic source regions are never maritime. Air masses are commonly described according to their source regions.
- Some air masses are also labelled *K* or *W*. *K* indicates that the air mass is cooler than the terrain it is moving across and *W* that it is warmer than the terrain it is moving across.

Air masses

Classification of air masses

Group	Subgroup	Source region	Properties at source
Polar (including arctic)	continental polar (cP)	Arctic, northern Eurasia, northern North America, Antarctic	cold, dry, and stable
	maritime polar (mP)	oceans poleward of 40 to 50 degrees	cool, moist, and unstable
Tropical (including equatorial)	continental tropical (cT)	low latitude deserts	hot, dry, and stable
	maritime tropical (mT)	tropical and subtropical oceans	warm, moist, and unstable

Principal air masses affecting North America

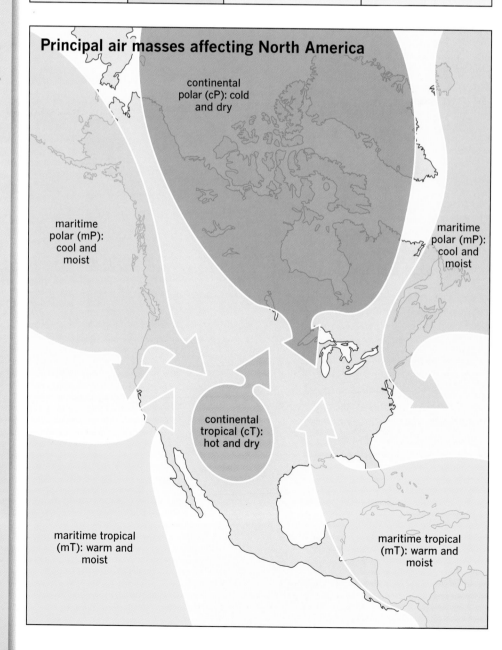

continental polar (cP): cold and dry

maritime polar (mP): cool and moist

maritime polar (mP): cool and moist

maritime tropical (mT): warm and moist

continental tropical (cT): hot and dry

maritime tropical (mT): warm and moist

Air masses over North America: winter

Key words

air mass
continental polar
  (cP)
fog
leeward
maritime polar
  (cP)

maritime tropical
  (mT)
precipitation
source region

Winter air masses

- Air mass source regions are subject to different climatic conditions from season to season.
- In winter, continental Polar (cP) air masses form over the very dry and very cold interior of Canada. These air masses are intensively cooled by radiant cooling from the snow-covered surface.
- Southward surges of winter cP air masses produce freezing conditions and clear skies across a large part of the continent. These air masses rarely reach the western seaboard.
- In winter, maritime Tropical (mT) air masses originating over the Gulf of Mexico and the tropical Atlantic encounter cP air masses as they move inland. Dense fog or prolonged light rain is often the result. This is the zone of air-mass mixing that covers the eastern seaboard, the southeast and the Gulf of Mexico.
- Maritime Polar (mP) air masses are formed over the north Pacific. They are relatively warmer and moister than the winter cP air masses they encounter along the western seaboard or to the leeward side of the western highlands. This zone of interaction produces frequent and heavy precipitation throughout the winter.

→ direction of movement

☐ continental polar air (cP)

☐ maritime polar air (mP)

☐ maritime tropical air (mT)

☐ zone of air mass mixing and interaction

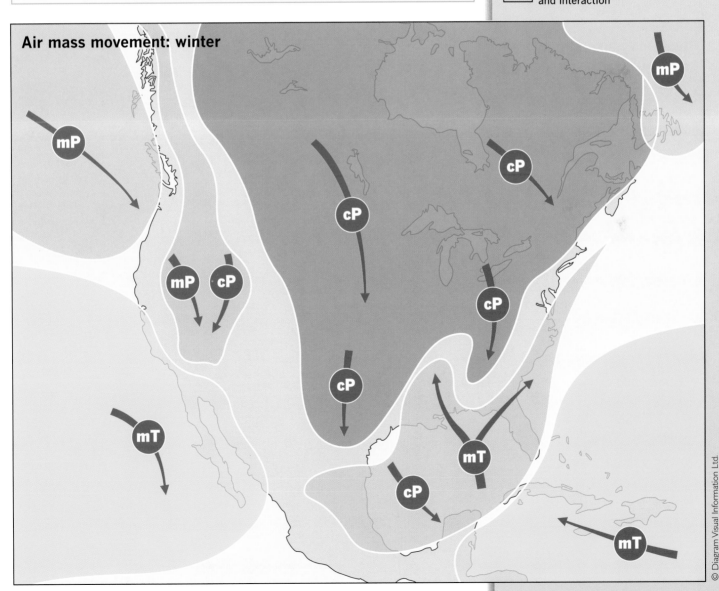

Air mass movement: winter

Air masses over North America: summer

© Diagram Visual Information Ltd.

Key words

air mass
continental polar
(cP)
continental
tropical (cT)
maritime polar
(mP)

maritime tropical
(mT)
precipitation
source region

direction of movement

continental polar air (cP)

maritime polar air (mP)

continental tropical air (cT)

maritime tropical air (mT)

zone of air mass mixing
and interaction

Summer air masses

- Air mass source regions are subject to different climatic conditions from season to season.
- In summer, continental Polar (cP) air masses form over terrain that is dry but intensively heated during the long days. These air masses are heated by the surface but receive little moisture.
- As summer cP air masses move southward across the heart of the continent they are slowly warmed and moistened, becoming more unstable the farther south they travel.
- In summer, maritime Tropical (mT) air masses that form over the Gulf of Mexico and the tropical Atlantic move much

farther inland than they do in the winter. This is because of the much greater sea-to-land pressure gradients over this region that exist in the summer.
- Summer mT air masses become even warmer and more unstable as they travel across land. These mT air masses are responsible for most precipitation in the United States east of the Rocky Mountains.
- In the summer, maritime Polar (mP) air masses originate over a north Pacific that is cooler than the continental landmass. These air masses push cool stable air along the western seaboard.

Air mass movement: summer

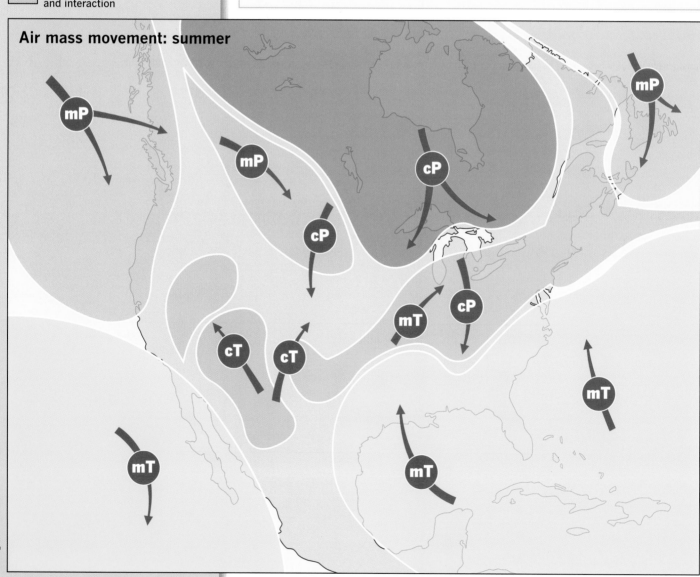

Cyclones and anticyclones

Cyclone in cross section

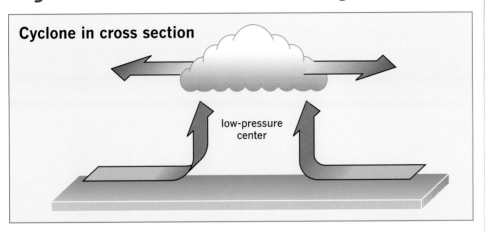

low-pressure center

Anticyclone in cross section

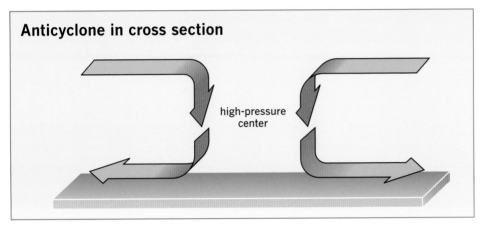

high-pressure center

Cyclonic winds

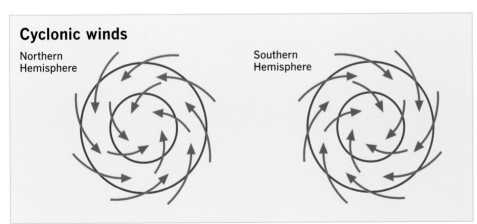

Northern Hemisphere

Southern Hemisphere

Anticyclonic winds

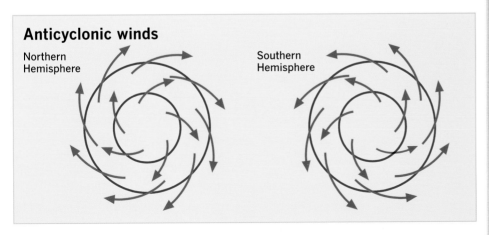

Northern Hemisphere

Southern Hemisphere

Key words

anticyclone
anticyclonic wind
convergence
Coriolis effect
cyclone

cyclonic wind
divergence

Convergence and divergence

- Due to the nature of global air circulation there are always regions where winds converge and others where they diverge.
- Where winds converge, air is forced upwards and low-pressure centers result. Where they diverge, air is forced downwards to replace the air moving away. High-pressure centers result.
- Ascending air tends to cool and its water vapor is likely to condense, producing clouds, storms, and precipitation.
- Descending air tends to be warmed and dried so that the development of clouds and precipitation is less likely.

Cyclonic and anticyclonic winds

- Because Earth rotates, airflows are subject to the Coriolis effect.
- The Coriolis effect results in winds that follow curved paths. Winds curve to the left in the Northern Hemisphere and to the right in the Southern Hemisphere.
- The combination of curving wind paths and the inflow and outflow of wind due to convergence or divergence results in *cyclonic winds* and *anticyclonic winds*.
- *Cyclonic winds* are winds that spiral inwards to a low-pressure zone.
- *Anticyclonic winds* are winds that spiral outwards from a high-pressure zone.

© Diagram Visual Information Ltd.

Key words

air mass	occluded front
Coriolis effect	polar circle
cyclogenesis	polar front
cyclone	tropics
front	
midlatitude	

Midlatitude cyclones

- *Midlatitude* or *frontal cyclones* are cyclonic storms that develop in latitudes between the tropics and the polar circles.
- They are the dominant determiners of weather across these regions of Earth, and develop where warm moist air masses from lower latitudes encounter cold dry air masses from higher latitudes. These zones of mixing air masses are known as the *polar fronts*.
- Midlatitude cyclones develop in a predictable series of stages. This development is known as *cyclogenesis*.

Cyclogenesis

- A midlatitude cyclone begins to develop at a weak disturbance along the front between a cold polar air mass and a warm tropical air mass.
- The warmer air is forced to rise over the cooler air mass. As the warm air rises, it follows a curved path as determined by the *Coriolis effect*.
- At the same time, cooler air begins to flow into the area behind the moving warm air, also following a curved path determined by the Coriolis effect.
- As these movements of air continue and become more pronounced, the characteristic rotating wind systems of a cyclone become evident.
- Because cold fronts move about twice as rapidly as warm fronts, the cold front in a cyclone eventually circles behind and catches up with the advancing warm front. This results in an *occluded front*. The cyclone dissipates within one or two days of an occluded front forming.
- The entire process from cyclogenesis to dissipation usually lasts between three and ten days.

Life cycle of a cyclone

A cyclone in three dimensions

A kink forms on the polar front.

A cyclone deepens; warm and cold fronts enclose a sector of warm, moist air.

A mature cyclone has developed, with its associated clouds and weather.

→ warm air

→ cold air

A cyclone as shown on a weather chart

A kink forms on the polar front.

A cyclone deepens; warm and cold fronts enclose a sector of warm, moist air.

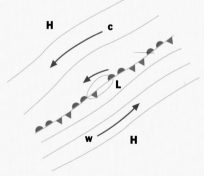

A mature cyclone has developed, with its associated clouds and weather.

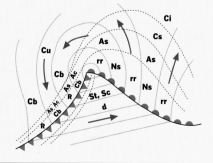

⌒⌒ warm front

▲▲▲ cold front

H	high pressure	**Cs**	cirrostratus
L	low pressure	**As**	altostratus
c	cold sector	**Ns**	nimbostratus
w	warm sector	**Cu**	cumulus
d	drizzle	**Cb**	cumulonimbus
rr	light rain	**Ac**	altocumulus
R	heavy rain	**St**	stratus
Ci	cirrus	**Sc**	stratocumulus

Cyclonic weather

Midlatitude cyclone

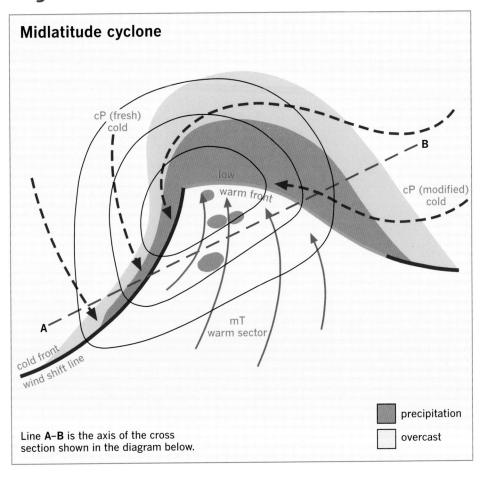

Line **A–B** is the axis of the cross section shown in the diagram below.

■ precipitation
□ overcast

Key words

air mass
cyclone
front
midlatitude
precipitation

tropical cyclone
warm sector

Cyclonic weather

- Cyclones are the prime producers of weather in the midlatitude regions.
- In a mature midlatitude cyclone in the Northern Hemisphere a warm moist front is advancing northwest over a retreating cold air mass. At the same time a cold front is advancing southeast under a retreating warm air mass.
- The warm air between these two fronts is known as the *warm sector*.
- Both the advancing warm air and the warm air being uplifted by the advancing cold air are rising. Warm rising air tends to produce clouds and precipitation.
- Precipitation and winds associated with a midlatitude cyclone are rarely as severe as those associated with tropical cyclones.

Midlatitude cyclone: cross section

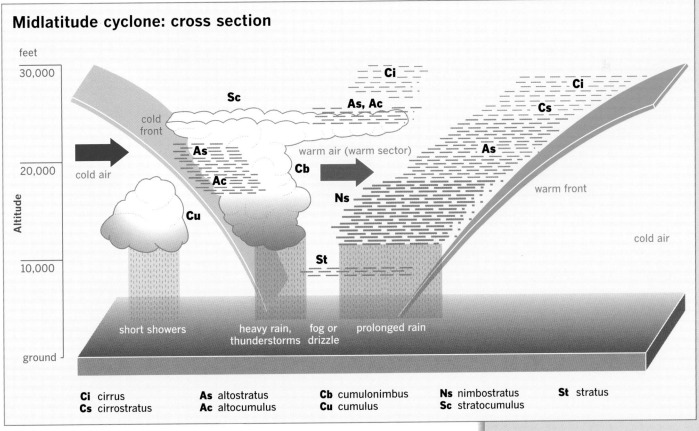

Ci cirrus
Cs cirrostratus
As altostratus
Ac altocumulus
Cb cumulonimbus
Cu cumulus
Ns nimbostratus
Sc stratocumulus
St stratus

Key words

air mass	polar
cold occlusion	tropical
cyclone	warm occlusion
front	warm sector
midlatitude	
occluded front	

Occluded fronts

- In a mature midlatitude cyclone in the Northern Hemisphere a warm moist front is advancing northwest over a retreating cold air mass. At the same time a cold front is advancing southeast under a retreating warm air mass.
- The warm air between these two fronts is known as the *warm sector*.
- Cold fronts tend to advance more rapidly than warm fronts. Eventually, the advancing cold front catches up with the advancing warm front. An *occluded front* is the result of this collision.
- When an occlusion occurs the cold air mass in front of the advancing warm front and the cold air mass behind the advancing cold front are joined. At this point, all the warm air is forced to rise.
- One of the cold air masses is usually warmer than the other cold air mass, although both are colder than the warm air mass that is occluded.
- The advancing cold air mass will rise over the retreating cold air mass or undercut it depending on their relative temperatures.
- When the advancing cold air mass undercuts the retreating cold air mass because it is cooler, a *cold occlusion* is formed.
- When the advancing cold air mass rises above the retreating cold air mass because it is warmer, a *warm occlusion* is formed.
- Clouds and precipitation may be formed as the uplifted retreating air or advancing air is cooled further as it gains altitude.
- Occluded fronts generally dissipate within one or two days and the front between cold polar air and warm tropical air becomes stable again.

Occluded fronts

Occlusion as shown on a weather chart

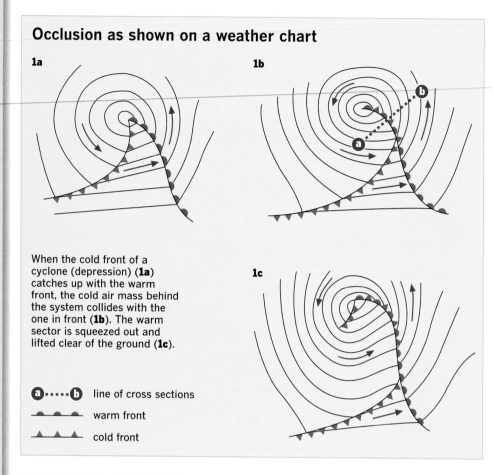

1a

1b

1c

When the cold front of a cyclone (depression) (**1a**) catches up with the warm front, the cold air mass behind the system collides with the one in front (**1b**). The warm sector is squeezed out and lifted clear of the ground (**1c**).

ⓐ·····ⓑ line of cross sections

━●━●━●━ warm front

━▲━▲━▲━ cold front

Cross sections of occluded fronts

2a Warm occlusion

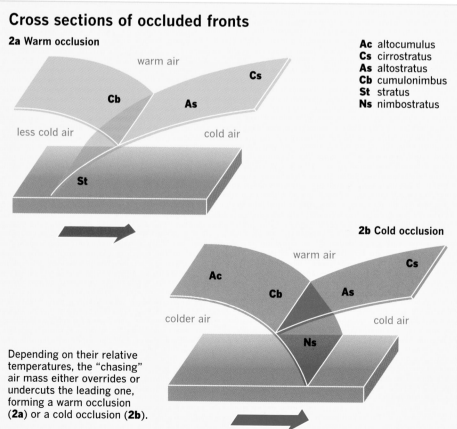

warm air

Cs

Cb

As

less cold air

cold air

St

Ac altocumulus
Cs cirrostratus
As altostratus
Cb cumulonimbus
St stratus
Ns nimbostratus

2b Cold occlusion

warm air

Cs

Ac

Cb

As

colder air

cold air

Ns

Depending on their relative temperatures, the "chasing" air mass either overrides or undercuts the leading one, forming a warm occlusion (**2a**) or a cold occlusion (**2b**).

World's hottest places, by continent/region

Key words

sea level

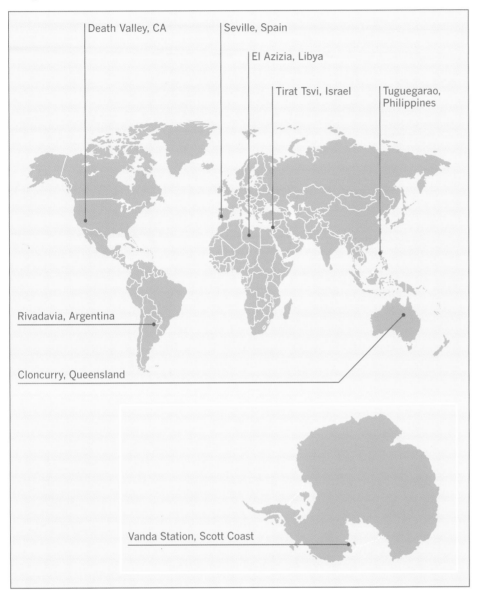

Death Valley, CA

Seville, Spain

El Azizia, Libya

Tirat Tsvi, Israel

Tuguegarao, Philippines

Rivadavia, Argentina

Cloncurry, Queensland

Vanda Station, Scott Coast

Death Valley

- Death Valley is a depression in the Mojave Desert of Southern California, southeast of the Sierra Nevada mountains.
- Badwater Basin in Death Valley holds the record as the lowest point in the Western Hemisphere at 282 feet (86 m) below sea level.
- The highest temperature ever officially recorded in the United States, 134°F (56.7°C), occurred at a location in Death Valley. This is also the second-highest temperature ever officially recorded anywhere in the world.
- Much of the valley is surrounded by high mountains. This, combined with the low elevation of the valley, means that heated air in the valley cannot easily escape. The bare rock of the valley sides also radiates a great deal of heat, compounding the extreme temperatures.
- Death Valley is the only known place in the Western Hemisphere where nighttime temperatures often exceed 100°F (38°C).

Location	Continent/region	Height above/ below sea level in feet (meters)		Maximum temperature °F (°C)		Date
El Azizia, Libya	Africa	367	(112)	136	(57.8)	13 Sep 1922
Death Valley, CA	North America	–178	(–54)	134	(56.7)	10 Jul 1913
Tirat Tsvi, Israel	Middle East	–722	(–220)	129	(53.9)	21 Jun 1942
Cloncurry, Queensland	Australia	622	(190)	128	(53.3)	16 Jan 1889
Seville, Spain	Europe	26	(7.9)	122	(50.0)	4 Aug 1881
Rivadavia, Argentina	South America	676	(206)	120	(48.9)	11 Dec 1905
Tuguegarao, Philippines	Pacific	72	(21.9)	108	(42.2)	29 Apr 1912
Vanda Station, Scott Coast	Antarctica	49	(14.9)	59	(15.0)	5 Jan 1974

Key words

albedo
geomagnetic
    South Pole
sea level
solar radiation

World's coldest places, by continent/region

Antarctica

- Antarctica has the coldest average temperatures of any region on Earth.
- The lowest air temperature at Earth's surface ever officially recorded, −128.6°F (−89.2°C), occurred at the Russian Vostok research station near the geomagnetic South Pole.
- The extremely cold temperatures common across Antarctica are due to three factors: lack of sunlight, elevation, and the high reflectiveness of the surface (also known as high *albedo*).
- For three months of the year there is almost no sunlight due to Earth's tilted axis of rotation. This is a factor the region has in common with the Arctic.
- Antarctica has the highest average elevation of any continent.
- Antarctica is covered with snow and ice that reflect up to 90 percent of the solar radiation that reaches the surface. In addition, the interior of Antarctica rarely has any cloud cover that could absorb solar radiation and radiate heat energy into the air.

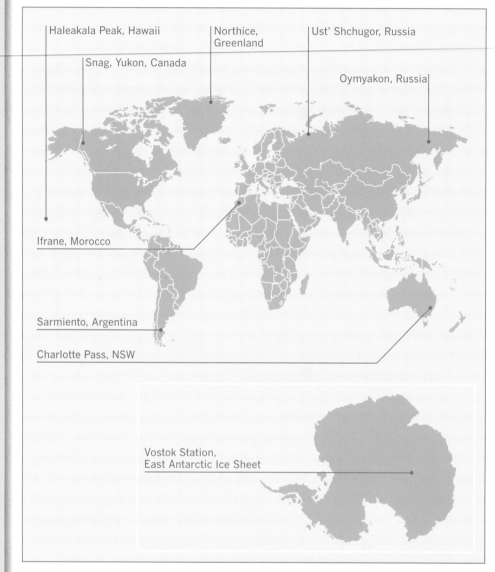

Haleakala Peak, Hawaii

Snag, Yukon, Canada

Northice, Greenland

Ust' Shchugor, Russia

Oymyakon, Russia

Ifrane, Morocco

Sarmiento, Argentina

Charlotte Pass, NSW

Vostok Station, East Antarctic Ice Sheet

Location	Continent/region	Height above/ below sea level in feet (meters)		Minimum temperature °F (°C)		Date
Vostok Station, East Antarctic Ice Sheet	Antarctica	11,220	(3,420)	−128.6	(−89.2)	21 Jul 1983
Oimekon, Russia	Asia	2,625	(800)	−90	(−67.8)	6 Feb 1933
Northice, Greenland	North America	7,687	(2,343)	−87	(−66.1)	9 Jan 1954
Snag, Yukon, Canada	North America	2,120	(646)	−81.4	(−63.0)	3 Feb 1947
Ust' Shchugor, Russia	Europe	279	(85)	−67	(−55.0)	Date unknown
Sarmiento, Argentina	South America	879	(268)	−27	(−32.8)	1 Jun 1907
Ifrane, Morocco	Africa	5,364	(1,635)	−11	(−23.9)	11 Feb 1935
Charlotte Pass, NSW	Australia	5,758	(1,755)	−9.4	(−23.0)	29 Jun 1994
Haleakala Peak, Hawaii	Pacific	9,750	(2,972)	−14	(−10.0)	2 Jan 1961

World's wettest places, by continent/region

Key words

monsoon
precipitation
prevailing wind
sea level

Cherrapunji

- Cherrapunji is a town in the Indian state of Meghalaya. It is 4,232 feet (1,290 m) above sea level.
- The area around Cherrapunji receives the greatest annual average rainfall of any location on Earth at about 460 inches (1,170 cm).
- In 2001–02 Cherrapunji received 483 inches (1,226 cm). In 1860–61 it is recorded as having received 901 inches (2,290 cm), though this figure is disputed by modern meteorologists.
- The extreme precipitation received in this region is due to the Asian *monsoon*.
- A monsoon is a seasonal reversal in the direction of prevailing winds caused by the large seasonal variation in temperature over landmasses compared to adjacent oceans.
- During the dry season the prevailing winds in the area blow from the land toward the ocean and little rain falls. During the wet season the prevailing winds blow from the ocean toward the land.
- These winds carry warm moist air that rises as it reaches highlands. As the air rises, its water vapor condenses and forms heavy precipitation.

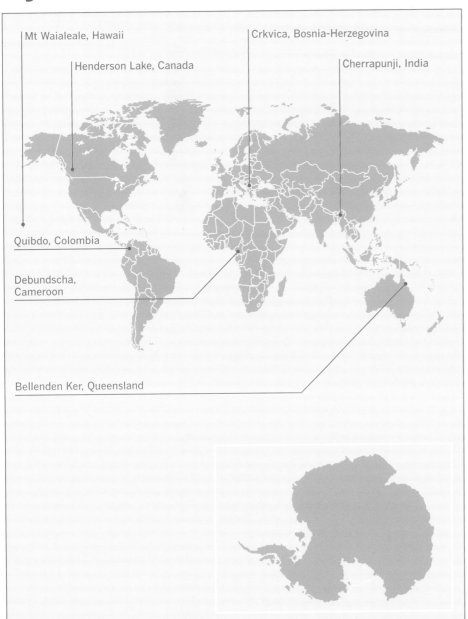

Mt Waialeale, Hawaii
Henderson Lake, Canada
Crkvica, Bosnia-Herzegovina
Cherrapunji, India
Quibdo, Colombia
Debundscha, Cameroon
Bellenden Ker, Queensland

Location	Continent/region	Height above/below sea level in feet (meters)		Highest average annual rainfall in inches (centimeters)	
Cherrapunji, India	Asia	4,232	(1,290)	483.0	(1,226.8)
Mt Waialeale, Hawaii	Pacific	5,148	(1,569)	460.0	(1,168.4)
Debundscha, Cameroon	Africa	30	(9)	405.0	(1,028.7)
Quibdo, Colombia	South America	120	(37)	354.0	(899.2)
Bellenden Ker, Queensland	Australia	5,102	(1,555)	340.0	(863.6)
Henderson Lake, Canada	North America	12	(4)	256.0	(650.0)
Crkvica, Bosnia-Herzegovina	Europe	3,337	(1,017)	183.0	(464.8)

© Diagram Visual Information Ltd.

Key words

ocean current
precipitation
sea level
windward

Atacama Desert

- The Atacama Desert stretches along the coast of Chile between the Pacific Ocean and the Andes Mountains.
- Between 1964 and 2001 a weather station at Quillagua in the Atacama Desert recorded an average annual rainfall figure of 0.02 inches (0.5 mm). This is the lowest, consistent average annual rainfall recorded on Earth.
- It is estimated that some locations in the Atacama Desert have received no rain at all for at least 400 years.
- The driest parts of the desert lie between the Pacific coastal range of mountains in the west and the foothills of the Andes range in the east.
- The cold Humboldt ocean current that flows along the coast of Chile cools moist air approaching the coast from the Pacific Ocean. This causes much of the water vapor to condense and precipitate over the coastal water.
- The little water vapor that reaches the coast tends to be precipitated on the windward (eastern) side of the Pacific coastal range and rarely reaches the desert areas inland.

World's driest places, by continent/region

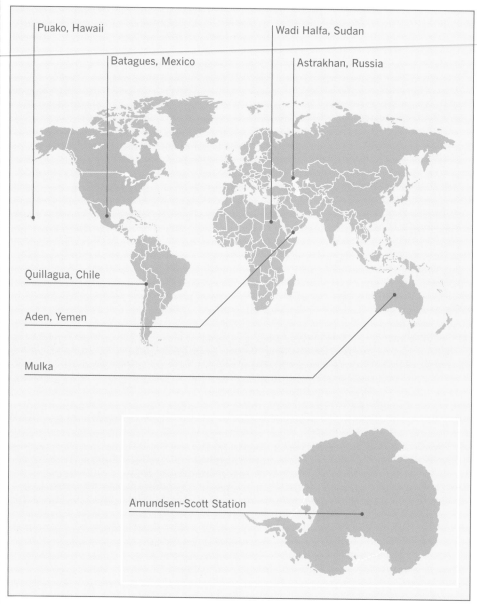

Puako, Hawaii

Batagues, Mexico

Wadi Halfa, Sudan

Astrakhan, Russia

Quillagua, Chile

Aden, Yemen

Mulka

Amundsen-Scott Station

Location	Continent/region	Height above/below sea level in feet (meters)		Lowest average annual rainfall in inches (centimeters)	
Quillagua, Chile	South America	95	(29)	0.02	(0.05)
Wadi Halfa, Sudan	Africa	410	(125)	0.1	(0.25)
Amundsen-Scott Station	Antarctica	9,186	(2,800)	0.8	(2.03)
Batagues, Mexico	North America	16	(5)	1.2	(3.05)
Aden, Yemen	Middle East	22	(7)	1.8	(4.57)
Mulka	Australia	160	(49)	4.05	(10.28)
Astrakhan, Russia	Europe	45	(14)	6.4	(16.26)
Puako, Hawaii	Pacific	5	(1.5)	8.9	(22.60)

Rainfall records: USA

Record rainfall in 24 hours

Figures indicate the highest total rainfall during a 24-hour period (inches) at a National Weather Service weather station. Figures apply to a single location in each state only: they are not statewide averages.

Key words

precipitation

5–10 inches (13–25 cm)	20–25 inches (50–63 cm)
10–15 inches (25–38 cm)	25–30 inches (63–76 cm)
15–20 inches (38–50 cm)	30+ inches (76+ cm)

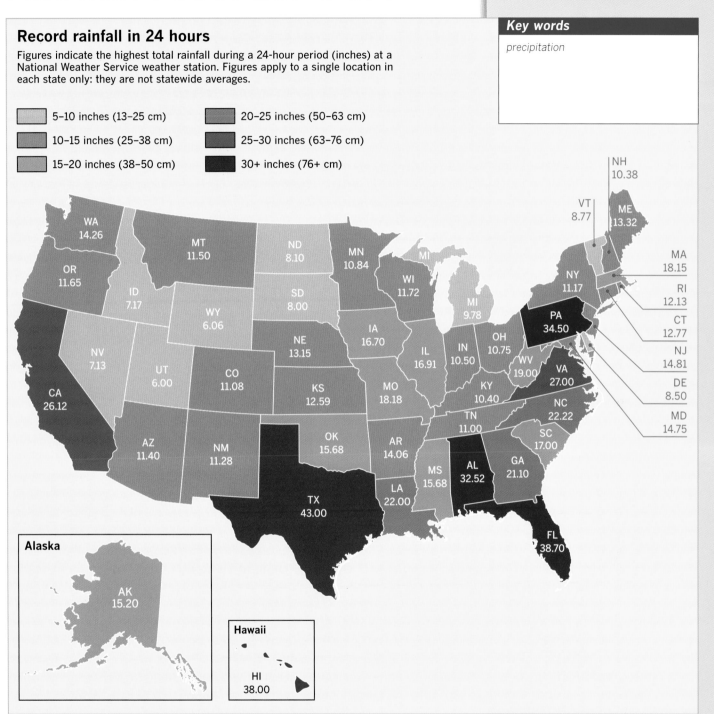

NH 10.38
VT 8.77
ME 13.32
MA 18.15
RI 12.13
CT 12.77
NJ 14.81
DE 8.50
MD 14.75

WA 14.26
MT 11.50
ND 8.10
MN 10.84
MI
WI 11.72
NY 11.17
OR 11.65
ID 7.17
SD 8.00
MI 9.78
PA 34.50
WY 6.06
IA 16.70
OH 10.75
WV 19.00
VA 27.00
NV 7.13
NE 13.15
IL 16.91
IN 10.50
UT 6.00
CO 11.08
KS 12.59
MO 18.18
KY 10.40
NC 22.22
CA 26.12
TN 11.00
SC 17.00
AZ 11.40
NM 11.28
OK 15.68
AR 14.06
MS 15.68
AL 32.52
GA 21.10
LA 22.00
TX 43.00
FL 38.70

Alaska

AK 15.20

Hawaii

HI 38.00

U.S. weather data

- The National Weather Service (NWS) is the branch of the National Oceanic and Atmospheric Administration (NOAA) responsible for collecting data about the weather across the United States.
- The NWS utilizes a network of more than 600 automated weather stations known as the Automated Service Observing System (ASOS). In addition a network of more than 11,000 volunteer weather observers known as the Cooperative Observer Program (COOP) with a variety of approved equipment also provides daily data.
- NWS data is collected and collated by the National Climatic Data Center (NCDC). The NCDC has the world's largest archive of weather data. It has comprehensive weather data of the geography of the United States for the last 150 years.

Highest total annual rainfall: USA

Highest total annual rainfall

Figures indicate the highest total rainfall during a year (inches) at a National Weather Service weather station. Readings apply to a single location in each state only: they are not statewide averages.

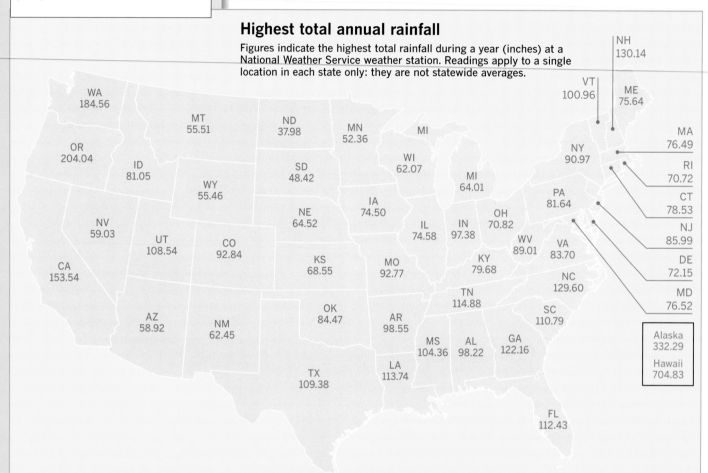

State	Year	Weather station	Elevation: feet
Alabama	1961	Citronelle	331
Alaska	1976	MacLeod Harbor	40
Arizona	1978	Hawley Lake	8,180
Arkansas	1957	Newhope	850
California	1909	Monumental	2,420
Colorado	1897	Ruby	10,000
Connecticut	1955	Burlington	460
Delaware	1948	Lewes	10
Florida	1966	Wawahitchka	50
Georgia	1959	aKukui	3,600
Hawaii	1982	Roland	5,788
Idaho	1933	New Burnside	4,150
Illinois	1950	Marengo	560
Indiana	1890	Muscatine	570
Iowa	1851	Blaine	680
Kansas	1993	Russelville	1,530
Kentucky	1950	New Orleans (Audubon)	590
Louisiana	1991	Brunswick	6
Maine	1845	Towson	70
Maryland	1971	New Salem	390
Massachusetts	1996	Adrian	845
Michigan	1881	Fairmont	770
Minnesota	1993	Waveland	1,187
Mississippi	1991	Portageville	8
Missouri	1957		280

State	Year	Weather station	Elevation: feet
Montana	1953	Summit	5,210
Nebraska	1869	Omaha	980
Nevada	1969	Mount Rose Resort	7,300
New Hampshire	1969	Mount Washington	6,260
New Jersey	1882	Peterson	100
New Mexico	1941	White Tail	7,450
New York	1996	Slide Mountain	2,649
North Carolina	1964	Rosman	2,220
North Dakota	1944	Milnor	2,600
Ohio	1870	Little Mountain	1,187
Oklahoma	1957	Kiamichi Tower	2,350
Oregon	1996	Laurel Mountain	3,590
Pennsylvania	1952	Mount Pocono	1,910
Rhode Island	1983	Kingston	100
South Carolina	1994	Jocassee	2,500
South Dakota	1946	Deadwood	4,550
Tennessee	1957	Haw Knob	4,900
Texas	1873	Clarksville	440
Utah	1983	Alta	8,760
Vermont	1996	Mount Mansfield	3,950
Virginia	1996	Philpott Dam	1,123
Washington	1931	Wynoochee Oxbow	670
West Virginia	1926	Bayard	2,381
Wisconsin	1884	Embarrass	808
Wyoming	1945	Grassy Lake Dam	7,240

Lowest total annual rainfall: USA

Lowest total annual rainfall

Figures indicate the lowest total rainfall during a year (inches) at a National Weather Service weather station.
Readings apply to a single location in each state only: they are not statewide averages.

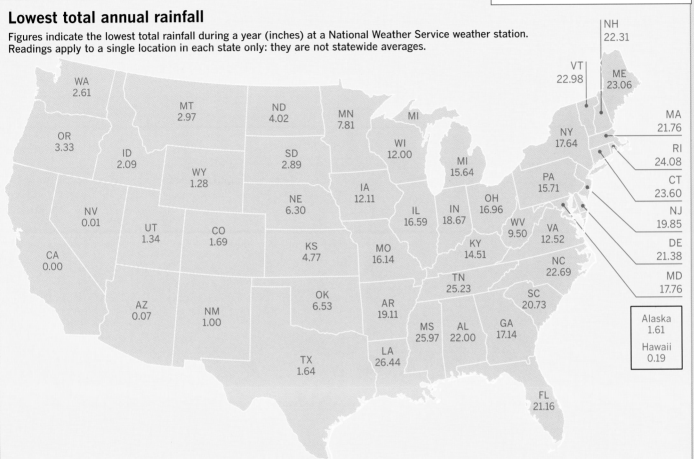

State	Year	Weather station	Elevation: feet
Alabama	1954	Primrose Farm	180
Alaska	1935	Barrow	31
Arizona	1956	Davis Dam	660
Arkansas	1936	Index	300
California	1929	Death Valley	−282
Colorado	1939	Buena Vista	7,980
Connecticut	1965	Baltic	140
Delaware	1965	Dover	30
Florida	1989	Conch Key	6
Georgia	1954	Swainsboro	320
Hawaii	1953	Kawaihae	75
Idaho	1947	Grand View	2,360
Illinois	1956	Keithsburg	540
Indiana	1934	Brooksville	630
Iowa	1958	Cherokee	1,360
Kansas	1956	Johnson	3,270
Kentucky	1968	Jeremiah	1,160
Louisiana	1936	Shreveport	170
Maine	1930	Machias	30
Maryland	1930	Picardy	1,030
Massachusetts	1965	Chatham Light Station	20
Michigan	1936	Crosswell	730
Minnesota	1936	Angus	870
Mississippi	1936	Yazoo City	120
Missouri	1956	La Belle	770

State	Year	Weather station	Elevation: feet
Montana	1960	Belfry	4,040
Nebraska	1931	Hull	4,400
Nevada	1898	Hot Springs	4,072
New Hampshire	1930	Bethlehem	1,440
New Jersey	1965	Canton	20
New Mexico	1910	Hermanas	4,540
New York	1941	Lewiston	320
North Carolina	1930	Mount Airy	1,070
North Dakota	1934	Parshall	1,930
Ohio	1963	Elyria	730
Oklahoma	1956	Regnier	4,280
Oregon	1939	Warm Springs Reservoir	3,330
Pennsylvania	1965	Breezewood	1,350
Rhode Island	1965	Block Island	40
South Carolina	1954	Rock Hill	667
South Dakota	1936	Ludlow	2,850
Tennessee	1941	Halls	310
Texas	1956	Presidio	2,580
Utah	1974	Myton	5,080
Vermont	1941	Burlington	330
Virginia	1941	Moores Creek Dam	1,950
Washington	1930	Wahluke	416
West Virginia	1930	Upper Tract	1,540
Wisconsin	1937	Plum Island	590
Wyoming	1960	Lysite	5,260

Tropical cyclones

Key words

atmospheric pressure	latent heat
cyclone	midlatitude
eye	precipitation
front	tropical cyclone
hurricane	typhoon

Tropical cyclone structure

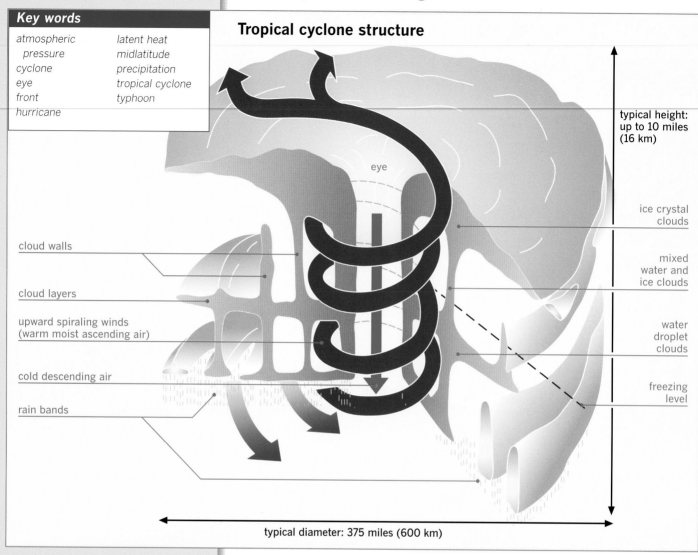

eye

cloud walls

cloud layers

upward spiraling winds
(warm moist ascending air)

cold descending air

rain bands

typical height:
up to 10 miles
(16 km)

ice crystal
clouds

mixed
water and
ice clouds

water
droplet
clouds

freezing
level

typical diameter: 375 miles (600 km)

Tropical cyclones

- *Tropical cyclones* are intense cyclonic storms that develop over the tropical oceans. They are known as *hurricanes* around the Atlantic, *cyclones* in India and Australia, and *typhoons* in the north Pacific. *Tropical cyclone* is the internationally agreed term for all storms of this type.
- Hurricanes are smaller than midlatitude cyclones and do not have associated fronts. They do, however, produce more concentrated precipitation and higher wind speeds than midlatitude cyclones.
- A hurricane is powered by latent heat energy released by the condensation of water vapor. They require a constant supply of warm moist air to develop. Hurricanes only therefore develop over oceans with a surface temperature of at least 79.7°F (26.5°C).
- The center of a hurricane is an extreme low-pressure zone. The lowest surface atmospheric pressure ever recorded for a hurricane was 870 millibars (average surface atmospheric pressure is about 1,013 millibars). Hurricanes have an average surface atmospheric pressure reading at their centers of about 950 millibars.

- Wind speeds in a hurricane are directly related to surface atmospheric pressure with lower pressure generating higher wind speeds.
- To qualify as a hurricane, a storm must have a surface atmospheric pressure of 980 millibars or lower, and wind speeds greater than 73 miles per hour (118 kmph).
- Hurricanes usually develop a distinctive *eye* at their low-pressure centers. The eye is a well of descending air 12 to 30 miles (20–50 km) wide that creates clear skies. The highest wind speeds and the heaviest precipitation are found in the wall of cloud immediately surrounding the eye.
- The layers of cloud surrounding the eye are organized bands of thunderstorms formed as warm moist air is drawn up and around the low pressure center.
- Hurricanes quickly disperse when they make landfall or pass over cooler waters because they are no longer being supplied with latent heat energy.

Saffir-Simpson scale

© Diagram Visual Information Ltd.

Saffir-Simpson hurricane strength categories

Category	Maximum sustained wind speed			Minimum surface pressure (mb)	Storm surge		
	mph	meters/ sec	knots		feet	meters	
1	74–96	33–43	64–83	more than 980	3–5	1.0–1.5	Damage primarily to unanchored mobile homes, shrubbery, and trees. Some coastal road flooding and minor pier damage.
2	97–111	43–50	84–97	965–979	6–8	1.8–2.4	Some roofing material, door, and window damage to buildings. Considerable damage to shrubbery and trees. Considerable damage to mobile homes. Low-lying escape routes flooded 2–4 hours before arrival of hurricane center.
3	112–131	50–98	97–114	945–964	9–12	2.7–3.7	Some structural damage to small residences and utility buildings. Many trees blown down. Low-lying escape routes flooded 3–5 hours before arrival of hurricane center. Coastal flooding destroys smaller structures.
4	132–155	59–69	115–135	920–944	13–18	3.9–5.5	Extensive curtainwall failures and complete roof failures on some small residences. Low-lying escape routes flooded 3–5 hours before arrival of hurricane center. Major damage to lower floors of coastal structures.
5	more than 156	more than 70	more than 136	below 920	more than 18	more than 5.5	Complete roof failure on many residences and industrial structures. Some complete building failures. Major damage to all structures less than 15 feet above sea level

Key words

cyclone
hurricane
Saffir-Simpson
  scale

storm surge
typhoon

Principal hurricane tracks and regional names

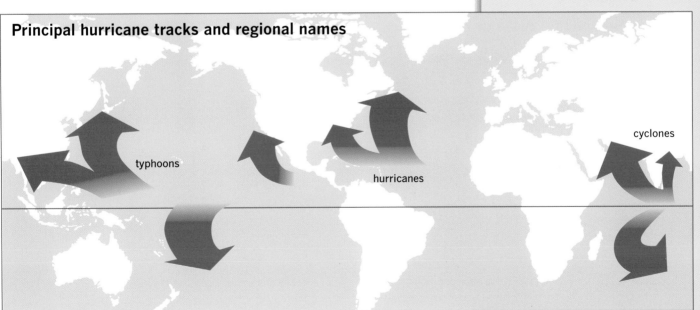

typhoons

hurricanes

cyclones

U.S. hurricanes 1950–2005: categories 1 and 2

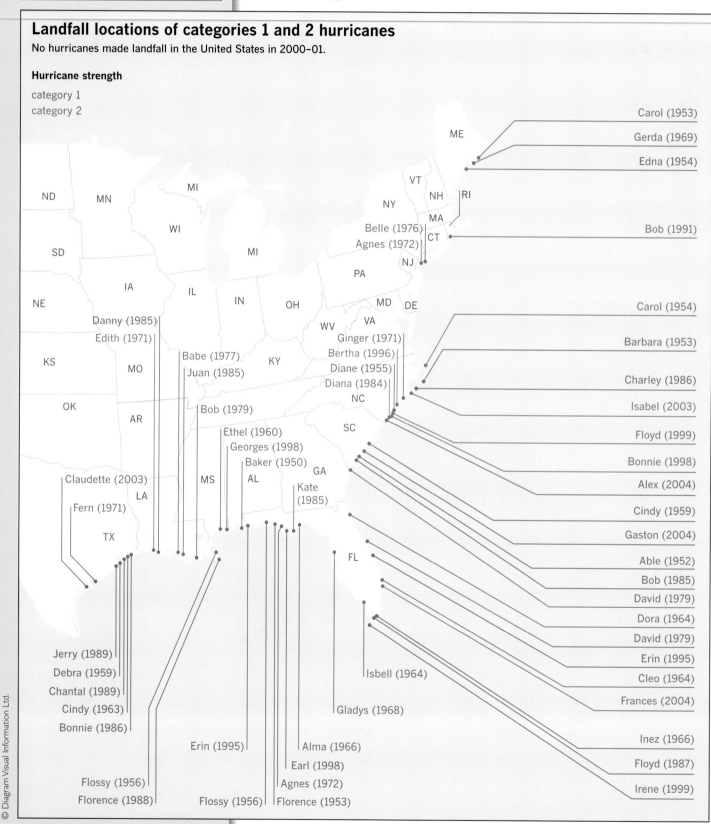

Landfall locations of categories 1 and 2 hurricanes

No hurricanes made landfall in the United States in 2000–01.

Hurricane strength

category 1
category 2

ND
MN
MI
ND
SD
WI
MI
NE
IA
IL
IN
OH
KS
MO
KY
OK
AR
LA
TX
MS
AL
GA
FL
VT
NY
NH
RI
MA
CT
NJ
PA
MD
DE
WV
VA
NC
SC
ME

Carol (1953)
Gerda (1969)
Edna (1954)

Bob (1991)

Belle (1976)
Agnes (1972)

Danny (1985)
Edith (1971)
Babe (1977)
Juan (1985)
Bob (1979)
Ethel (1960)
Georges (1998)
Baker (1950)
Kate (1985)

Ginger (1971)
Bertha (1996)
Diane (1955)
Diana (1984)

Carol (1954)
Barbara (1953)
Charley (1986)
Isabel (2003)
Floyd (1999)
Bonnie (1998)
Alex (2004)
Cindy (1959)
Gaston (2004)
Able (1952)
Bob (1985)
David (1979)
Dora (1964)
David (1979)
Erin (1995)
Cleo (1964)
Frances (2004)

Inez (1966)
Floyd (1987)
Irene (1999)

Claudette (2003)
Fern (1971)

Jerry (1989)
Debra (1959)
Chantal (1989)
Cindy (1963)
Bonnie (1986)

Erin (1995)

Alma (1966)

Earl (1998)

Isbell (1964)

Gladys (1968)

Flossy (1956)
Florence (1988)

Flossy (1956)

Agnes (1972)
Florence (1953)

U.S. hurricanes 1950–2005: categories 3, 4, and 5

Key words

hurricane
*Saffir-Simpson
 scale*

Landfall locations of categories 3, 4, and 5 hurricanes

No hurricanes made landfall in the United States in 2000–01.

Hurricane strength

category 3   category 5
category 4

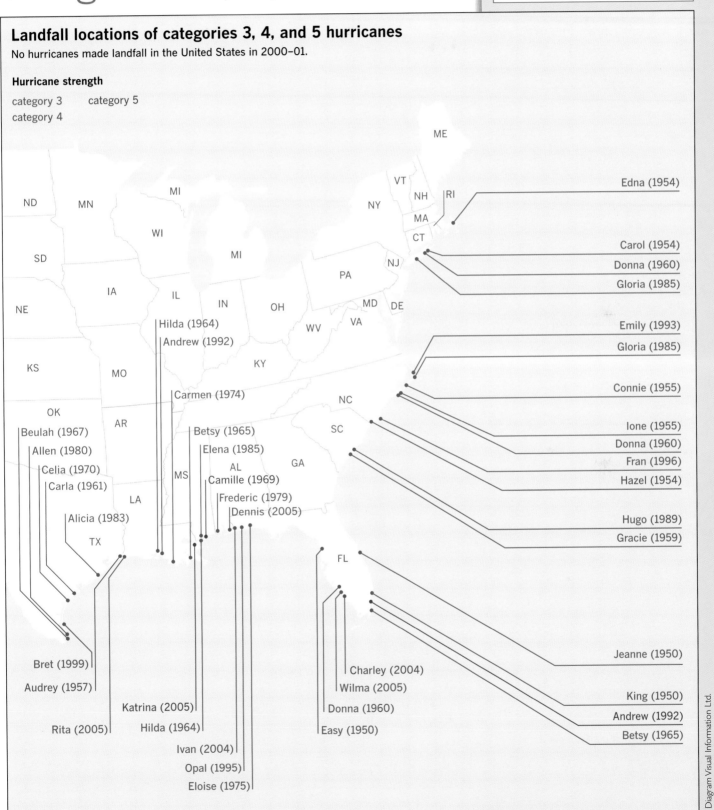

Edna (1954)

Carol (1954)
Donna (1960)
Gloria (1985)

Emily (1993)
Gloria (1985)

Connie (1955)

Ione (1955)
Donna (1960)
Fran (1996)
Hazel (1954)

Hugo (1989)
Gracie (1959)

Jeanne (1950)

King (1950)
Andrew (1992)
Betsy (1965)

Hilda (1964)
Andrew (1992)

Carmen (1974)

Beulah (1967)
Allen (1980)
Celia (1970)
Carla (1961)
Alicia (1983)

Betsy (1965)
Elena (1985)
Camille (1969)
Frederic (1979)
Dennis (2005)

Bret (1999)
Audrey (1957)

Katrina (2005)
Rita (2005)   Hilda (1964)
                Ivan (2004)
                Opal (1995)
                Eloise (1975)

Charley (2004)
Wilma (2005)
Donna (1960)
Easy (1950)

Key words

cyclone   tropical cyclone
hurricane
precipitation
storm surge
tornado

Hurricane energy

- A mature hurricane can release energy at a rate of 600,000,000,000,000 watts, which is two hundred times greater than the rate of global electricity generation.
- The most deadly hurricanes are not always the most powerful. Many hurricanes remain over the ocean, where only ships are at risk. Many others make landfall in sparsely populated areas or have become much weaker by the time they reach a coastline.
- Nations such as the United States and Japan are wealthy enough to have well-organized hurricane warning and response procedures in place that usually save many lives.
- The greatest death tolls occur in densely populated regions that are poorly prepared. The deadliest tropical cyclone on record was a category 2 storm that struck the Ganges Delta region of Bangladesh in 1970. It is estimated that 200,000–500,000 people were killed.

Hurricane damage

- Hurricanes that make landfall cause death and destruction by four mechanisms.
- High winds can cause structures to collapse and send debris flying through the air at high speeds. Vehicles are also commonly blown over or forced off roads.
- Heavy precipitation can cause rivers to flood very rapidly and very often causes landslides.
- The very low pressure of the storm center can cause sea levels to rise by tens of feet. This combines with a further surge in seawater caused by high winds. Together these are known as a *storm surge* and are the deadliest aspect of a hurricane.
- Tornadoes can develop around the perimeter of the storm.

Deadliest U.S. hurricanes

Ranking	Area hit (storm name*)	Year	Category	Deaths
1	Galveston, Texas	1900	4	8,000+
2	Lake Okeechobee, Florida	1928	4	1,836
3	New Orleans, Louisiana (Katrina)	2005	5	1,600+
4	South Texas and Florida Keys	1919	4	600–900
5	New England	1938	3	600
6	Florida Keys	1935	5	408
7	SW Louisiana/N Texas (Audrey)	1957	4	390
8	Northeast U.S.A.	1944	3	390
9	Grand Isle, Louisiana	1909	4	350
10	New Orleans, Louisiana	1915	4	275
11	Galveston, Texas	1915	4	275
12	Mississippi/Louisiana (Camille)	1969	5	256
13	Florida/Mississippi/Alabama	1926	4	243
14	Northeast USA (Diane)	1955	1	184
15	Southeast Florida	1906	2	164
16	Mississippi/Alabama	1906	3	134
17	Northeast USA (Agnes)	1972	1	122
18	S Carolina/N Carolina (Hazel)	1954	4	95
19	SE Florida/SE Louisiana (Betsy)	1965	3	75
20	Northeast USA (Carol)	1954	3	60
21	Florida/Louisiana/Mississippi	1947	4	51
22	Florida/Eastern USA (Donna)	1960	4	50
23	Georgia/S Carolina/N Carolina	1940	2	50
24	Texas (Carla)	1961	4	46
25	Velasco, Texas	1909	3	41
26	Freeport, Texas	1932	4	40
27	South Texas	1933	3	40
28	Louisiana (Hilda)	1964	3	38
29	Southwest Louisiana	1918	3	34
30	Southwest Florida	1910	3	30

* Naming of Atlantic hurricanes began in 1950

Retired hurricane names

Chronological list of retired hurricane names

Year	Name
1954	Carol
1954	Hazel
1955	Connie
1955	Diane
1955	Ione
1955	Janet
1957	Audrey
1960	Donna
1961	Carla
1961	Hattie
1963	Flora
1964	Cleo
1964	Dora
1964	Hilda
1965	Betsy
1966	Inez
1967	Beulah
1968	Edna
1969	Camille
1970	Celia
1972	Agnes
1974	Carmen
1974	Fifi
1975	Eloise
1977	Anita
1979	David
1979	Frederic
1980	Allen
1983	Alicia
1985	Elena
1985	Gloria
1988	Gilbert
1988	Joan
1989	Hugo

Year	Name
1990	Diana
1990	Klaus
1991	Bob
1992	Andrew
1995	Luis
1995	Marilyn
1995	Opal
1995	Roxanne
1996	Cesar
1996	Fran
1996	Hortense
1998	Georges
1998	Mitch
1999	Floyd
1999	Lenny
2000	Keith
2001	Allison
2001	Iris
2001	Michelle
2002	Isidore
2002	Lili
2003	Fabian
2003	Isabel
2003	Juan
2004	Charley
2004	Frances
2004	Ivan
2004	Jeanne
2005	Dennis
2005	Katrina
2005	Rita
2005	Stan
2005	Wilma

Key words

hurricane
latitude
longitude
typhoon

Naming hurricanes

- The modern practice of naming hurricanes began with the tradition of naming hurricanes affecting the West Indies for the Saints' days on which they occurred.
- Hurricanes are named because names cause less confusion than numbers or longitude and latitude designations when there is more than one active hurricane in a region.
- The practice of giving hurricanes and typhoons names became widespread among U.S. meteorologists during World War II.
- A formal system of naming hurricanes was introduced in the United States in 1950 based on the U.S.-phonetic alphabet system ("Able, Baker, Charlie," etc.) This was abandoned when a new international phonetic alphabet was introduced in 1953. U.S. meteorologists began using pre-selected lists of female names from that year.
- The practice of using only female names for hurricanes ended in 1978 for Eastern North Pacific storms and in 1979 for Atlantic and Caribbean storms. Lists of alternating male and female names are now used.

Retiring names

- Names are occasionally removed from the cyclical lists of storm names. This usually happens when a particularly deadly or damaging storm occurs in a particular region.
- The nation most affected by the storm may petition to have the name removed from the lists as a mark of respect for the dead and to avoid potential confusion in legal cases arising from the event.
- A new name beginning with the same letter is added to the list. The new name is either French, Spanish, or English, depending on the language spoken by the petitioning country.

Key words

hurricane

Atlantic and Caribbean hurricane names 2006–11

Atlantic and Caribbean hurricane names

- Hurricanes occurring in the Atlantic and Caribbean are named from a set of six lists, each with 21 names.
- The first hurricane in a particular year is given the first name on that year's list and so on.
- If all the names on a list are used, subsequent hurricanes are designated by letters of the Greek alphabet. This occured for the first time during 2005.
- Even if all the names are not used, the first hurricane of the following year is given the first name on the following year's list.
- At the end of six years, the lists are recycled. The list for 2006 can be used again in 2012.

Eastern North Pacific hurricane names

- Hurricanes occurring in the Eastern North Pacific are named in the same way as hurricanes in the Atlantic and Caribbean, but a different set of six lists is used. These lists contain 24 names each.
- The Eastern North Pacific hurricane name lists will also be reused starting in 2011.

Central North Pacific hurricane names

- Hurricanes occurring in the Central North Pacific are named according to a single list of 48 names.
- Each storm is given the next name on the list until the end of the list is reached. The list is not restarted at the beginning of each year.
- When the last name has been used, the same sequence is used again.

Atlantic, Gulf of Mexico, and Caribbean					
2006	**2007**	**2008**	**2009**	**2010**	**2011**
Alberto	Andrea	Arthur	Ana	Alex	Arlene
Beryl	Barry	Bertha	Bill	Bonnie	Bret
Chris	Chantal	Cristobal	Claudette	Colin	Cindy
Debby	Dean	Dolly	Danny	Danielle	Don
Ernesto	Erin	Edouard	Erika	Earl	Emily
Florence	Felix	Fay	Fred	Fiona	Franklin
Gordon	Gabrielle	Gustav	Grace	Gaston	Gert
Helene	Humberto	Hanna	Henri	Hermine	Harvey
Isaac	Ingrid	Iko	Ida	Igor	Irene
Joyce	Jerry	Josephine	Joaquin	Julia	Jose
Kirk	Karen	Kyle	Kate	Karl	Katia
Leslie	Lorenzo	Lili	Larry	Lisa	Lee
Michael	Melissa	Marco	Mindy	Matthew	Maria
Nadine	Noel	Nana	Nicholas	Nicole	Nate
Oscar	Olga	Omar	Odette	Otto	Ophelia
Patty	Pablo	Paloma	Peter	Paula	Philippe
Rafael	Rebekah	Rene	Rose	Richard	Rina
Sandy	Sebastien	Sally	Sam	Shary	Sean
Tony	Tanya	Teddy	Teresa	Tomas	Tammy
Valerie	Van	Vicky	Victor	Virginie	Vince
William	Wendy	Wilfred	Wanda	Walter	Whitney

Eastern and Central North Pacific hurricane names 2006–11

		Eastern North Pacific			
2006	2007	2008	2009	2010	2011
Aletta	Alvin	Alma	Andres	Agatha	Adrian
Bud	Barbara	Boris	Blanca	Blas	Beatriz
Carlotta	Cosme	Cristina	Carlos	Celia	Calvin
Daniel	Dalila	Douglas	Dolores	Darby	Dora
Emilia	Erick	Elida	Enrique	Estelle	Eugene
Fabio	Flossie	Fausto	Felicia	Frank	Fernanda
Gilma	Gil	Genevieve	Guillermo	Georgette	Greg
Hector	Henriette	Hernan	Hilda	Howard	Hilary
Ileana	Ivo	Iselle	Ignacio	Isis	Irwin
John	Juliette	Julio	Jimena	Javier	Jova
Kristy	Kiko	Kenna	Kevin	Kay	Kenneth
Lane	Lorena	Lowell	Linda	Lester	Lidia
Miriam	Manuel	Marie	Marty	Madeline	Max
Norman	Narda	Norbert	Nora	Newton	Norma
Olivia	Octave	Odile	Olaf	Orlene	Otis
Paul	Priscilla	Polo	Patricia	Paine	Pilar
Rosa	Raymond	Rachel	Rick	Roslyn	Ramon
Sergio	Sonia	Simon	Sandra	Seymour	Selma
Tara	Tico	Trudy	Terry	Tina	Todd
Vicente	Velma	Vance	Vivian	Virgil	Veronica
Willa	Wallis	Winnie	Waldo	Winifred	Wiley
Xavier	Xina	Xavier	Xina	Xavier	Xina
Yolanda	York	Yolanda	York	Yolanda	York
Zeke	Zelda	Zeke	Zelda	Zeke	Zelda

Central North Pacific	
Circular list	
Akoni	Alika
Ema	Ele
Hana	Huko
Io	Ioke
Keli	Kika
Lala	Lana
Moke	Maka
Nele	Neki
Oka	Oleka
Peke	Peni
Uleki	Ulia
Wila	Wali
Aka	Ana
Ekeka	Ela
Hali	Halola
Ioalana	Iune
Keoni	Kimo
Li	Loke
Mele	Malla
Nona	Niala
Oliwa	Oko
Paka	Pali
Upana	Ulika
Wene	Walaka

Tornadoes

Key words

Fujita-Pearson scale
hurricane
tornado

Tornadoes

- A *tornado* is a rapidly rotating column of air that stretches from a cloud base to the ground.
- Tornadoes often form a twisting funnel-shaped cloud, but these are not always present.
- Tornadoes are among the most destructive and deadly of all weather phenomena. They are associated with winds that can be in excess of 300 miles per hour (480 kmph).
- They form in association with large thunderstorms and hurricanes.
- Tornadoes occur all over the world, but more are recorded in the United States than in any other country.
- The intensity of a tornado is given according to the Fujita-Pearson Tornado scale.

Fujita-Pearson tornado scale

Category	Wind speed miles per hour (kmph)	Damage
F0	<73 (<115)	Light damage. Some damage to branches, signposts, and chimneys.
F1	73-112 (116-180)	Moderate damage. Mobile homes pushed off foundations. Vehicles forced from roads.
F2	113-157 (181-250)	Considerable damage. Roofs torn off, railroad cars overturned, vehicles lifted from roads. Light missiles generated.
F3	158-206 (251-330)	Severe damage. Roofs and walls collapsed. Trains overturned. Most trees uprooted.
F4	207-260 (331-415)	Devastating damage. Well-constructed houses leveled. Vehicles lifted and thrown. Heavy missiles generated.
F5	261-318 (416-510)	Incredible damage. Most building leveled. Automobile-sized missiles generated.

Tornado frequency across the United States

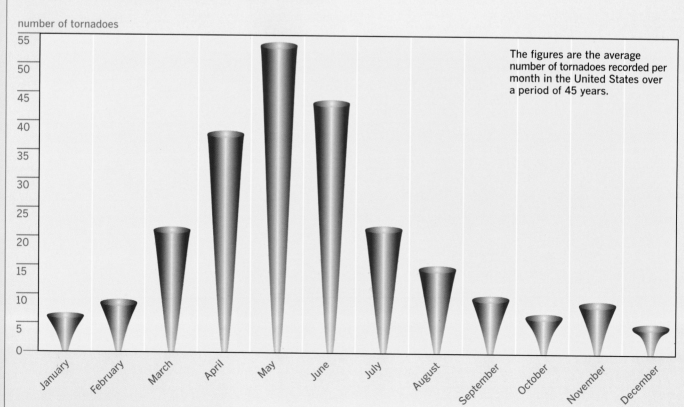

number of tornadoes

The figures are the average number of tornadoes recorded per month in the United States over a period of 45 years.

Tornado distribution

Tornado tracks during the super outbreak of April 3, 1974

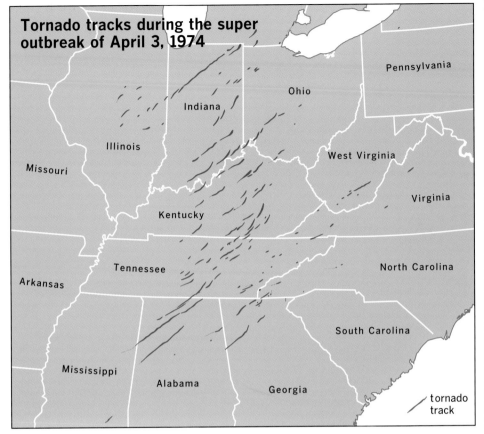

Pennsylvania

Ohio

Indiana

Illinois

Missouri

West Virginia

Kentucky

Virginia

Tennessee

North Carolina

Arkansas

South Carolina

Mississippi

Alabama

Georgia

/ tornado track

Key words

Fujita-Pearson scale
tornado
tornado outbreak

Tornado frequency

● About 1,000 tornadoes occur within the United States each year. This can be compared to the total of about 100,000 thunderstorms that also form over the United States each year.

● On average, these 1,000 tornadoes kill about 50 people per year.

● A *tornado outbreak* refers to a twenty-four hour period in which six or more tornadoes occur. During the "super outbreak" of April 3, 1974, 148 tornadoes occurred in 13 states, including six category F5 and 23 category F4 storms. Three hundred and fifteen people were killed and 5,484 were injured.

Tornado territory

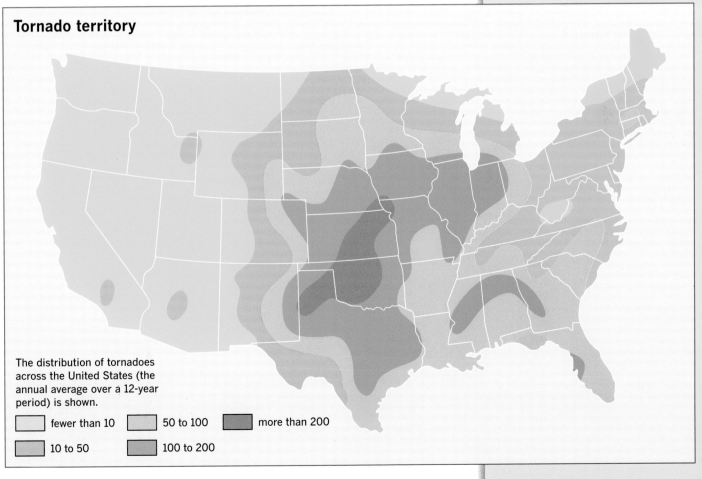

The distribution of tornadoes across the United States (the annual average over a 12-year period) is shown.

	fewer than 10		50 to 100		more than 200
	10 to 50		100 to 200		

© Diagram Visual Information Ltd.

Key words
hurricane

Major hurricanes

● Until Hurricane Katrina in 2005, Hurricane Andrew was the most costly storm ever to have struck the United States.

● Rated category 5, with sustained winds of up to 143 knots (264 kmph), it crossed the Bahamas and arrived at the Florida coast on August 23, 1992. Between August 23 and 26, Andrew plowed through Florida and Louisiana, almost totally destroying the Florida towns of Homestead and Florida City. It destroyed 63,000 homes in Florida and 44,000 in Louisiana. The total cost amounted to about $27 billion.

● Hurricane Floyd was a category 4 storm, with winds of 126 knots (233 kmph), that moved along the east coast between September 15 and 17, 1999, causing damage in North Carolina, Virginia, Pennsylvania, and New Jersey costing about $6 billion.

● Hurricane Georges was almost as costly, destroying property worth $5.9 billion in Louisiana, Mississippi, Alabama, and Florida between September 21 and 28, 1998. Before reaching the Gulf coast George had crossed the Caribbean, killing 250 people in the Dominican Republic and 27 in Haiti.

● Hurricanes are fierce windstorms, but they also deliver torrential rain and storm surges caused by a combination of low air pressure, onshore winds, and high tides. Most of the damage they cause is due to flooding, mudslides, and landslides, rather than a result of their winds.

● Hurricane Katrina (August 2005) will probably turn out to be the costliest hurricane to date.

The cost of U.S. wind storms

Event	Date	Summary	US$ cost*	Deaths
Hurricane Katrina	Aug 2005	Category 5. The largest recorded hurricane of its type.	75.0 billion+	1,600+
Hurricane Ivan	Sep 2004	Category 3. Significant wind and flood damage across AL and FL.	12.0 billion+	52
Hurricane Frances	Sep 2004	Category 2. Significant wind and flood damage across Florida.	9.0 billion+	38
Hurricane Isabel	Sep 2003	Category 2. Considerable storm damage in NC, VA, and MD.	5.0 billion+	55
Ohio-Tennessee tornadoes	May 2003	Record 400 tornadoes in one week over MS, OH, TN, and other parts of the south east.	3.4 billion+	51
Hurricane Floyd	Sep 1999	Category 2. Severe wind and flood damage in eastern NC.	6.0 billion+	75
Arkansas-Tennessee tornadoes	Jan 1999	Two outbreaks of tornadoes in six days across AR and TN.	1.3 billion	17
Hurricane Georges	Sep 1998	Category 2. Hit Puerto Rico, Florida Keys, and Gulf coast areas of LA, MS, AL, and FL.	5.9 billion	16
Hurricane Fran	Sep 1996	Category 3. North Carolina and Virginia.	5.0 billion+	37
Hurricane Opal	Oct 1995	Category 3. Florida Panhandle, AL, western GA, eastern TN western NC, and SC.	3.0 billion+	27
Hurricane Marilyn	Sep 1995	Category 2. Extreme damage in U.S. Virgin Islands.	2.1 billion	13
Hurricane Iniki	Sep 1992	Category 4. Extensive damage on Kauai, HI.	1.8 billion	7
Hurricane Andrew	Aug 1992	Category 4. Extensive damage in Florida and Louisiana.	27.0 billion	58
Hurricane Bob	Aug 1991	Category 2. Hit coastal NC, Long Island, and New England.	1.5 billion	18

*Actual damage costs at the time. Figures are not adjusted for inflation and should not be used to compare one event with another.

The cost of U.S. floods

Event	Date	Summary	US$ cost*	Deaths
Texas-Louisiana floods	Jun 2001	Rainfall of 30–40 inches produced by tropical storm Allison causes severe flooding in central Texas and Louisiana. Further damage in MS, FL, VA, and PA.	5.0 billion	43
Texas floods	Oct–Nov 1998	Severe flooding across Texas after two consecutive rainstorms of 10–20 inches.	1.0 billion	31
Northern plains floods	Apr–May 1997	Extensive flooding across North Dakota, South Dakota, and Minnesota due to exceptionally heavy spring snowmelt.	3.7 billion	11
Mississippi-Ohio Valley floods	Mar 1997	Severe flooding associated with tornadoes across AR, MO, MS, TN, IL, IN, KY, OH, and WV.	1.0 billion	67
West Coast floods	Winter 1996–97	Combination of heavy rains and snowmelt caused severe flooding in CA, WA, OR, ID, NV, and MT.	3.0 billion	36
Pacific Northwest floods	Feb 1996	Persistent heavy rains combined with snowmelt caused floods across OR, WA, ID, and western MT.	1.0 billion	9
Southern states floods	May 1995	Torrential rain, hailstorms, and tornadoes across TX, OK, LA and MS. Dallas and New Orleans worst affected.	5.0–6.0 billion	32
California floods	Jan–Mar 1995	Extended period of winter storms caused wind damage and periodic flooding throughout California.	3.0 billion+	27
Texas floods	Oct 1994	Much of southeast Texas affected by floods caused by heavy rains and thunderstorms.	1.0 billion	19
Tropical storm Alberto	Jul 1994	Torrential rains (up to 25 inches) caused by tropical storm Alberto led to flooding in GA, AL, and Florida Panhandle.	1.0 billon	32
Midwest floods	Summer 1993	Widespread and severe flooding across central USA.	21.0 billion	48

*Actual damage costs at the time. Figures are not adjusted for inflation and should not be used to compare one event with another.

Major floods

- From June to August 1993 the Missouri and Mississippi rivers and their tributaries overflowed their banks. The resulting floods affected Illinois, Iowa, Kansas, Minnesota, Missouri, Nebraska, North Dakota, South Dakota, and Wisconsin. Fifty people lost their lives and the damage cost an estimated $21 billion.
- Storms in May 1995 brought torrential rain and hail, as well as tornadoes, across large parts of Texas, Oklahoma, southeastern Louisiana, and southern Mississippi. Dallas and New Orleans were hit hardest, with 10–25 inches (250–635 mm) of rain falling in the space of five days. The damage to property cost $5–6 billion and 32 people died.
- Rainstorms on October 17 and 18, 1998, caused floods that covered one quarter of Texas. The damage amounted to $1 billion.
- Winter rain and snow can also cause severe flooding and the low temperatures increase the risk to life.
- The worst winter floods of modern times began in December 1996 and continued through early January, affecting parts of California, Idaho, Nevada, Oregon, and Washington. States of emergency were declared in more than 90 counties and at least 125,000 people had to be evacuated from their homes. The damage cost about $3 billion.
- Hurricane Katrina (August 2005) resulted in the worst flooding of a U.S. city ever, when New Orleans' defensive levees were breached by storm surge waters resulting in huge loss of life and severe damage to low-lying areas of the city.

Key words

atmosphere	sublimation
latent heat	
latent heat of evaporation	
latent heat of melting	

Latent heat

- *Latent heat* refers to the amount of energy in the form of heat that is needed for a material to undergo a change of state from solid to liquid ("latent heat of melting") or from liquid to gas ("latent heat of evaporation").
- In meteorology, the latent heat of melting and of evaporation for water is critical for understanding the transfer of heat between the atmosphere, the oceans, and Earth's surface.
- The energy added or removed affects only the physical change of state: the temperature of the substance does not change.
- Latent heat is expressed in calories per gram (cal/gm).

heat absorbed

heat released

change of state

Energy and change of state

Changes requiring the addition of heat energy (endothermic processes)

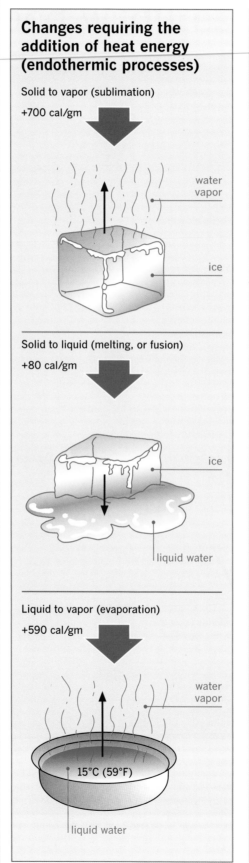

Solid to vapor (sublimation)

+700 cal/gm

water vapor

ice

Solid to liquid (melting, or fusion)

+80 cal/gm

ice

liquid water

Liquid to vapor (evaporation)

+590 cal/gm

water vapor

15°C (59°F)

liquid water

Changes involving the release of heat energy (exothermic processes)

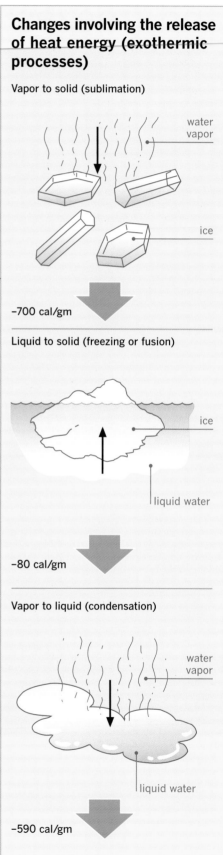

Vapor to solid (sublimation)

water vapor

ice

−700 cal/gm

Liquid to solid (freezing or fusion)

ice

liquid water

−80 cal/gm

Vapor to liquid (condensation)

water vapor

liquid water

−590 cal/gm

Instruments: temperature and humidity

Key words

dry bulb
  thermometer
hygrograph
maximum
  thermometer
minimum
  thermometer
thermograph
thermometer
wet bulb
  thermometer

Dry bulb thermometer   Wet bulb thermometer

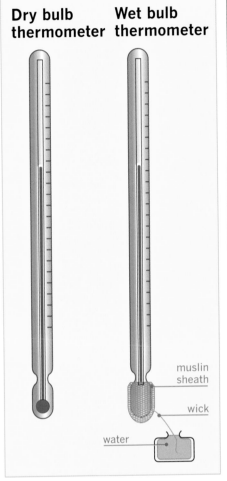

muslin sheath

wick

water

Maximum thermometer   Minimum thermometer

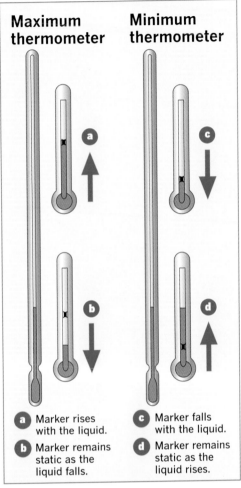

a Marker rises with the liquid.

b Marker remains static as the liquid falls.

c Marker falls with the liquid.

d Marker remains static as the liquid rises.

Thermograph

The coiled bimetal strip contracts or relaxes as the temperature causes one of the metals to expand or contract more than the other. These contractions are translated into vertical movements by a system of levers.

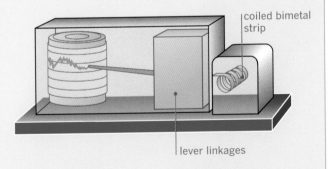

coiled bimetal strip

lever linkages

Hygrograph

Strands of hair expand or contract as humidity increases or decreases. These contractions and expansions are translated into vertical movements by a system of levers.

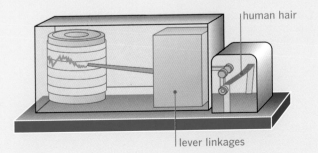

human hair

lever linkages

Thermometers

- Thermometers are used by meteorologists to measure temperature and temperature change.
- A basic weather station typically uses four thermometers; a *dry bulb thermometer*, a *wet bulb thermometer*, a *minimum thermometer*, and a *maximum thermometer*.
- A dry bulb thermometer is used to measure air temperature. The liquid inside the thermometer expands or contracts as the air heats or cools the thermometer.
- A wet bulb thermometer is used to relate air temperature to humidity. The bulb in a wet bulb thermometer is wrapped in a wet muslin sheath. The water in the muslin evaporates most rapidly when the air is at its driest. This evaporation causes cooling, so the wet bulb thermometer shows a lower temperature than the dry bulb under the same conditions. The difference in these temperatures indicates relative humidity.
- A minimum thermometer records the lowest temperature reached over a period of time. A marker inside the column of the thermometer moves with the liquid as long as it is cooling. The marker does not move when the liquid is warming.
- A maximum thermometer records the highest temperature reached over a period of time. A marker inside the column of the thermometer moves with the liquid as long as it is moving in one direction (warming). The marker does not move when the liquid is moving in the other direction (cooling).
- All four thermometers are kept out of the direct rays of the Sun and a few feet above the ground.

Instruments: atmospheric pressure

Key words

aneroid
  barometer
atmospheric
  pressure
barometer

mercury
  barometer
thermometer

Barometers

- Barometers are used to measure atmospheric pressure.
- There are two common types of barometer: the *mercury barometer* and the *aneroid barometer*.
- A mercury barometer contains a column of mercury about 30 inches (76 cm) tall in a narrow tube that has sufficient height for the column to increase in height by a few inches. One end of the tube is open and immersed in a reservoir of mercury. The surface of the mercury in the reservoir is exposed to the atmosphere. As atmospheric pressure increases, the weight of the air pushes the column of mercury further up the tube. As atmospheric pressure decreases, the decreasing weight of the air allows the column of mercury to descend under the influence of gravity. A scale alongside the column of mercury allows atmospheric pressure to be read.
- An aneroid barometer contains a sealed chamber that is partially evacuated. As atmospheric pressure increases, the chamber is compressed. As atmospheric pressure decreases the chamber expands. These expansions and contractions cause sprung levers to move. The movements of these levers are translated into movements of a pointer on a calibrated scale.
- A *barograph* is a barometer that records atmospheric pressure either continually or at set intervals to show changes in atmospheric pressure.

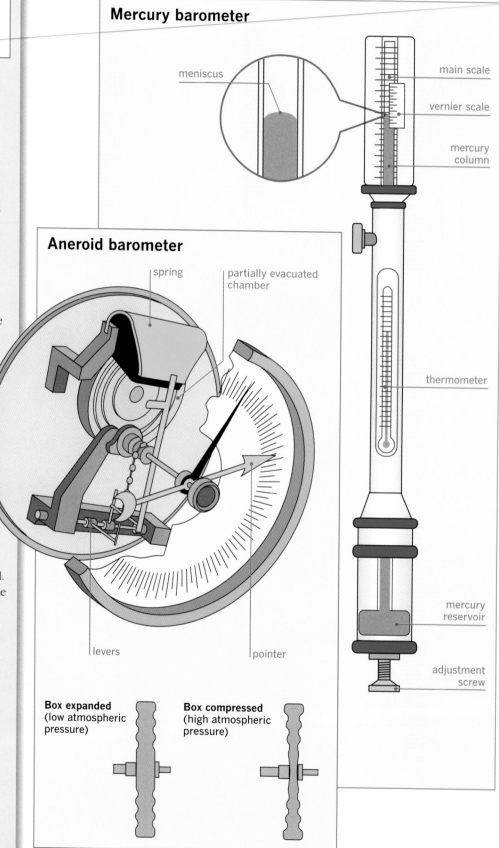

Mercury barometer

meniscus

main scale

vernier scale

mercury column

thermometer

mercury reservoir

adjustment screw

Aneroid barometer

spring

partially evacuated chamber

levers

pointer

Box expanded (low atmospheric pressure)

Box compressed (high atmospheric pressure)

Instruments: Sun, wind, and rainfall

Key words

anemometer
Campbell-Stokes
  recorder
cup anemometer
rainfall gauge

sunshine
  recorder

Campbell-Stokes recorder

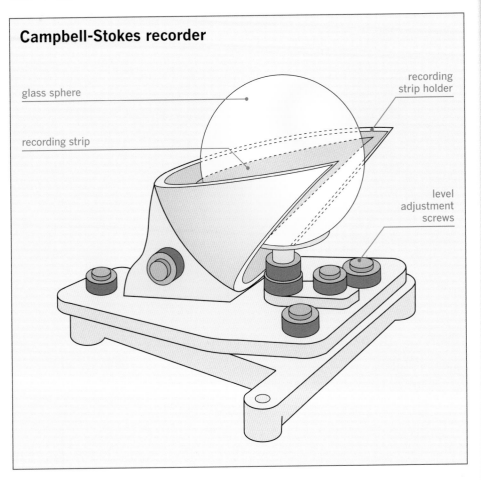

glass sphere

recording strip

recording strip holder

level adjustment screws

Cup anemometer

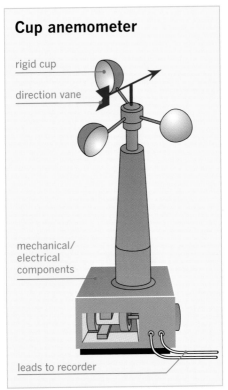

rigid cup

direction vane

mechanical/ electrical components

leads to recorder

Rainfall gauge

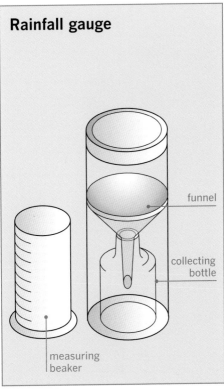

funnel

collecting bottle

measuring beaker

Sunshine recorders

- Sunshine recorders are used to measure the amount of sunshine or the amount and intensity of sunshine that occurs during a particular period.
- The *Campbell-Stokes recorder* is a sunshine recorder that measures both the amount and intensity of sunshine.
- A spherical lens focuses the Sun's rays onto a sensitive strip of treated paper inside the device. The focused light burns an impression onto the paper.
- The length of the burned trace indicates the duration of the sunlight and the depth and breadth of the trace indicate the intensity.

Anemometers

- Anemometers are used to measure wind speed.
- The *cup anemometer* has three or four rigid cups mounted symmetrically around a freely rotating vertical axis. Wind pushes against the cups and causes the axis to rotate. Mechanical and electronic components in the base of the device measure the rate of rotation of the axis and translate this into a wind speed.
- Other types of anemometer use propellers, or measure the change in resistance of a wire carrying an electrical current, or the change in the velocity of sound, caused by the movement of air.

Rainfall gauges

- Rainfall gauges are used to measure the amount and sometimes the intensity of rain.
- Rain is collected using a container with a known diameter. The collected water is measured in a narrow-diameter measuring beaker so that the column of water is relatively tall and therefore easier to measure.

Key words

atmospheric	radiosonde
pressure	balloon
humidity	
pilot balloon	
radiosonde	

Instruments: weather balloons

Weather balloons

- Weather balloons are used by meteorologists to gather information about weather conditions at different altitudes in the atmosphere.
- There are two basic forms of weather balloon: *pilot balloons* and *radiosonde balloons*.
- Pilot balloons are used to measure wind speeds and directions in the upper atmosphere. A pilot balloon is filled with helium so that it rises through the atmosphere. A theodolite is used to measure its position at set intervals throughout its flight. The horizontal and vertical movements of the balloon can be translated into data about the wind conditions it is encountering.
- Radiosonde balloons are helium- or hydrogen-filled balloons that carry instrument packages, known as "radiosondes," into the upper atmosphere.
- Radiosondes typically include instruments to measure temperature, humidity, and pressure, and some also measure wind speed and direction.
- As the balloon carrying the radiosonde ascends, it expands, because atmospheric pressure decreases with altitude while the pressure within the balloon remains the same.
- Radiosonde balloons are designed to survive to altitudes of between six and 22 miles (10 and 35 km). Above their design altitudes, the balloons burst and their radiosondes fall back to the surface under a parachute.
- Radiosondes typically transmit the data they collect while they are in the air. This data is received by a ground station where it is analyzed by meteorologists. The radiosonde is recovered and reused if possible.
- Radiosonde balloons may also carry radar reflectors so that they can easily be tracked by radar.

Pilot balloon

theodolite

balloon

computer data storage

Radiosonde balloon

balloon

radar reflector and parachute

radio transmitter

humidity recorder

temperature recorder

pressure recorder

radiosonde

instrument batteries

ground station receiver

Instruments: weather satellites

Key words

atmosphere	pole
geostationary	weather satellite
orbit	
latitude	
longitude	

Geostationary Operational Environment Satellite (GOES)

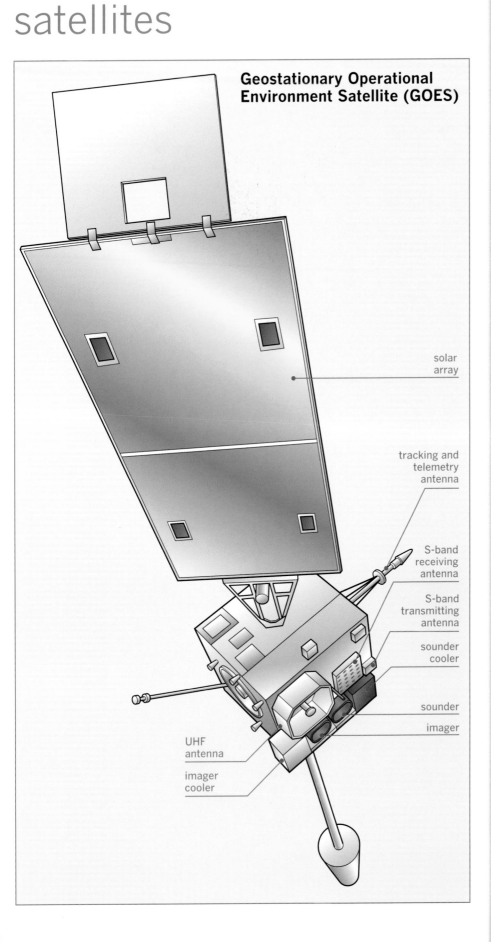

solar array

tracking and telemetry antenna

S-band receiving antenna

S-band transmitting antenna

sounder cooler

sounder

imager

UHF antenna

imager cooler

Weather satellites

- The first dedicated meteorological satellite was the *Television and Infrared Observation Satellite 1* (*TIROS 1*) launched in April 1960.
- Since that time, Earth-orbiting meteorological satellites have become one of the most important and comprehensive sources of information for meteorologists.

National Oceanic and Atmospheric Administration

- The National Oceanic and Atmospheric Administration (NOAA) manages the United States' meteorological satellites.
- NOAA operates two meteorological satellites in *geostationary orbit*. A geostationary orbit is an Earth orbit that maintains a satellite's position over a fixed point on Earth's surface.
- These satellites are designated Geostationary Operational Environment Satellites (GOES). *GOES 10* (or *GOES West*) and *GOES 12* (or *GOES East*) are currently in service.
- Operational GOES satellites continually view about one third of Earth. Together, the two GOES satellites continually view Earth at all latitudes between longitudes 20° W and 165° E.
- GOES satellites carry two primary meteorological instruments: an *imager* and a *sounder*.
- The imager detects radiant energy and reflected solar energy from Earth's surface and atmosphere.
- The sounder measures temperature and moisture at all altitudes through Earth's atmosphere.
- NOAA also operates a series of secondary meteorological satellites in orbits that pass close to Earth's North and South poles.

© Diagram Visual Information Ltd.

Key words

okta
synoptic chart

Synoptic chart

- Weather stations report conditions to a forecasting center at regular intervals. This data is plotted on a *synoptic chart*. It would be impractical to write a description of the weather at each weather station on the chart, so international standard weather map symbols are used.
- Wind direction is shown by the angle of a line drawn from the circle that indicates the location of the weather station. The absence of a wind symbol means the air is calm.
- The amount of the sky covered by cloud is measured in eighths, called *oktas*, and shown by a circle that is open or partly or completely filled.
- There are nine symbols to indicate present weather conditions. The absence of a symbol means no precipitation and no haze or fog.
- There are 12 symbols to indicate cloud type, but there are several ways to draw the symbols for cirrus, cirrostratus, and altocumulus.
- A front is shown as a line drawn where the front touches the surface. A cold front is indicated by triangles and a warm front by semicircles, both on the forward edge of the moving front. Triangles and semicircles on alternate sides of the line indicate a front that is not moving. Alternating triangles and semicircles show fronts that are occluding.

Weather map symbols

Wind speed and direction

The shaft indicates the direction the wind is blowing from.

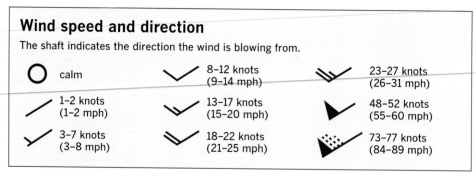

Cloud cover

Cloud cover is indicated in eighths.

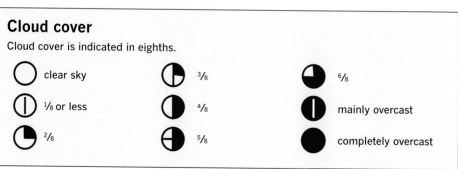

Weather conditions at time of observation

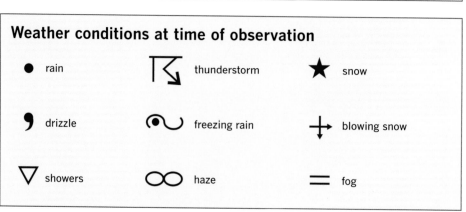

Cloud types visible

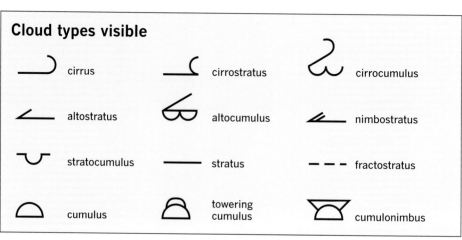

Fronts and pressure centers

 cold front   occluded front   (H)/(L) high/low pressure center

warm front   stationary front

Weather station data plot

Weather station data

- Data from each weather station are plotted in a standardized way. Symbols show wind, cloud, and present and past weather conditions. Numbers show pressures and temperatures. Atmospheric pressure is shown in millibars, but in simplified form and with decimal points removed for clarity: 1,014.8 mb appears as 148 and 2.8 mb as 28. The Celsius scale is often used to report temperatures, kilometers for visibility, meters for cloud base, and millimeters for precipitation amounts.

- Each item of information is placed in a particular position around the cloud-cover symbol that marks the location of the weather station. The complete record is known as a station model and because the contents of the model are standardized according to rules agreed by the World Meteorological Organization, a meteorologist can extract information quickly from any weather station on the chart. A weather forecaster calculates the direction the weather is moving in and its speed, then uses the station models to predict where those conditions will be at the end of the forecast period.

Key words

station model

Station models

- An enormous amount of information can be carried in the symbol cluster for a single weather-reporting station. This type of cluster, or *station model*, is used only for the most detailed analytical charts. A simpler version is used for most daily weather maps.

Station model symbol cluster

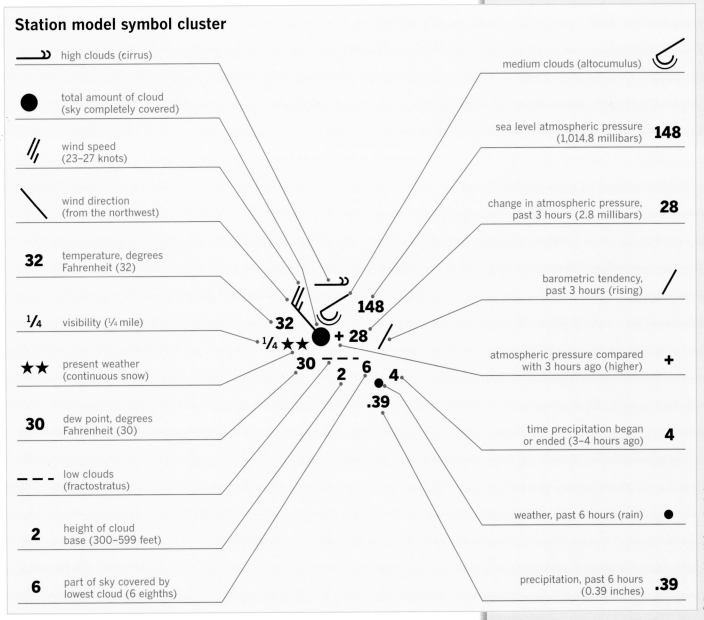

- high clouds (cirrus)
- total amount of cloud (sky completely covered)
- wind speed (23–27 knots)
- wind direction (from the northwest)
- **32** temperature, degrees Fahrenheit (32)
- **¹/₄** visibility (¹/₄ mile)
- ★★ present weather (continuous snow)
- **30** dew point, degrees Fahrenheit (30)
- – – – low clouds (fractostratus)
- **2** height of cloud base (300–599 feet)
- **6** part of sky covered by lowest cloud (6 eighths)

- medium clouds (altocumulus)
- sea level atmospheric pressure (1,014.8 millibars) **148**
- change in atmospheric pressure, past 3 hours (2.8 millibars) **28**
- barometric tendency, past 3 hours (rising) /
- atmospheric pressure compared with 3 hours ago (higher) **+**
- time precipitation began or ended (3–4 hours ago) **4**
- weather, past 6 hours (rain) ●
- precipitation, past 6 hours (0.39 inches) **.39**

© Diagram Visual Information Ltd.

Simplified weather map

Key words

synoptic chart

Synoptic chart

- Forecasters usually plot just the key elements of each station's detailed report when preparing synoptic charts. This chart shows a low-pressure system over Texas. Note the clear skies behind the system and the heavy cloud cover in the warm sector between the warm and cold weather fronts.

Weather station data

- The simplified synoptic chart shows a weak frontal depression moving in a northeasterly direction. This is the open stage of the frontal system, where air behind the cold front has not yet started to push beneath the warm air.
- In the warm sector between the fronts the sky is overcast. The easterly or southeasterly winds back (change direction in a counterclockwise direction) to southerly as the fronts approach, but winds remain easterly on either side of the warm front. Wind speeds range from 8–22 knots (14.8–40.7 kmph): a gentle to strong breeze.

- Skies are clearer to the west, behind the cold front, and the temperature is up to 20°F lower in the cooler air. Winds are from a more westerly direction and somewhat stronger, up to 27 knots (50 kmph), which is almost gale force.
- Ahead of the warm front, in the northern part of the region, a gentle to strong breeze blows from the east. Skies are overcast and temperatures cool. The dew point and air temperatures are the same, making very low cloud or fog likely.
- Near the center of the depression, where pressure is lowest, the sky is overcast and a moderate breeze is blowing from the north.

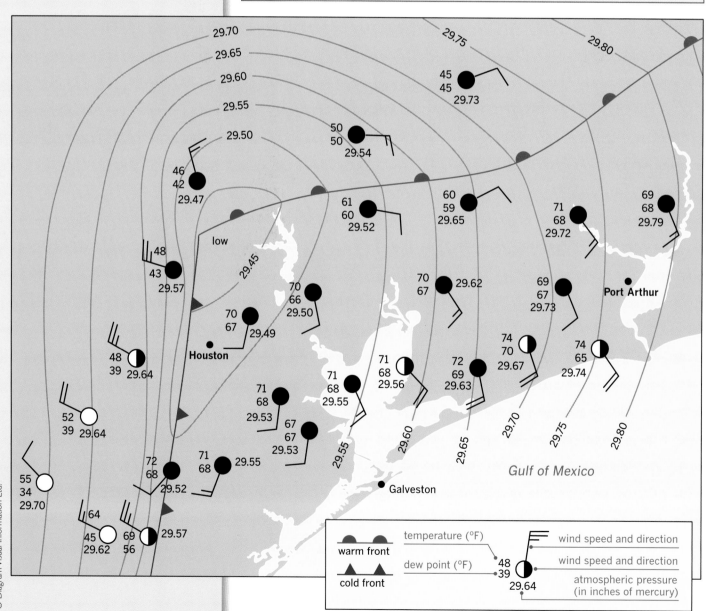

Climate regions of the world

Climate types

- *Climate* refers to the typical weather that a place experiences over many years. Different parts of the world can be described as having very dry, wet, hot, or cold climates. Climates affect very large areas of the world and those of particular regions are determined mainly, but not entirely, by latitude.

- There have been many schemes to classify climates. The classification most widely used today was developed between 1884 and 1916 by the German climatologist Wladimir Peter Köppen (1846–1940). The map below is based on the Köppen classification.

- Köppen divided climates into six principal types designated by the letters A through F, with highland climates forming a seventh. Within these categories, additional letters provide further information about climates. For example, Edmonton, Alberta, has cold winters, short, cool summers, and precipitation throughout the year; it is designated Dfc in the Köppen scheme. D indicates a cold, northern climate with winter temperatures below 26.6°F (–3°C) and temperatures above 50°F (10°C) in the warmest month.

Key words

climate
Köppen
  classification
latitude
polar

temperate
tropical

Locations of climate types

Each of the locations indicated on the map has a climate typical of one of the major climate regions on Earth.

Addis Ababa, Ethiopia
Amsterdam, The Netherlands
Buenos Aires, Argentina
Cloncurry, Queensland, Australia
Edmonton, Alberta, Canada
Eismitte, Greenland
Krasnoyarsk, Siberia, Russia
Manama, Bahrain
Manaus, Brazil
Mexico City, Mexico
Ouagadougou, Burkina Faso
Montreal, Quebec, Canada

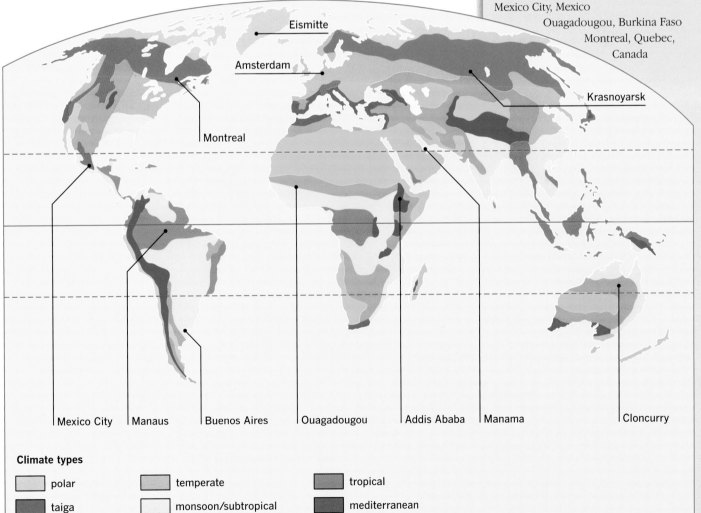

Climate types

polar	temperate	tropical
taiga	monsoon/subtropical	mediterranean
highland	savanna/steppe	desert

Climate types: 1

Climate diagrams

- A climate diagram shows the temperature and precipitation throughout the year in a particular place.
- In Addis Ababa, Ethiopia, the temperature varies little through the year, indicating a low latitude, but it is never very hot, indicating a high elevation. Addis Ababa has a highland climate (H) with a pronounced summer rainy season.
- Amsterdam, Netherlands, shows much greater seasonal variation in temperature, but precipitation spread fairly evenly through the year. It has a maritime west coast climate (Cfb).
- Bahrain has hot summers, mild winters, and it is very dry. It has the climate of a hot desert (Bwh).
- Buenos Aires has warm summers, mild winters, and precipitation spread evenly through the year. It has a humid subtropical climate (Cwa).
- Cloncurry, Australia, has hot summers, mild winters, and rain falls mainly in summer. This is a savanna climate (Aw).
- Edmonton, Canada, has very cold winters, cool summers, and more precipitation in summer than in winter. It has a subpolar climate (Dfc).

ⓐ average monthly temperature

ⓑ average monthly rainfall

Locator map

Addis Ababa Ethiopia (1)

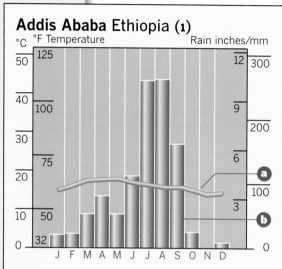

Buenos Aires Argentina (4)

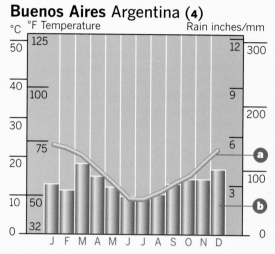

Amsterdam Netherlands (2)

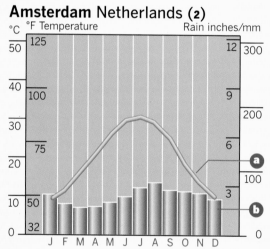

Cloncurry Australia (5)

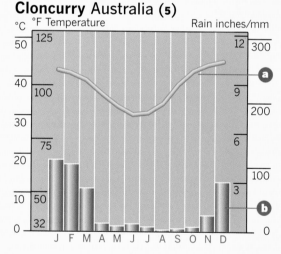

Bahrain (3)

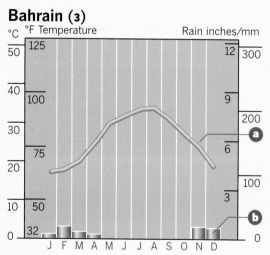

Edmonton Canada (6)

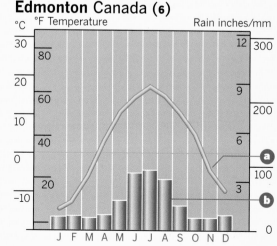

Climate types: 2

Locator map

a average monthly temperature
b average monthly rainfall

Climate diagrams

- Eismitte lies near the center of the ice sheet that covers most of Greenland, at 71° N and 250 miles (402 km) from the coast. It is a bitterly cold, extremely dry place, with a polar icecap climate of perpetual frost (EF). Even in the middle of summer the temperature barely rises above freezing.
- Krasnoyarsk, Russia, has very cold winters, cool summers, and little precipitation. It has a dry, steppe climate (BSk).
- Manaus, Brazil, has a typical tropical rainforest climate (Af). It is hot all year, with little seasonal variation, and rainfall is high, especially in summer.
- Mexico City, Mexico, has a highland climate (H). The temperature varies little through the year, but the weather is seldom extremely hot, despite Mexico lying in the tropics. Winters are dry.
- Ouagadougou, Burkina Faso, lies between the tropical forests of the African west coast and the Sahara to the north. It is warm all year and no rain falls between November and February. It has a dry, low-latitude, steppe climate (BSh).
- Montreal, Canada, has cold winters, short cool summers, and precipitation is spread evenly through the year. It has a continental humid climate (Dfb).

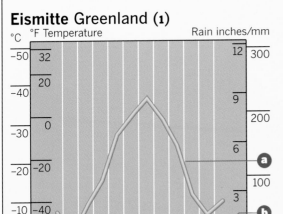

Eismitte Greenland (1)

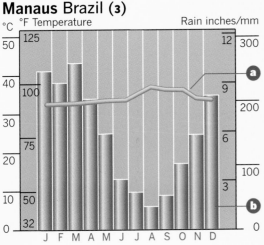

Manaus Brazil (3)

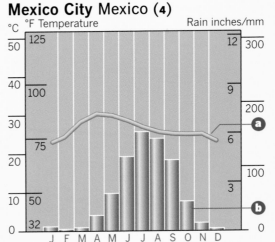

Mexico City Mexico (4)

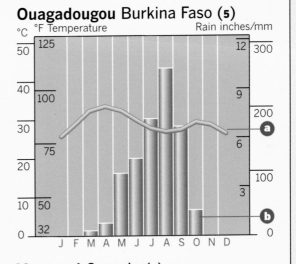

Ouagadougou Burkina Faso (5)

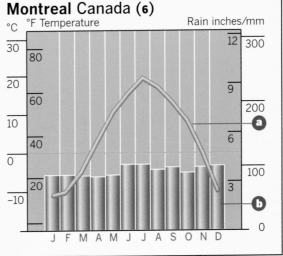

Montreal Canada (6)

© Diagram Visual Information Ltd.

Vertical temperature zones

© Diagram Visual Information Ltd.

Key words

latitude
life zone
snow line
temperate
tropical

Life zones

- Climatic conditions tend to change with altitude. On a large mountain there is typically a range of climatic conditions at differing altitudes.
- These are often referred to as *life zones* because they can be defined by the life forms that live in them, particularly the types of vegetation.
- The most obvious of these life zones begins at the *snow line*. Above the snow line there is permanent snow and ice, and almost no vegetation is able to survive.
- The typical pattern of life zones found on mountains differs with latitude. In the tropics, temperatures are generally higher and have less seasonal variation. This results in snow lines at higher altitudes.
- High-altitude regions below the snow line of a tropical mountain may experience frosts almost every night, but daytime temperatures are high enough to prevent permanent ice forming.

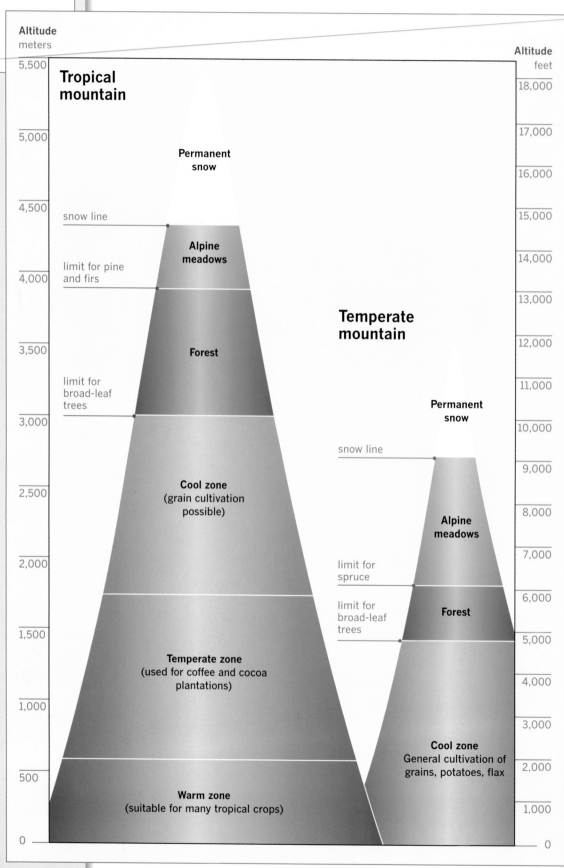

Altitude
meters

Altitude
feet

Tropical mountain

Permanent snow

snow line

Alpine meadows

limit for pine and firs

Forest

limit for broad-leaf trees

Cool zone (grain cultivation possible)

Temperate zone (used for coffee and cocoa plantations)

Warm zone (suitable for many tropical crops)

Temperate mountain

Permanent snow

snow line

Alpine meadows

limit for spruce

limit for broad-leaf trees

Forest

Cool zone General cultivation of grains, potatoes, flax

meters	feet
5,500	18,000
	17,000
5,000	16,000
	15,000
4,500	14,000
4,000	13,000
3,500	12,000
	11,000
3,000	10,000
2,500	9,000
	8,000
2,000	7,000
	6,000
1,500	5,000
	4,000
1,000	3,000
500	2,000
	1,000
0	0

U.S. coastal and inland temperature ranges

Key words

climate
latitude

Pacific Coast

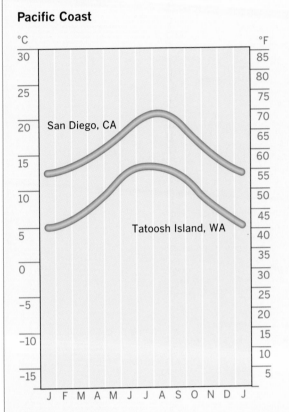

San Diego, CA

Tatoosh Island, WA

Atlantic Coast

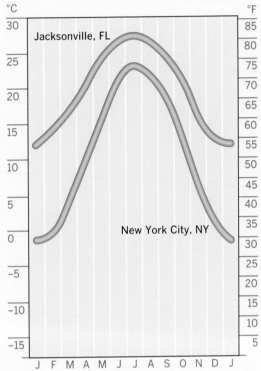

Jacksonville, FL

New York City, NY

Rocky Mountains

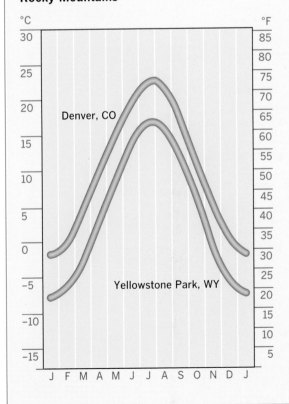

Denver, CO

Yellowstone Park, WY

Mississippi Valley

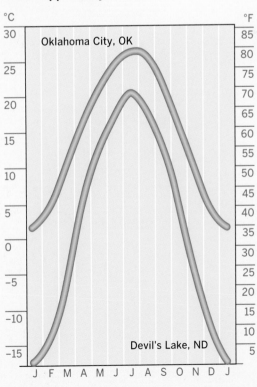

Oklahoma City, OK

Devil's Lake, ND

Coastal and inland climate

- The western coast of the United States receives air that has crossed the Pacific Ocean, giving this region a maritime climate in which contact with the sea surface cools the air in summer and warms it in winter, preventing seasonal extremes of temperature. This is reflected in the shallow curve for the temperatures at San Diego and Tatoosh Island.

- Places on the Atlantic coast receive air that has crossed the continent. They therefore have more continental climates, with a larger seasonal temperature range. Their climates are nonetheless influenced by the proximity of the ocean, especially in winter, preventing extreme cold.

- The continental climates of places far from the coast produce a much wider temperature range. Devil's Lake is in approximately the same latitude as Tatoosh Island, and Oklahoma City lies at about the same latitude as San Diego.

U.S. winter and summer temperatures

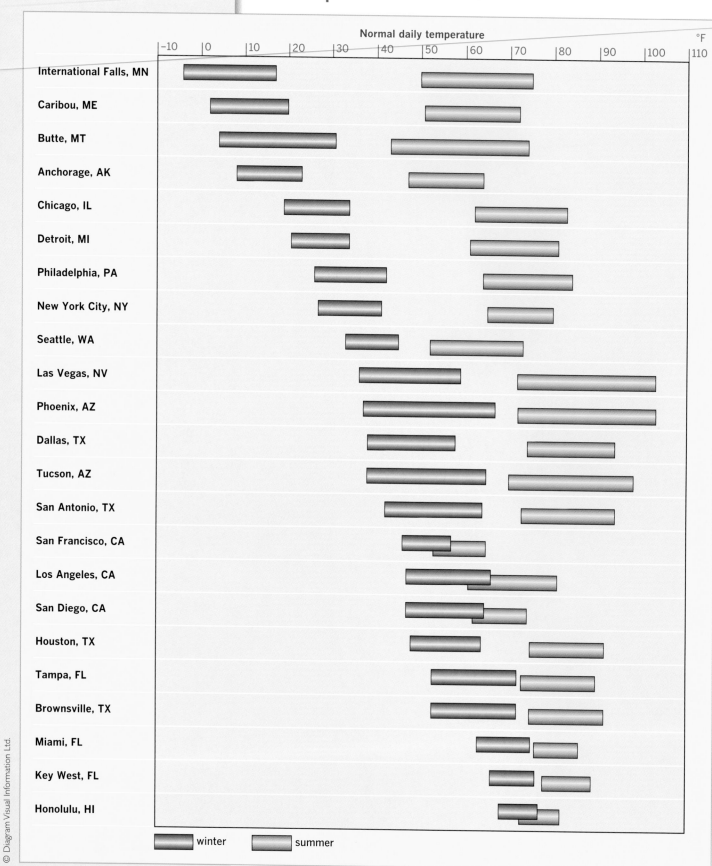

Normal daily temperature

International Falls, MN
Caribou, ME
Butte, MT
Anchorage, AK
Chicago, IL
Detroit, MI
Philadelphia, PA
New York City, NY
Seattle, WA
Las Vegas, NV
Phoenix, AZ
Dallas, TX
Tucson, AZ
San Antonio, TX
San Francisco, CA
Los Angeles, CA
San Diego, CA
Houston, TX
Tampa, FL
Brownsville, TX
Miami, FL
Key West, FL
Honolulu, HI

−10 |0 |10 |20 |30 |40 |50 |60 |70 |80 |90 |100 |110 °F

winter   summer

Frost-free days: world

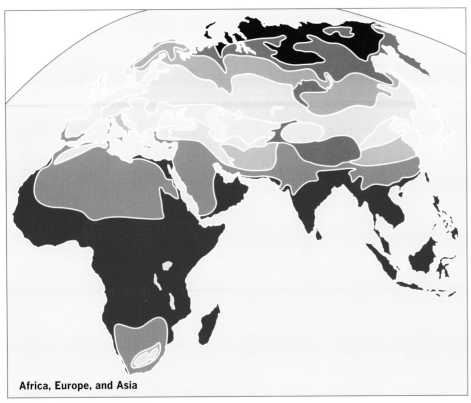

Africa, Europe, and Asia

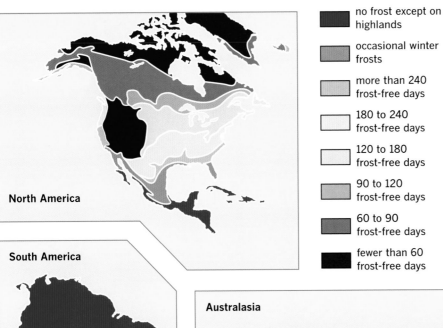

North America

South America

Australasia

■ no frost except on highlands

■ occasional winter frosts

□ more than 240 frost-free days

□ 180 to 240 frost-free days

□ 120 to 180 frost-free days

■ 90 to 120 frost-free days

■ 60 to 90 frost-free days

■ fewer than 60 frost-free days

Key words

growing season
latitude
tropical

First and last frosts

● Farmers and horticulturists cannot cultivate frozen ground and when the ground is frozen there is no liquid water for plant roots to absorb, so plants are unable to grow.

● Commercial growers need to sow seed as early as possible in spring and continue growing as late as possible into the fall.

● After the ground thaws in spring there is a risk of late frosts, and early frosts can occur long before the ground freezes at the onset of winter. Temperatures below freezing damage crop plants by killing flowers and tender shoots in spring, and by destroying fruits before they have set seed in the autumn. Consequently, the length of the agricultural and horticultural growing season does not depend on the time that elapses between the spring thaw and winter freeze, but on the time from the date of the last frost of early spring until the first frost of the fall.

● The number of frost-free days varies with latitude and elevation, but it is only tropical climates that never experience frost. Everywhere else, as the map shows, freezing temperatures restrict crop production to a greater or lesser extent.

Key words
jet stream
polar
polar front
tornado
tropical

Wind patterns

- In winter, polar air covers most of the central and eastern United States. Prevailing winds are from the west, but undulations in the polar front frequently draw very cold air southward from the far north, producing northerly winds over Canada and the northern states that swing to a west-to-east direction as they approach the front.

- In summer the entire pattern shifts northward and all of the coterminous United States lies beneath tropical air. The jet stream is weaker in summer (with an average wind speed of about 32 knots, 60 kmph) than in winter (average speed 67 knots, 125 kmph). Weather systems move more slowly. Winds are lighter and there are long periods of settled weather—but with a risk of severe storms.

- To the north of the polar front, Canada experiences winds bringing cold air from the Arctic that become westerly as they approach the front. On the southern side of the front, the United States experiences winds from three directions. Cool, dry air enters from the west, across the mountains. Hot, dry air moves northward from Mexico across Texas and New Mexico, where its temperature rises further through contact with the hot ground. Warm, very moist air enters from the Gulf of Mexico. These airflows meet across the Great Plains, where the moist Gulf air forms a layer trapped between two layers of dry air. From time to time this highly unstable situation breaks down to produce violent storms, bringing tornadoes to the region known as Tornado Alley.

Seasonal winds over the USA

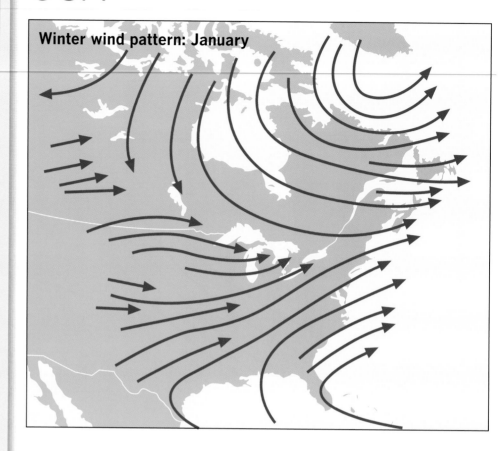

Winter wind pattern: January

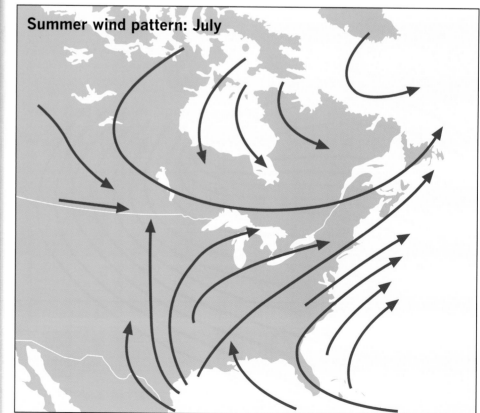

Summer wind pattern: July

Climate regions of the oceans

Key words

climate
gyre
latitude
polar
tropical

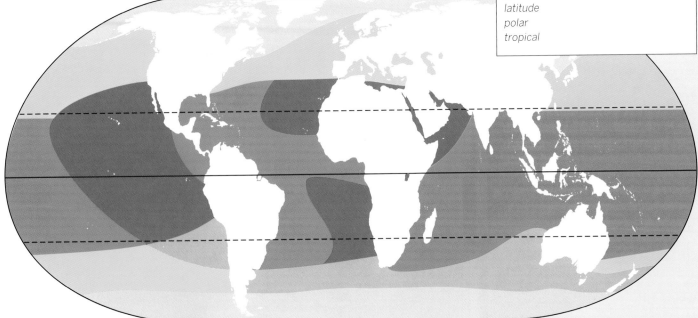

- warm tropical ocean
- cool tropical ocean
- cold polar ocean
- warm temperate ocean
- cool temperate ocean

Surface currents

- The sea surface moves, as the prevailing winds drag the water along: from east to west in the tropics, and from west to east in middle latitudes. The wind creates surface currents that turn as they approach continents, their direction reversing as they move from the influence of the tropical easterly winds to that of the midlatitude westerlies. The currents move in circles called gyres in each of the ocean basins, moving clockwise in the Northern Hemisphere and counterclockwise in the Southern Hemisphere. The gyres transport warm water away from the equator and carry cool water toward the equator. This circulation also produces regions of relatively warmer or cooler seas resembling the climatic zones on land.

← warm currents   ← cold currents

Ocean temperatures

- Tropical climates are warmer than those of high latitudes and this difference affects the oceans as well as the continents. By late summer the surface of the tropical oceans is often warmer than 85°F (29°C), while the polar oceans are only slightly above freezing.

- Warm water moves from east to west on both sides of the equator. As the currents carry water away from the equator they make the western sides of the oceans warmer than the eastern, where cool water is moving toward the equator. When warm currents enter the Arctic Ocean the pattern reverses, the eastern side becoming the warmer.

© Diagram Visual Information Ltd.

Key words

ice age
greenhouse gas

The Carboniferous-Permian ice age

320 million years ago

- Around 320 million years ago, toward the end of the Carboniferous and during the early Permian periods, large parts of the world plunged into an ice age that lasted for 70 million years. Ice sheets eventually covered most of what are now Antarctica, southern Australia, India, southern Africa, and eastern South America. There was also an ice sheet near what is now Siberia, which was then near the North Pole.

- At the time, the continents of the present-day Southern Hemisphere, together with India, were joined together forming a supercontinent known as *Gondwana*. Early in the Permian, the northern continents had been joined with Gondwana in a single landmass known as *Pangaea* (Greek for "all land"). The Carboniferous-Permian ice age gripped the southern part of Pangaea. During the Permian much of the center of Pangaea became a vast hot desert.

- Farther north, Pangaean coastal regions were marshy in many places. Plants growing there included ferns, seed ferns, and relatives of modern club mosses. Ancestors of coniferous and flowering plants were starting to appear in the drier areas inland. Insects flew among the plants and the first reptiles fed on the vegetation.

- The movement of the continents pushed Gondwana across the South Pole, triggering a drop in temperature that allowed ice sheets to form and spread.

- The amount of carbon dioxide in the air fell during the Carboniferous. Carbon dioxide is a greenhouse gas and its reduction may also have allowed the temperature to decrease. Carbon dioxide was removed as dying swamp plants fell into the mud and slowly changed into coal instead of decomposing and returning their carbon to the air.

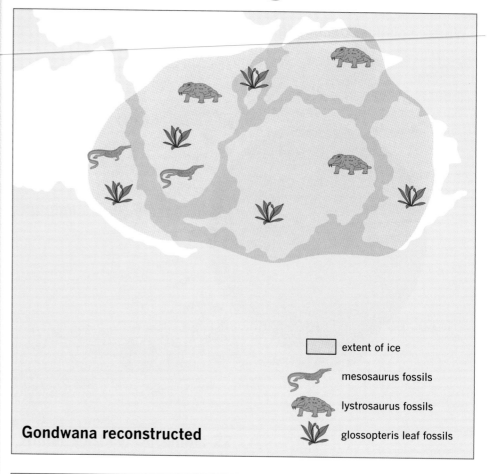

Gondwana reconstructed

☐ extent of ice

mesosaurus fossils

lystrosaurus fossils

glossopteris leaf fossils

Early Permian glaciation

☐ extent of ice sheets   ← direction of ice movement

The Pleistocene ice age

Ice ages

- The most recent ice age, known as the Pleistocene or simply "the Ice Age," lasted from 1.8 million–10,000 years ago.
- Ice sheets advanced across the Northern Hemisphere four times in this period, each time producing a *glaciation*. Episodes of warmer climates between glaciations are known as *interglacials*. At present we are living in the Holocene interglacial.
- The most recent glaciation, known as the Wisconsinian, began about 70,000 years ago. The ice sheets reached their maximum extent about 20,000 years ago. By 15,000 years ago the ice was starting to retreat and by 10,000 years ago the ice sheet that had once covered northern Eurasia covered only part of Scandinavia. The Laurasian ice sheet of North America covered only the northeastern part of the continent. The glaciation had ended.

Glaciations

From the earliest (**1**) to the most recent (**4**), the principal glaciations of the Ice Age are known by the following names in North America and Europe:

	North America	Europe
4	Wisconsinian	Würm
3	Illinoisan	Riss
2	Kansan	Mindel
1	Nebraskan	Günz

Present day   ice cover

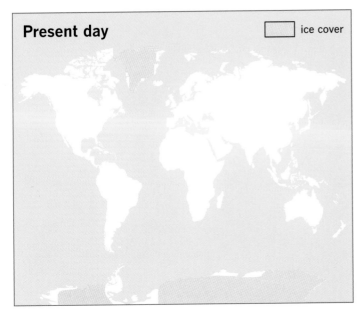

10,000 years ago

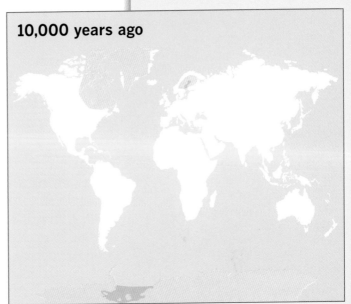

15,000 years ago

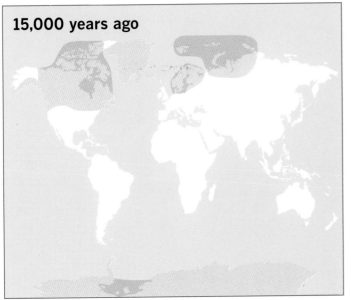

20,000 years ago

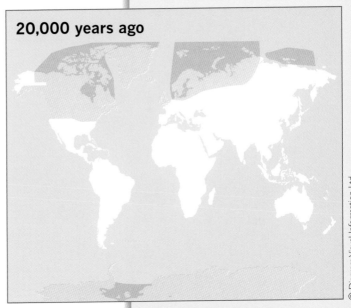

Key words

ice age

Maximum ice cover: North America

Laurentide ice sheet

- Ice sheets advanced and retreated repeatedly during the Pleistocene epoch.
- The Laurentide ice sheet of North America was the biggest ice sheet in the world. At its greatest extent the Laurentide stretched from the Rocky Mountains to Nova Scotia and Newfoundland. The whole of the Arctic Ocean was frozen and the ice sheet covered all of Canada. Ice covered the sea between North America and Greenland. Northern and central Alaska escaped the ice, perhaps because the climate was too dry for snow to accumulate, but southern Alaska was covered.
- The southern boundary of the Laurentide ice sheet ran from about where Vancouver is today to Massachusetts, but with a large extension around the Great Lakes, where the ice reached southern Illinois.

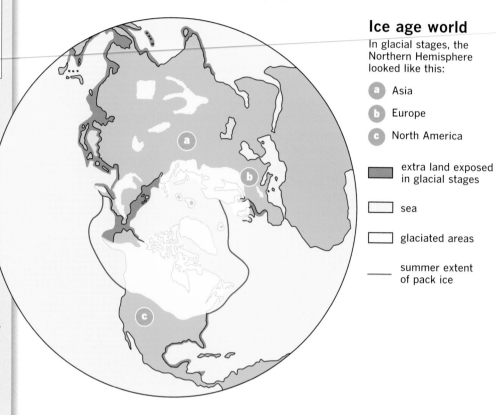

Ice age world

In glacial stages, the Northern Hemisphere looked like this:

- **a** Asia
- **b** Europe
- **c** North America

▦	extra land exposed in glacial stages
▢	sea
▢	glaciated areas
—	summer extent of pack ice

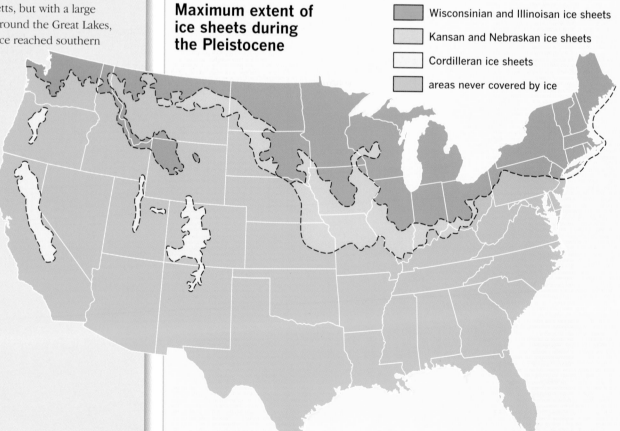

Maximum extent of ice sheets during the Pleistocene

▦	Wisconsinian and Illinoisan ice sheets
▦	Kansan and Nebraskan ice sheets
▢	Cordilleran ice sheets
▦	areas never covered by ice

Maximum ice cover: Europe

Key words

ice age

Ice age world

In glacial stages, the Northern Hemisphere looked like this:

a Asia

b Europe

c North America

▨ extra land exposed in glacial stages

☐ sea

☐ glaciated areas

— summer extent of pack ice

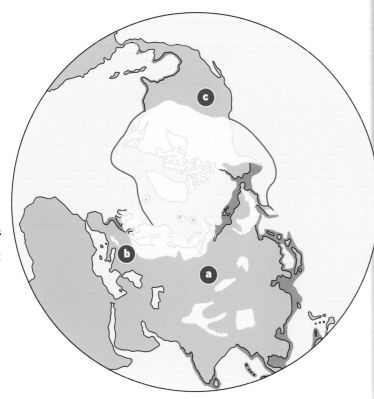

Fennoscandian ice sheet

● The ice sheet over Eurasia was smaller than the Laurentide, but similar in other respects. It is often called the Fennoscandian, but particular sections have names of their own, the largest being the Scandinavian.

● At its greatest extent the ice stretched from the Laptev Sea, at about 120° E, to the western coast of Ireland. There were smaller ice sheets in eastern Siberia, but the climate was too dry for the entire region to be covered by ice.

● Most of Britain lay beneath ice as far south as a line from the Bristol Channel to the Wash. In continental Europe the ice covered central Germany and Poland. Smaller glaciers and ice sheets formed in the Alps, Pyrenees, and Caucasus.

Mountain ice caps

a Alps

b Pyrenees

c Caucasus

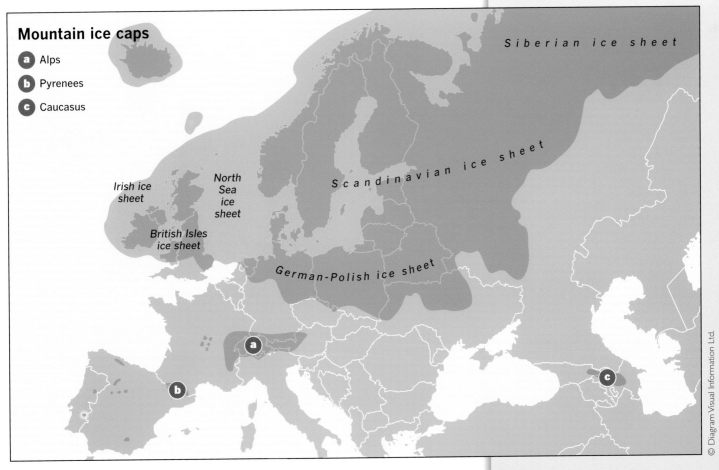

Siberian ice sheet

Scandinavian ice sheet

Irish ice sheet

North Sea ice sheet

British Isles ice sheet

German-Polish ice sheet

City name • City name
A general description of each city (two on each page), its location, and general climate.

Elevation
● The cities' average heights above sea level in feet and meters.

Latitude
● The cities' locations in degrees and minutes north or south.

Köppen climate
● The Köppen climate code and description of each city's location.

Key to world climate data
pages 111 to 152

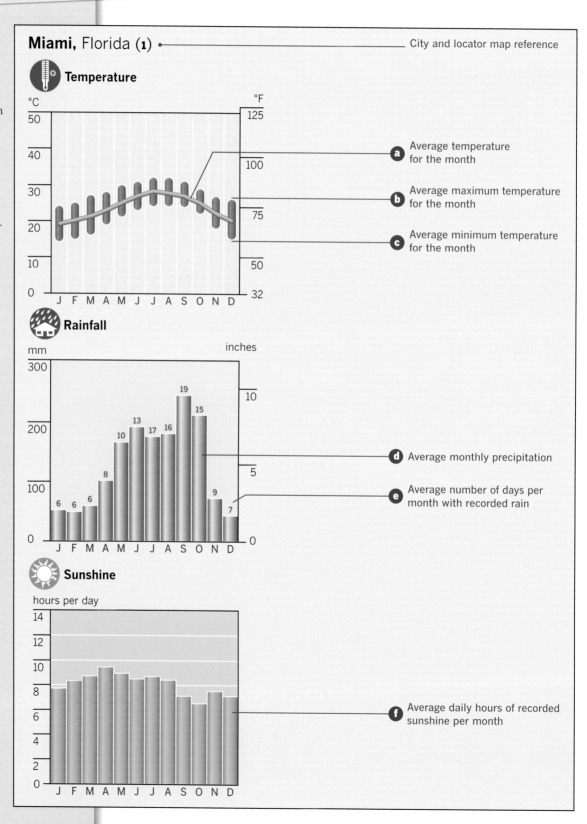

Miami, Florida (1) ———————————————— City and locator map reference

Temperature

°C ————————————————————— °F

a Average temperature for the month

b Average maximum temperature for the month

c Average minimum temperature for the month

Rainfall

mm ——————— inches

d Average monthly precipitation

e Average number of days per month with recorded rain

Sunshine

hours per day

f Average daily hours of recorded sunshine per month

Anchorage • Cheyenne

North America 1

Average recorded monthly features

a Temperature
b Maximum temperature
c Minimum temperature
d Precipitation
e Days with rain
f Daily hours of sunshine

Locator map

Anchorage • Cheyenne

- Anchorage is sheltered from the extreme conditions further inland, but its climate is little influenced by the ocean.
- Cheyenne has a dry climate, but avoids extreme heat because of its high elevation.

Elevation
- Anchorage: 132 feet (40 m).
- Cheyenne: 6,139 feet (1,871 m).

Latitude
- Anchorage: 61°14' N
- Cheyenne: 41°09' N

Köppen climate
- Anchorage Cfb (maritime west coast, no dry season, mild winters, cool to warm summers).
- Cheyenne: BSk (midlatitude steppe climate, semiarid, cool).

Anchorage, Alaska (1)

Temperature

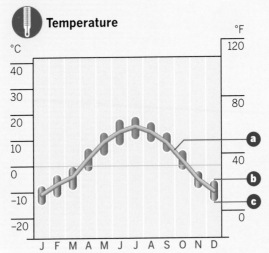

Rainfall

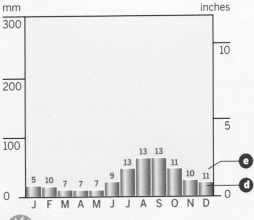

Sunshine

hours per day

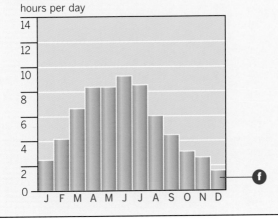

Cheyenne, Wyoming (2)

Temperature

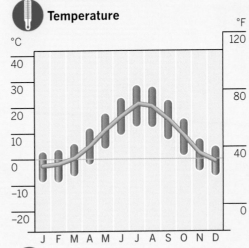

Rainfall

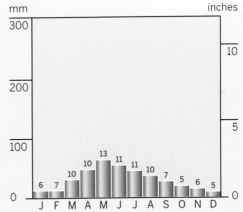

Sunshine

hours per day

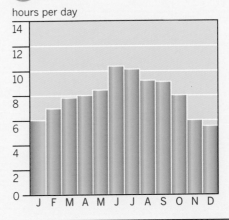

Chicago • Churchill

North America 2

Chicago • Churchill
- Chicago has a very changeable climate, strongly influenced by the Great Lakes.
- Churchill has a cold, dry climate, but sometimes enjoys high temperatures during the brief summer.

Average recorded monthly features
- **a** Temperature
- **b** Maximum temperature
- **c** Minimum temperature
- **d** Precipitation
- **e** Days with rain
- **f** Daily hours of sunshine

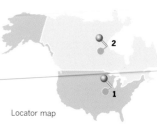

Locator map

Elevation
- Chicago: 823 feet (251 m)
- Churchill: 43 feet (13 m)

Latitude
- Chicago: 41°53' N
- Churchill: 58°47' N

Köppen climate
- Chicago: Dfa (humid continental, hot summers, cold winters).
- Churchill: Dfc (subarctic, short cool summers, long cold winters, dry).

Chicago, Illinois (1)

Temperature

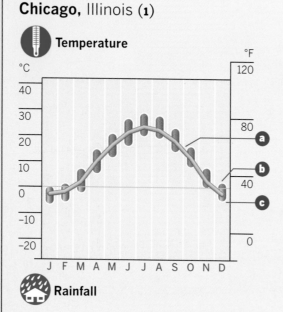

Rainfall

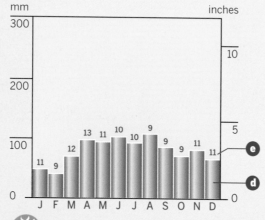

Sunshine

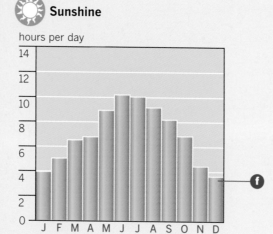

Churchill, Canada (2)

Temperature

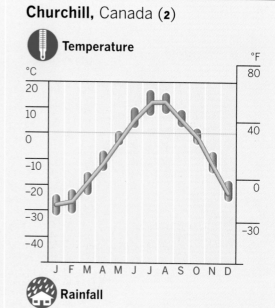

Rainfall

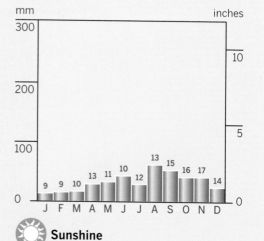

Sunshine

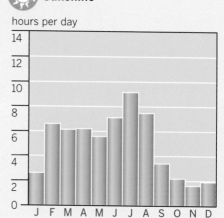

Edmonton • Houston

North America 3

Average recorded monthly features

- **a** Temperature
- **b** Maximum temperature
- **c** Minimum temperature
- **d** Precipitation
- **e** Days with rain
- **f** Daily hours of sunshine

Locator map

Edmonton • Houston

- Edmonton has a dry, cool, prairie climate, but with chinook winds raising average winter temperatures.
- Houston has a hot, moist climate and occasionally experiences hurricanes.

Elevation
- Edmonton: 2,199 feet (677 m)
- Houston: 41 feet (13 m)

Latitude
- Edmonton: 53°35' N
- Houston: 29°46' N

Köppen climate
- Edmonton: BSk (midlatitude cold steppe, semiarid, cool or cold).
- Houston: Cfa (humid subtropical, no dry season, hot summers, mild winters).

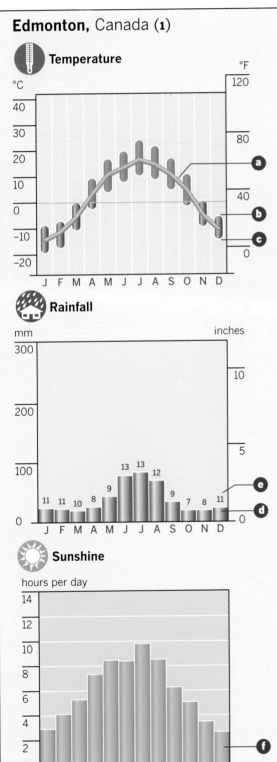

Edmonton, Canada (1)

Temperature

Rainfall

Sunshine

hours per day

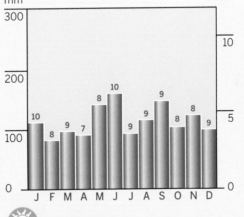

Houston, Texas (2)

Temperature

Rainfall

Sunshine

hours per day

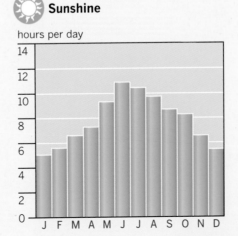

Los Angeles • Mexico City

Los Angeles • Mexico City

- Los Angeles has a climate dominated by the semipermanent region of high pressure over the ocean.
- Mexico City has a tropical climate with a summer rainy season, but avoids extreme heat because of its elevation.

Elevation

- Los Angeles: 312 feet (95 m)
- Mexico City: 7,575 feet (2,309 m)

Latitude

- Los Angeles: 34°03' N
- Mexico City: 19°24' N

Köppen climate

- Los Angeles: Csa (Mediterranean, hot, dry summers, mild winters).
- Mexico City: H (highland climate, cool due to elevation).

North America 4

Average recorded monthly features

a Temperature
b Maximum temperature
c Minimum temperature
d Precipitation
e Days with rain
f Daily hours of sunshine

Locator map

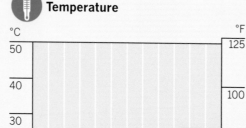

Los Angeles, California (1)

 Temperature

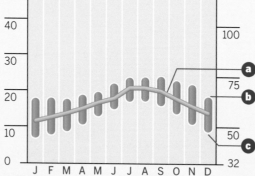

 Rainfall

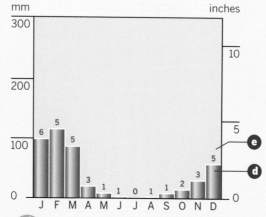

Sunshine

hours per day

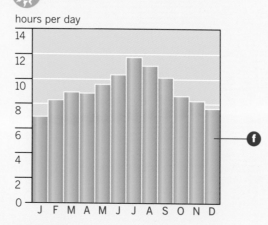

Mexico City, Mexico (2)

Temperature

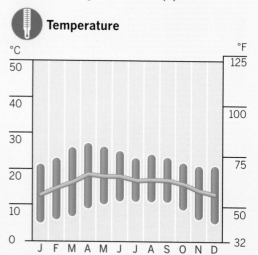

Rainfall

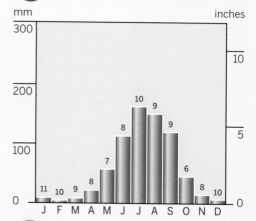

Sunshine

hours per day

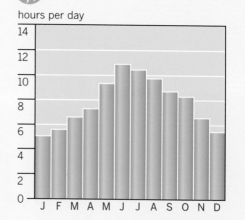

Miami • Montreal

North America 5

Average recorded monthly features

- **a** Temperature
- **b** Maximum temperature
- **c** Minimum temperature
- **d** Precipitation
- **e** Days with rain
- **f** Daily hours of sunshine

Locator map

Miami • Montreal

- Miami has a climate similar to that of the tropical savanna grasslands, but occasionally experiences hurricanes.
- Montreal has a moist, cool, maritime climate.

Elevation
- Miami: 25 feet (8 m)
- Montreal: 187 feet (57 m)

Latitude
- Miami: 25°48' N
- Montreal: 45°30' N

Köppen climate
- Miami: Aw (tropical savanna climate, hot with a summer rainy season).
- Montreal: Dfb (continental moist, short, warm summers, cold winters).

Miami, Florida (1)

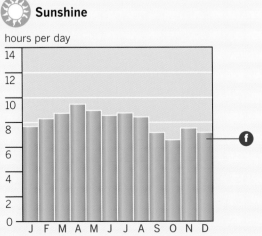

Montreal, Canada (2)

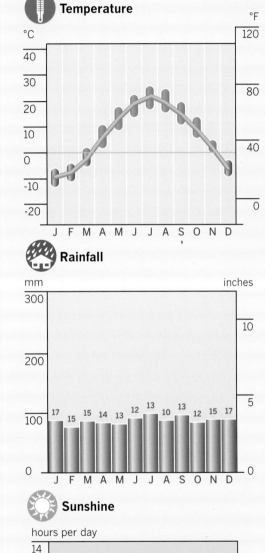

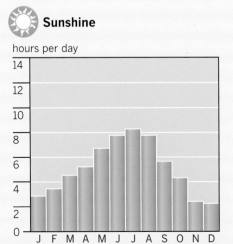

New York • San Francisco

North America 6

New York City• San Francisco

- New York has a warm, maritime climate, with hot summers but much snow in winter.
- San Francisco has a mild, equable climate, but frequent fogs in summer.

Elevation
- New York City: 131 feet (40 m)
- San Francisco: 52 feet (16 m)

Latitude
- New York City: 40°43' N
- San Francisco: 37°47' N

Köppen climate
- New York City: Dfb (humid continental, severe winter, no dry season, warm summer).
- San Francisco: Csb (Mediterranean, warm, dry summer, mild winter).

Average recorded monthly features

- **a** Temperature
- **b** Maximum temperature
- **c** Minimum temperature
- **d** Precipitation
- **e** Days with rain
- **f** Daily hours of sunshine

Locator map

New York City, New York (1)

Temperature

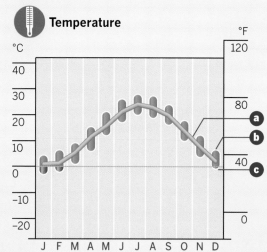

Rainfall

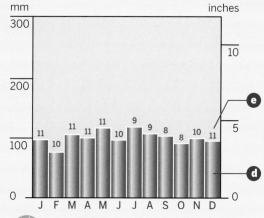

Sunshine

hours per day

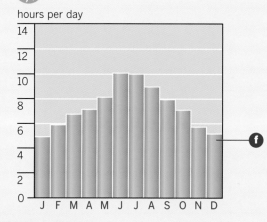

San Francisco, California (2)

Temperature

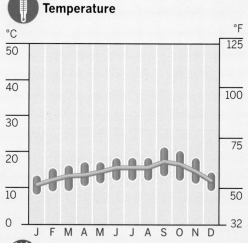

Rainfall

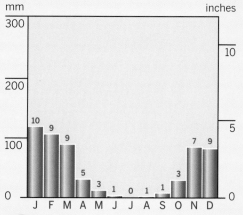

Sunshine

hours per day

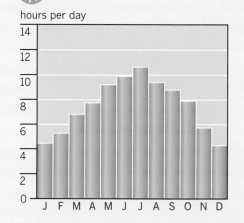

San José • St. Louis

North America 7

Average recorded monthly features

a Temperature
b Maximum temperature
c Minimum temperature
d Precipitation
e Days with rain
f Daily hours of sunshine

Locator map

San José • St. Louis

- San José has a tropical climate with a summer rainy season, but moderate temperatures owing to its elevation.
- St. Louis has hot summers, cool winters, and droughts are common.

Elevation
- San José: 3,760 feet (1,146 m)
- St. Louis: 568 feet (173 m)

Latitude
- San José: 9°56' N
- St. Louis: 38°28' N

Köppen climate
- San José: Aw (tropical rainforest, with summer rainy season).
- St. Louis: Dfa (humid continental with long, hot summers, cold winters, no dry season).

San José, Costa Rica (1)

Temperature

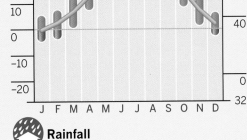

Rainfall

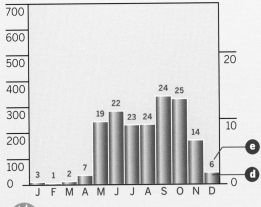

Sunshine

hours per day

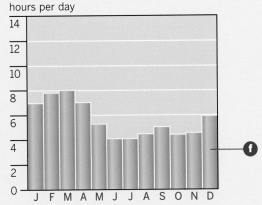

St. Louis, Missouri (2)

Temperature

Rainfall

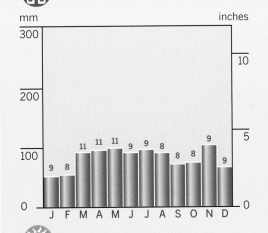

Sunshine

hours per day

WORLD CLIMATE DATA

Vancouver • Washington, D.C.

- Vancouver has a cool maritime climate: dry in summer, wet in winter.
- Washington has hot, humid summers and cool winters, often with heavy snow.

Elevation
- Vancouver: 45 feet (14 m)
- Washington: 72 feet (22 m)

Latitude
- Vancouver: 49°17' N
- Washington: 38°54' N

Köppen climate
- Vancouver: Cfc (maritime west coast, mild winter, cool summer, moist).
- Washington: Dfb (humid continental, severe winter, no dry season, warm summer).

Vancouver • Washington
North America 8

Average recorded monthly features

- **a** Temperature
- **b** Maximum temperature
- **c** Minimum temperature
- **d** Precipitation
- **e** Days with rain
- **f** Daily hours of sunshine

Locator map

Vancouver, Canada (1)

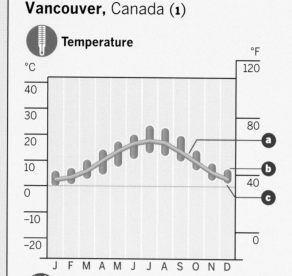

Temperature

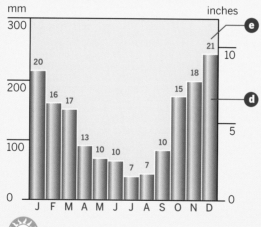

Rainfall

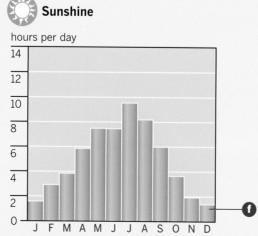

Sunshine

Washington, D.C. (2)

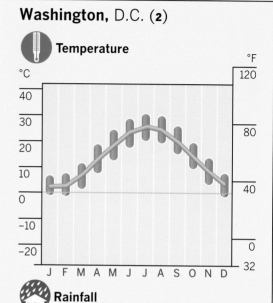

Temperature

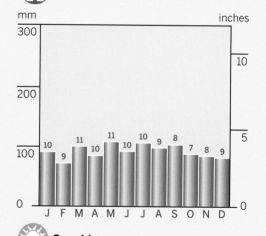

Rainfall

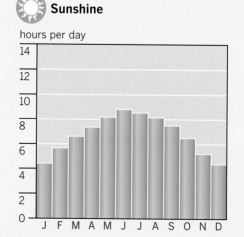

Sunshine

© Diagram Visual Information Ltd.

Antofagasta • Brasilia

South America 1

Average recorded monthly features

ⓐ Temperature   **ⓓ** Precipitation
ⓑ Maximum temperature   **ⓔ** Days with rain
ⓒ Minimum temperature   **ⓕ** Daily hours of sunshine

Locator map

Antofagasta • Brasilia
- Antofagasta has a cool desert climate, with very low rainfall and little change in temperature through the year.
- Brasilia has a tropical grassland climate with a summer rainy season and moderate temperatures owing to its elevation.

Elevation
- Antofagasta: 308 feet (94 m)
- Brasilia: 3,481 feet (1,061 m)

Latitude
- Antofagasta: 23°42' S
- Brasilia: 15°47' S

Köppen climate
- Antofagasta: BWh (hot desert).
- Brasilia: Aw (tropical savanna, hot all year, summer rainy season).

Antofagasta, Chile (1)

Temperature

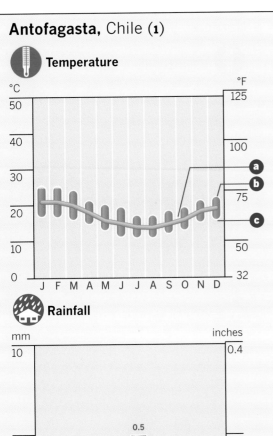

Rainfall

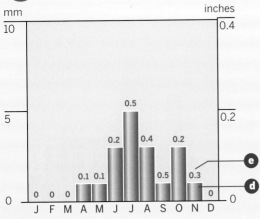

Sunshine

hours per day

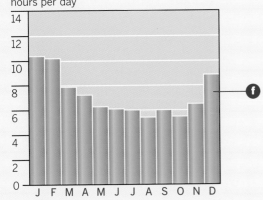

Brasilia, Brazil (2)

Temperature

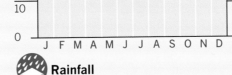

Rainfall

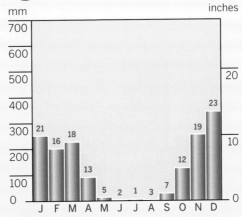

Sunshine

hours per day

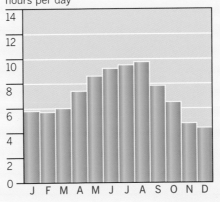

Manaus • Quito

- Manaus, in the Amazon Basin, has a hot, wet, tropical climate.
- Quito, almost on the equator but high above sea level has a climate often described as "perpetual spring."

Elevation

- Manaus: 144 feet (34 m)
- Quito: 9,446 feet (2,879 m)

Latitude

- Manaus: 3°08' S
- Quito: 0°13' S

Köppen climate

- Manaus: Af (tropical rain forest, hot and wet throughout the year).
- Quito: Aw (tropical savanna, cool, summer rainy season).

Manaus • Quito

South America 4

Average recorded monthly features

- **a** Temperature
- **b** Maximum temperature
- **c** Minimum temperature
- **d** Precipitation
- **e** Days with rain
- **f** Daily hours of sunshine

Locator map

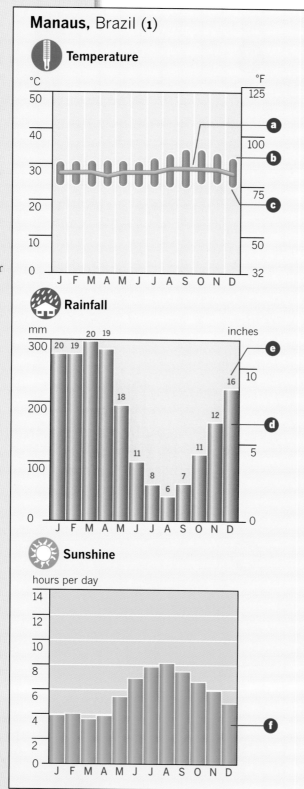

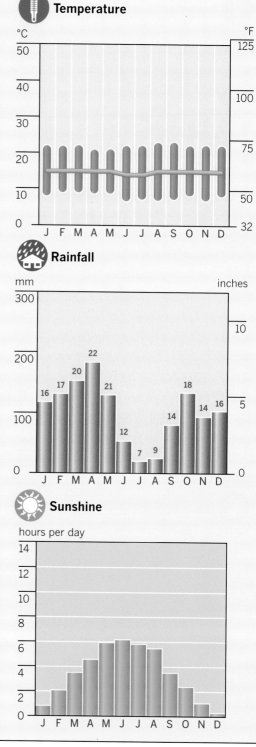

Rio de Janeiro • Santiago

E South America 5

Av **Average recorded monthly features**

- **a** **a** Temperature
- **b** **b** Maximum temperature
- **c** **c** Minimum temperature
- **d** Precipitation
- **e** Days with rain
- **f** Daily hours of sunshine

Locator map

Rio de Janeiro • Santiago

- Rio de Janeiro, on the coast of Brazil, has temperatures moderated by sea breezes, but humidity is often very high.
- Santiago, has warm, dry summers and mild winters with occasional frosts.

Elevation

- Rio de Janeiro: 20 feet (3 m)
- Santiago: 1,706 feet (520 m)

Latitude

- Rio de Janeiro: 22°55' S
- Santiago: 33°27' S

Köppen climate

- Rio de Janeiro: Cfa (humid subtropical, hot summer, mild winter, summer rainy season).
- Santiago: BWk (midlatitude desert, hot summer, mild winter, winter rainy season).

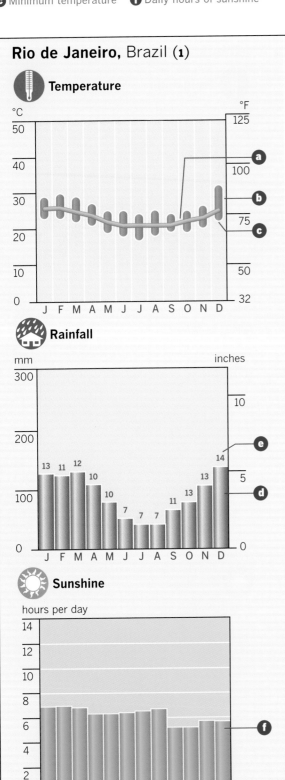

Rio de Janeiro, Brazil (1)

Temperature

Santiago, Chile (2)

Temperature

Rainfall

Rio de Janeiro days with rain: 13 11 12 10 10 7 7 7 11 13 13 14

Santiago days with rain: 0 0 1 1 5 6 6 5 3 3 1 0

Sunshine

hours per day

© Diagram Visual Information Ltd.

Lisbon • London

- Lisbon, on the Atlantic coast, has warm dry summers and mild winters.
- London has a maritime climate dominated by weather systems from the Atlantic, which make the weather very changeable.

Elevation
- Lisbon: 253 feet (77 m)
- London: 16 feet (5 m)

Latitude
- Lisbon: 38°43' N
- London: 51°28' N

Köppen climate
- Lisbon: Csb (Mediterranean, short, dry summer, mild winter).
- London: Cfb (maritime west coast, warm summer, mild winter, no dry season).

Lisbon • London

Europe 3

Average recorded monthly features
- **a** Temperature
- **b** Maximum temperature
- **c** Minimum temperature
- **d** Precipitation
- **e** Days with rain
- **f** Daily hours of sunshine

Locator map

Lisbon, Portugal (1)

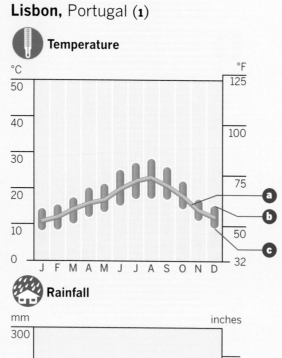

Temperature

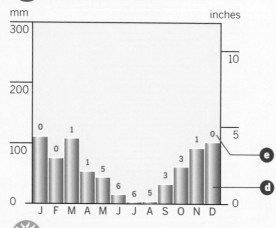

Rainfall

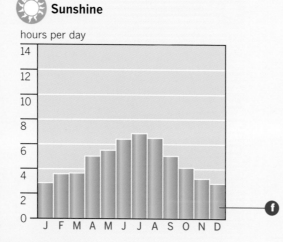

Sunshine
hours per day

London, England (2)

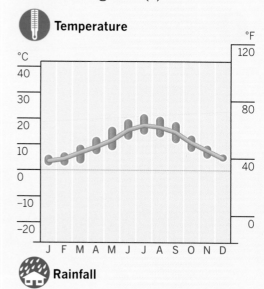

Temperature

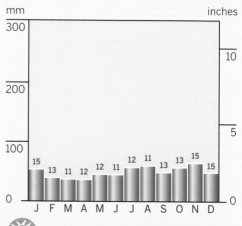

Rainfall

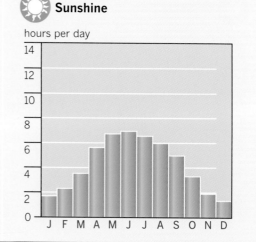

Sunshine
hours per day

Moscow • Palma

Europe 4

Average recorded monthly features

a Temperature
b Maximum temperature
c Minimum temperature
d Precipitation
e Days with rain
f Daily hours of sunshine

Locator map

Moscow • Palma

- Moscow has a moist continental climate, with warm summers and very cold winters.
- Palma, in the Balearic Islands, has a climate strongly influenced by the surrounding sea, giving it warm summers, mild winters, and low rainfall.

Elevation
- Moscow: 512 feet (156 m)
- Palma: 33 feet (10 m)

Latitude
- Moscow: 55°45' N
- Palma: 39°33' N

Köppen climate
- Moscow: Dfb (humid continental, short warm summer, very cold winter).
- Palma: Csa (Mediterranean, warm summer, mild winter, no dry season).

Moscow, Russia (1)

Temperature

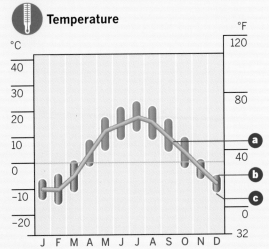

Rainfall

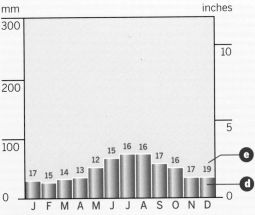

Sunshine

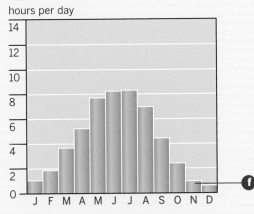

Palma, Mallorca, Spain (2)

Temperature

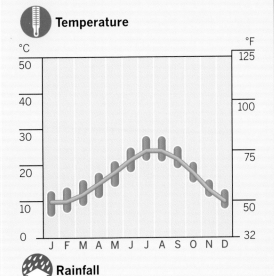

Rainfall

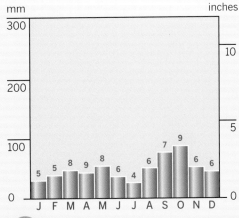

Sunshine

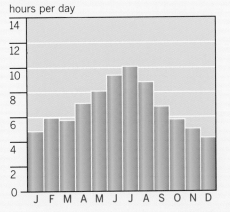

Paris • Reykjavik

Paris • Reykjavik
- Paris, on the central French plain, has warm summers, mild winters, and fairly low rainfall.
- Reykjavik, Iceland's capital, is also the country's main port, which remains ice-free all year because it lies in the path of the warm North Atlantic Current. The weather is very changeable.

Elevation
- Paris: 246 feet (75 m)
- Reykjavik: 59 feet (18 m)

Latitude
- Paris: 48°49' N
- Reykjavik: 64°08' N

Köppen climate
- Paris: Cfb (maritime west coast, warm summer, mild winter, no dry season).
- Reykjavik: Cfc (maritime west coast, short, cool summer, mild winter, no dry season).

Paris • Reykjavik

Europe 5

Average recorded monthly features
- **a** Temperature
- **b** Maximum temperature
- **c** Minimum temperature
- **d** Precipitation
- **e** Days with rain
- **f** Daily hours of sunshine

Locator map

Paris, France (1)

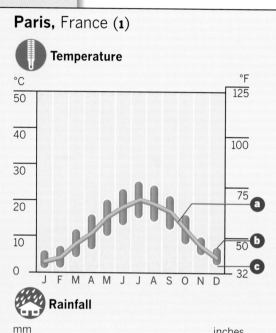

Reykjavik, Iceland (2)

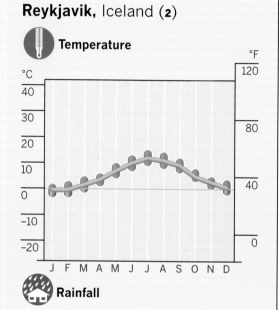

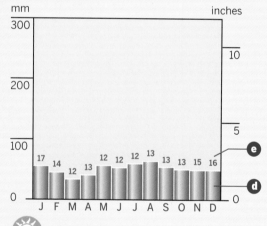

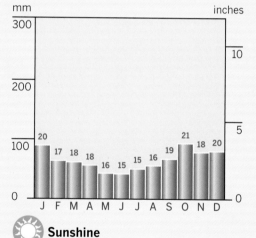

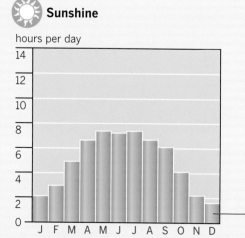

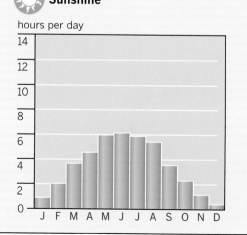

Rome • Santander

Europe 6

Average recorded monthly features

a Temperature
b Maximum temperature
c Minimum temperature
d Precipitation
e Days with rain
f Daily hours of sunshine

Locator map

Rome • Santander

- Rome is situated on a low-lying plain and has a typical Mediterranean climate, with hot, dry summers and mild winters.
- Santander, on Spain's northern coast, has a cool, moist climate influenced by depressions crossing the Atlantic.

Elevation
- Rome: 56 feet (17 m)
- Santander: 217 feet (66 m)

Latitude
- Rome: 41°54' N
- Santander: 43°28' N

Köppen climate
- Rome: Csa (Mediterranean, hot, dry summer, mild winter).
- Santander: Cfb (maritime west coast, warm summer, mild winter, wet through the year).

Rome, Italy (1)

Temperature

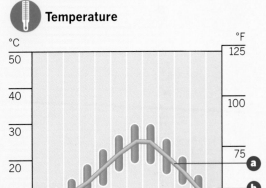

Rainfall

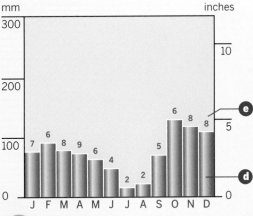

Sunshine

hours per day

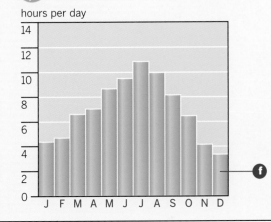

Santander, Spain (2)

Temperature

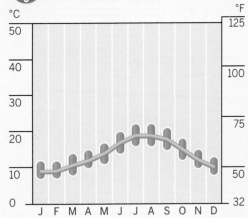

Rainfall

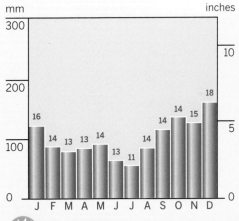

Sunshine

hours per day

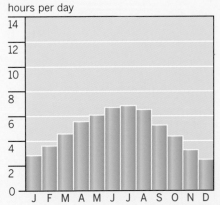

Shannon • Stockholm

Shannon • Stockholm

- Shannon, in western Ireland, is exposed to weather systems from the Atlantic and has a cool, wet climate.
- Stockholm, on Sweden's Baltic coast, has a continental climate moderated by the sea.

Elevation
- Shannon: 45 feet (14 m)
- Stockholm: 144 feet (44 m)

Latitude
- Shannon: 52°30' N
- Stockholm: 59°21' N

Köppen climate
- Shannon: Cfb (maritime west coast, warm summer, mild winter, wet throughout the year).
- Stockholm: Dfb (humid continental, short, warm summer, cold winter, moist all year).

Shannon • Stockholm

Europe 7

Average recorded monthly features

- **a** Temperature
- **b** Maximum temperature
- **c** Minimum temperature
- **d** Precipitation
- **e** Days with rain
- **f** Daily hours of sunshine

Locator map

Shannon, Ireland (1)

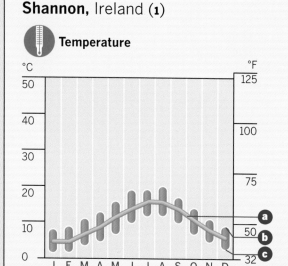

Temperature

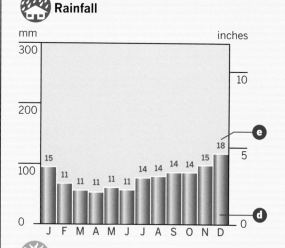

Rainfall

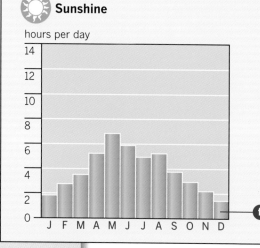

Sunshine

hours per day

Stockholm, Sweden (2)

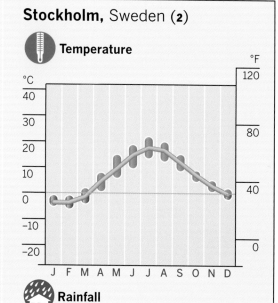

Temperature

Rainfall

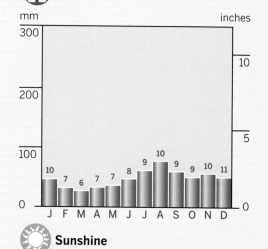

Sunshine

hours per day

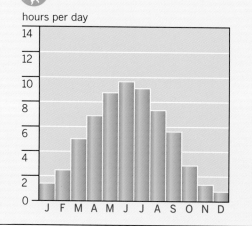

Beirut • Colombo

Asia and Middle East 2

Average recorded monthly features

a Temperature
b Maximum temperature
c Minimum temperature
d Precipitation
e Days with rain
f Daily hours of sunshine

Locator map

Beirut • Colombo

● Beirut, on the eastern coast of the Mediterranean, has hot summers that are humid at night but tempered by sea breezes by day, and mild winters.

● Colombo, in the south-western lowlands of Sri Lanka, has a tropical climate, and is hot all year with more rain in summer than in winter due to the Asian monsoon.

Elevation

● Beirut:
  111 feet (34 m)
● Colombo:
  24 feet (7 m)

Latitude

● Beirut: 33°54' N
● Colombo: 6°54' N

Köppen climate

● Beirut: Csa (Mediterranean, mild winter, hot dry summer).
● Colombo: Af (tropical rain forest, hot and wet all year).

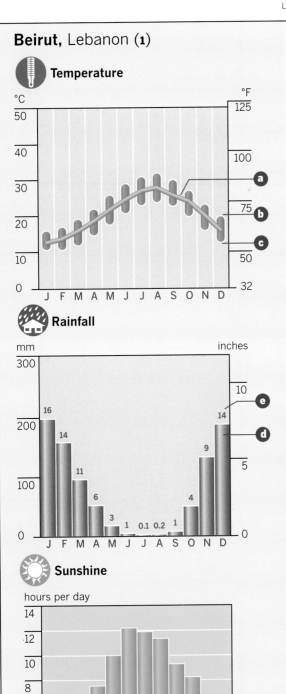

Beirut, Lebanon (1)

Temperature

Rainfall

Sunshine

Colombo, Sri Lanka (2)

Temperature

Rainfall

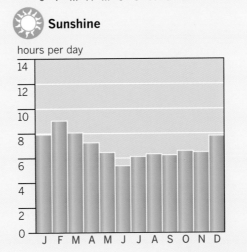

Sunshine

Harbin • Ho Chi Minh City

- Harbin, lying on a plain in northern China, has a continental climate with cool summers and cold winters.
- Ho Chi Minh City, in southern Vietnam, has a tropical climate influenced by the Asian monsoon.

Elevation
- Harbin: 564 feet (172 m)
- Ho Chi Minh City: 30 feet (9 m)

Latitude
- Harbin: 45°45' N
- Ho Chi Minh City: 10°47' N

Köppen climate
- Harbin: Dwa (humid continental, warm summer, cold winter, summer rainy season).
- Ho Chi Minh City: Aw (tropical savanna, hot all year, summer rainy season).

Harbin • Ho Chi Minh City
Asia and Middle East 3

Average recorded monthly features
- **a** Temperature
- **b** Maximum temperature
- **c** Minimum temperature
- **d** Precipitation
- **e** Days with rain
- **f** Daily hours of sunshine

Locator map

Harbin, China (1)

Temperature

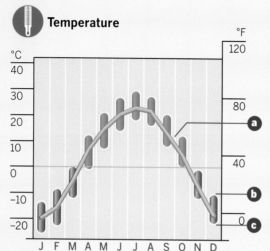

Rainfall

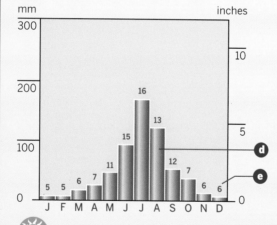

Sunshine

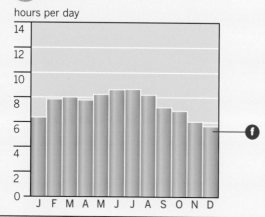

Ho Chi Minh City, Vietnam (2)

Temperature

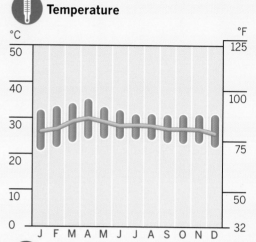

Rainfall

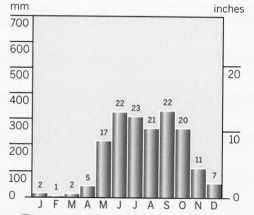

Sunshine

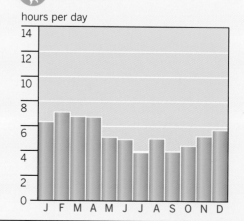

Hong Kong • Jakarta

Asia and Middle East 4

Average recorded monthly features

- **a** Temperature
- **b** Maximum temperature
- **c** Minimum temperature
- **d** Precipitation
- **e** Days with rain
- **f** Daily hours of sunshine

Locator map

Hong Kong • Jakarta

- Hong Kong, on the Chinese coast and including several islands, has a humid subtropical climate influenced by the Asian monsoon.
- Jakarta, on the coast of Java, Indonesia, has a wet equatorial climate.

Elevation

- Hong Kong: 109 feet (33 m)
- Jakarta: 26 feet (8 m)

Latitude

- Hong Kong: 22°18' N
- Jakarta: 6°11' S

Köppen climate

- Hong Kong: Cfa (humid subtropical, hot summer, mild winter, summer rainy season).
- Jakarta: Af (tropical rain forest, hot and wet, more rain in summer).

Hong Kong, China (1)

Temperature

°C / °F

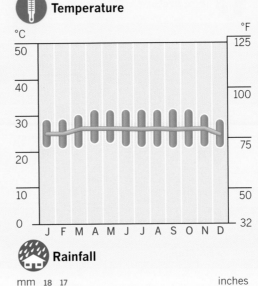

Rainfall

mm / inches

6, 8, 11, 11, 16, 21, 19, 17, 15, 8, 5, 5

J F M A M J J A S O N D

Sunshine

hours per day

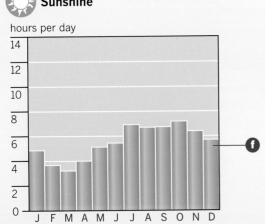

J F M A M J J A S O N D

Jakarta, Indonesia (2)

Temperature

°C / °F

J F M A M J J A S O N D

Rainfall

mm 18 17 / inches

15, 11, 9, 7, 5, 4, 5, 8, 12, 14

J F M A M J J A S O N D

Sunshine

hours per day

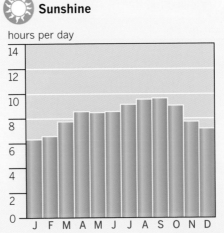

J F M A M J J A S O N D

Mumbai • New Delhi

- Mumbai (formerly Bombay) on India's western coastal plain, has an extreme monsoon climate with dry winters and wet summers.
- New Delhi, situated on the plains of northern India, has a fairly dry climate, and is hot in summer.

Elevation
- Mumbai: 37 feet (11 m)
- New Delhi: 714 feet (218 m)

Latitude
- Mumbai: 18°54' N
- New Delhi: 28°35' N

Köppen climate
- Mumbai: Am (tropical monsoon, hot all year, dry winter, wet summer).
- New Delhi: Aw (tropical savanna, hot, dry in winter).

Mumbai • New Delhi

Asia and Middle East 7

Average recorded monthly features
- **a** Temperature
- **b** Maximum temperature
- **c** Minimum temperature
- **d** Precipitation
- **e** Days with rain
- **f** Daily hours of sunshine

Locator map

Mumbai, India (1)

 Temperature

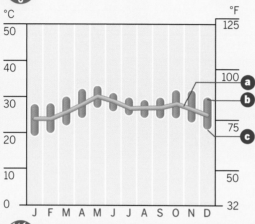

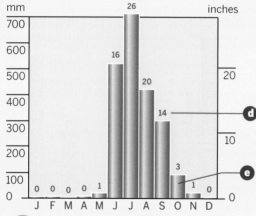 **Rainfall**

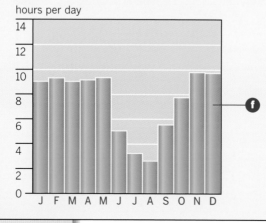

Sunshine

hours per day

New Delhi, India (2)

 Temperature

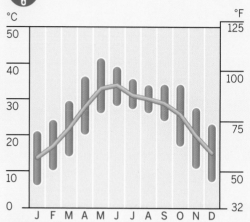

Rainfall

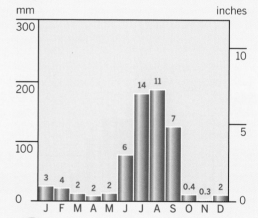

Sunshine

hours per day

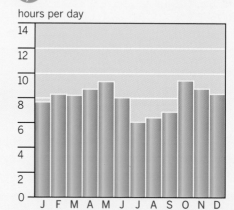

Shanghai • Singapore
Asia and Middle East 8

Average recorded monthly features

a Temperature **d** Precipitation
b Maximum temperature **e** Days with rain
c Minimum temperature **f** Daily hours of sunshine

Locator map

Shanghai • Singapore
- Shanghai, on the coast of central China, has hot summers, but winter nights can be frosty, and typhoons from the East China Sea occasionally cause damage.
- Singapore, at the tip of the Malayan Peninsula, has a typically hot, humid, equatorial climate.

Elevation
- Shanghai: 23 feet (7 m)
- Singapore: 33 feet (10 m)

Latitude
- Shanghai: 31°12' N
- Singapore: 1°18' N

Köppen climate
- Shanghai: Cfa (humid subtropical, hot, wet summer, mild winter, rain all year).
- Singapore: Af (tropical rain forest, hot and rainy all year).

Shanghai, China (1)

Temperature

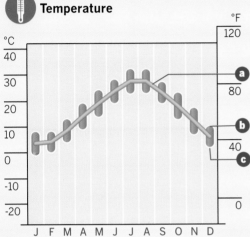

Rainfall

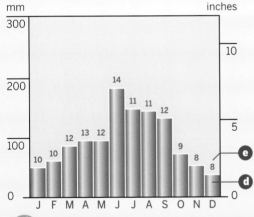

Sunshine

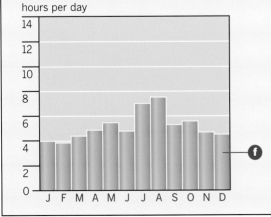

Singapore, Singapore (2)

Temperature

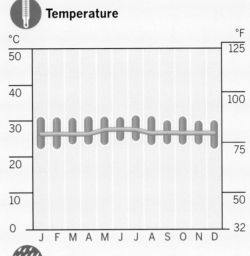

Rainfall

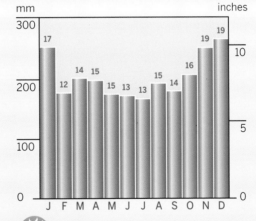

Sunshine

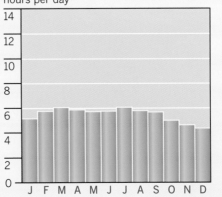

Tehran • Tokyo

Asia and Middle East 9

Locator map

Average recorded monthly features

a Temperature   **d** Precipitation
b Maximum temperature   **e** Days with rain
c Minimum temperature   **f** Daily hours of sunshine

Tehran • Tokyo

- Tehran, situated on a high plateau, has a dry climate with hot summers, but winters are cold because of its elevation.
- Tokyo, on the eastern coast of central Honshu, Japan, has a wet climate with warm, humid summers and mild winters.

Elevation

- Tehran: 4,002 feet (1,220 m)
- Tokyo: 19 feet (6 m)

Latitude

- Tehran: 35°41' N
- Tokyo: 35°41' N

Köppen climate

- Tehran: BWh (low-latitude desert, hot summers, cold winter, dry all year).
- Tokyo: Cfa (humid subtropical, hot summer, mild winter, rain all year, but more in summer).

Tehran, Iran (1)

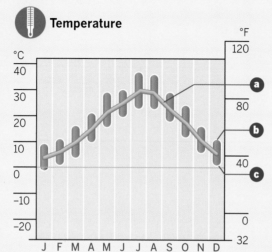

Temperature

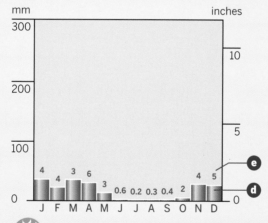

Rainfall

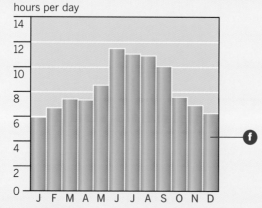

Sunshine

Tokyo, Japan (2)

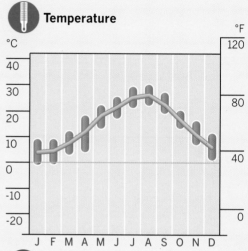

Temperature

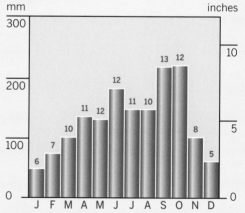

Rainfall

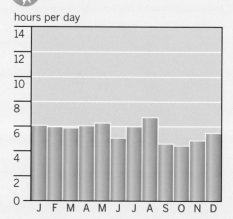

Sunshine

Ulaanbaatar • Verkhoyansk

Asia and Middle East 10

Average recorded monthly features

a Temperature
b Maximum temperature
c Minimum temperature
d Precipitation
e Days with rain
f Daily hours of sunshine

Locator map

Ulaanbaatar • Verkhoyansk

- Ulaanbaatar (formerly Ulan Bator), Mongolia, has an extreme continental climate, and is very dry with a wide range of temperature.

- Verkhoyansk, Russia, is at the Northern Hemisphere cold pole (the place with the lowest temperatures), and has a very cold and dry, extreme continental climate.

Elevation

- Ulaanbaatar: 4,347 feet (1,325 m)
- Verkhoyansk: 328 feet (100 m)

Latitude

- Ulaanbaatar: 47°55' N
- Verkhoyansk 67°34' N

Köppen climate

- Ulaanbaatar: BWk (midlatitude cold desert, cool summer, very cold winter).
- Verkhoyansk: Dfd (subarctic, short, cool summer, long, very cold winter, dry).

Ulaanbaatar, Mongolia (1)

Temperature

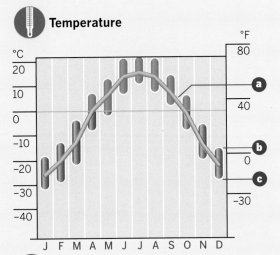

Rainfall

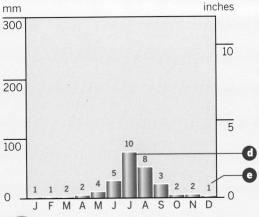

Sunshine

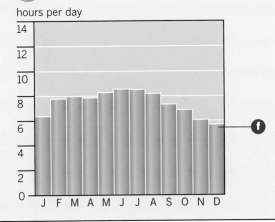

Verkhoyansk, Russia (2)

Temperature

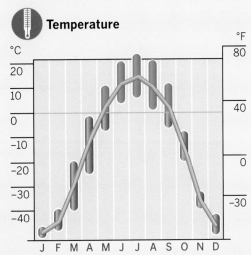

Rainfall

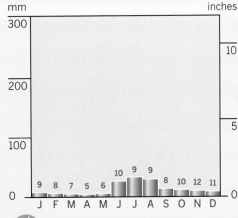

Sunshine

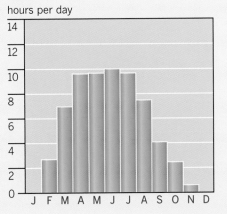

Addis Ababa • Cairo

- Addis Ababa, in the mountains of Ethiopia, has a healthy climate with little difference between summer and winter temperatures, but summer weather is humid and thunderstorms are frequent.
- Cairo, situated on the Nile in the Egyptian desert, has a hot, dry climate.

Elevation

- Addis Ababa: 8,038 feet (2,450 m)
- Cairo: 381 feet (116 m)

Latitude

- Addis Ababa: 9°20' N
- Cairo: 29°52' N

Köppen climate

- Addis Ababa: H (highland, moderate rainfall, cool because of elevation).
- Cairo: BWh (low latitude desert, hot and dry all year).

Addis Ababa • Cairo

Africa 1

Average recorded monthly features

- **a** Temperature
- **b** Maximum temperature
- **c** Minimum temperature
- **d** Precipitation
- **e** Days with rain
- **f** Daily hours of sunshine

Locator map

Addis Ababa, Ethiopia (1)

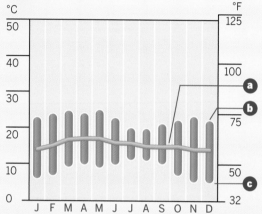
Temperature

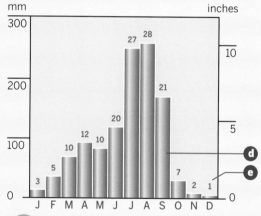
Rainfall

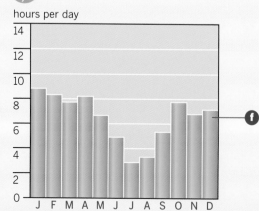
Sunshine

Cairo, Egypt (2)

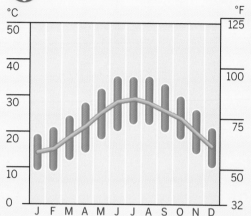
Temperature

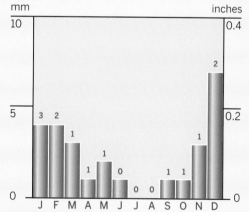
Rainfall

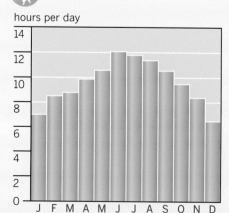
Sunshine

Cape Town • Casablanca

Africa 2

Average recorded monthly features

- **a** Temperature
- **b** Maximum temperature
- **c** Minimum temperature
- **d** Precipitation
- **e** Days with rain
- **f** Daily hours of sunshine

Locator map

Cape Town • Casablanca

- Cape Town, on the coast of South Africa, has a sunny, equable climate, with dry summers.
- Casablanca, on the Atlantic coast of Morocco, has moderate temperatures because of air from the ocean, and moderate winter rainfall.

Elevation

- Cape Town: 56 feet (17 m)
- Casablanca: 203 feet (62 m)

Latitude

- Cape Town: 33°54' S
- Casablanca: 33°19' N

Köppen climate

- Cape Town: Csb (Mediterranean, warm, dry summer, mild winter).
- Casablanca: Csa (Mediterranean, hot, dry summer, mild winter).

Cape Town, South Africa (1)

Temperature

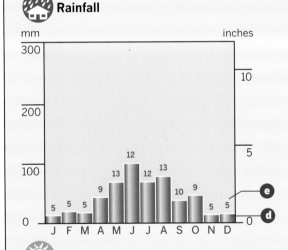

Rainfall

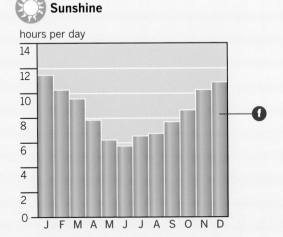

Sunshine

Casablanca, Morocco (2)

Temperature

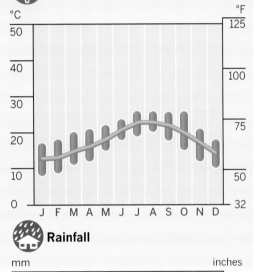

Rainfall

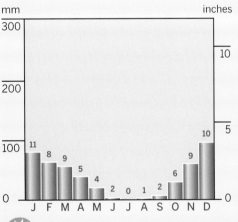

Sunshine

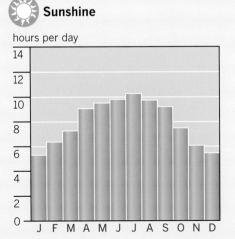

© Diagram Visual Information Ltd.

Johannesburg • Khartoum

- Johannesburg, situated on the high veldt grasslands of South Africa, has warm summers and mild winters.
- Khartoum, in the desert of northern Sudan, has an extremely hot, dry climate.

Elevation

- Johannesburg: 5,463 feet (1,665 m)
- Khartoum: 1,279 feet (390 m)

Latitude

- Johannesburg: 26°14' S
- Khartoum: 15°37' N

Köppen climate

- Johannesburg: BSh (low latitude steppe, warm all year, summer rainy season).
- Khartoum: BWh (low latitude desert, hot and dry all year).

Johannesburg • Khartoum

Africa 3

Average recorded monthly features

- **a** Temperature
- **b** Maximum temperature
- **c** Minimum temperature
- **d** Precipitation
- **e** Days with rain
- **f** Daily hours of sunshine

Locator map

Johannesburg, South Africa (1)

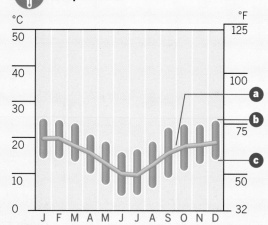

Khartoum, Sudan (2)

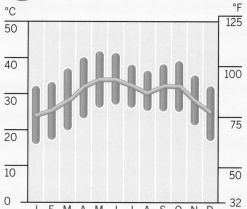

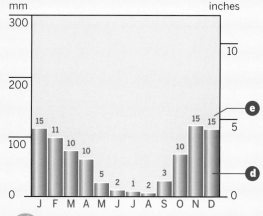

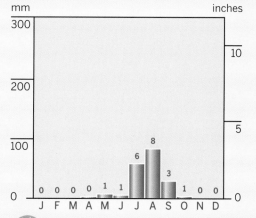

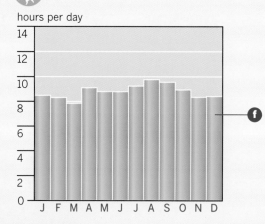

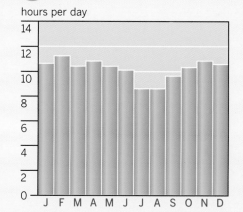

Kinshasa • Lagos

Africa 4

Average recorded monthly features

a Temperature
b Maximum temperature
c Minimum temperature
d Precipitation
e Days with rain
f Daily hours of sunshine

Locator map

Kinshasa • Lagos

- Kinshasa, in the Democratic Republic of the Congo, has an equatorial climate, with little seasonal change in temperature, but a dry winter season.
- Lagos, on the coast of Nigeria, is hot and humid all year, but has a winter dry season.

Elevation

- Kinshasa: 1,066 feet (322 m)
- Lagos: 10 feet (3 m)

Latitude

- Kinshasa: 4°20' S
- Lagos: 6°27' N

Köppen climate

- Kinshasa: Aw (tropical savanna, hot all year, summer rainy season).
- Lagos: Af (tropical rain forest, hot and wet all year, but most rain in summer).

Kinshasa, Dem. Rep. of Congo (1)

Temperature

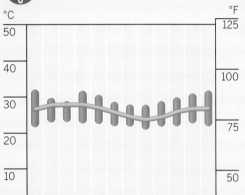

a
b
c

Rainfall

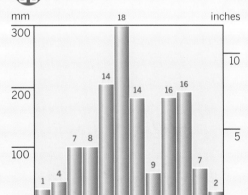

e
d

Sunshine

hours per day

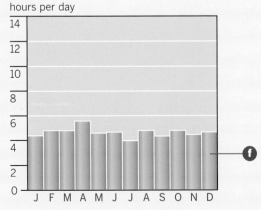

f

Lagos, Nigeria (2)

Temperature

Rainfall

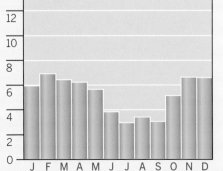

Sunshine

hours per day

Lusaka • Nairobi

- Lusaka, in the highlands of Zambia, has a tropical climate with moderate temperatures because of its elevation and little difference between summer and winter, but a summer rainy season.
- Nairobi, in the highlands of Kenya, is warm all year, but seldom hot because of its elevation.

Elevation
- Lusaka: 4,191 feet (1,277 m)
- Nairobi: 5,971 feet (1,820 m)

Latitude
- Lusaka: 15°25' S
- Nairobi: 1°16' S

Köppen climate
- Lusaka: Aw (tropical savanna, warm all year, dry in winter).
- Nairobi: BSh (low latitude steppe, warm all year, rainy seasons in spring and fall).

Lusaka • Nairobi

Africa 5

Average recorded monthly features

- **a** Temperature
- **b** Maximum temperature
- **c** Minimum temperature
- **d** Precipitation
- **e** Days with rain
- **f** Daily hours of sunshine

Locator map

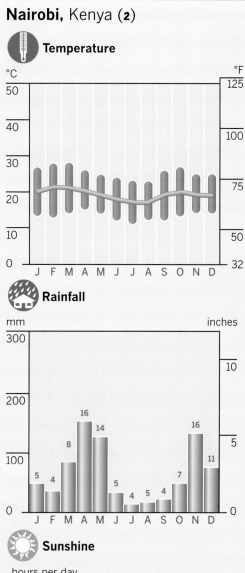

Lusaka, Zambia (**1**)

Temperature

Rainfall

- 19
- 18
- 12
- 3
- 1
- 0
- 0
- 0
- 0
- 3
- 10
- 18

Sunshine

hours per day

Nairobi, Kenya (**2**)

Temperature

Rainfall

- 5
- 4
- 8
- 16
- 14
- 5
- 4
- 5
- 4
- 7
- 16
- 11

Sunshine

hours per day

Saint-Denis • Timbuktu

Africa 6

Average recorded monthly features

a Temperature
b Maximum temperature
c Minimum temperature
d Precipitation
e Days with rain
f Daily hours of sunshine

Locator map

WORLD CLIMATE DATA

Saint-Denis • Timbuktu

● Saint-Denis, on the island of Réunion in the Indian Ocean, has a tropical climate strongly influenced by the surrounding ocean.

● Timbuktu, in central Mali, has a climate typical of the southern edge of the Sahara Desert. It is hot all year, with a short rainy season in summer.

Elevation

● Saint-Denis: 68 feet (21 m)
● Timbuktu: 988 feet (301 m)

Latitude

● Saint-Denis: 20°52' S
● Timbuktu: 16°46' N

Köppen climate

● Saint-Denis: Af (tropical rain forest, hot and wet all year).
● Timbuktu: BWh (low latitude desert, hot and dry all year).

Saint-Denis, Réunion (1)

Temperature

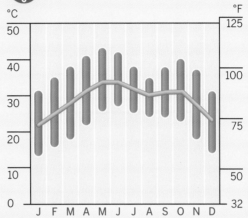

Rainfall

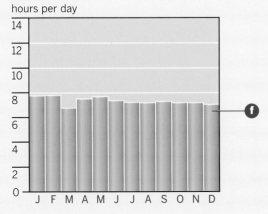

Sunshine

Timbuktu, Mali (2)

Temperature

Rainfall

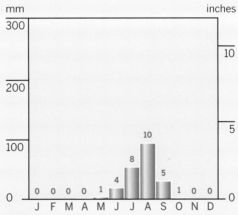

Sunshine

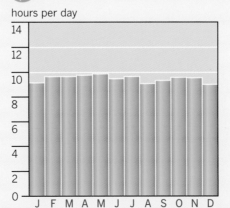

Tunis • Windhoek

- Tunis, on the coast of Tunisia, has a Mediterranean climate, with hot dry summers, and occasional snow in winter.
- Windhoek, in the highlands of Namibia, is warm throughout the year and has a little rain in winter.

Elevation
- Tunis: 217 feet (66 m)
- Windhoek: 5,669 feet (1,728 m)

Latitude
- Tunis: 36°47' N
- Windhoek: 22°34' S

Köppen climate
- Tunis: Csa (Mediterranean, hot, dry summer, mild winter).
- Windhoek: BSh (low latitude steppe, hot all year, semiarid).

Tunis • Windhoek
Africa 7

Average recorded monthly features

- **a** Temperature
- **b** Maximum temperature
- **c** Minimum temperature
- **d** Precipitation
- **e** Days with rain
- **f** Daily hours of sunshine

Locator map

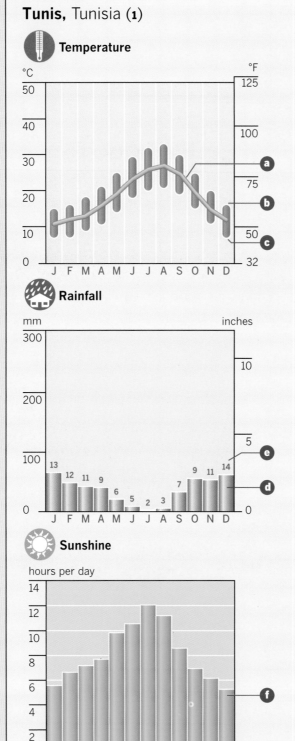

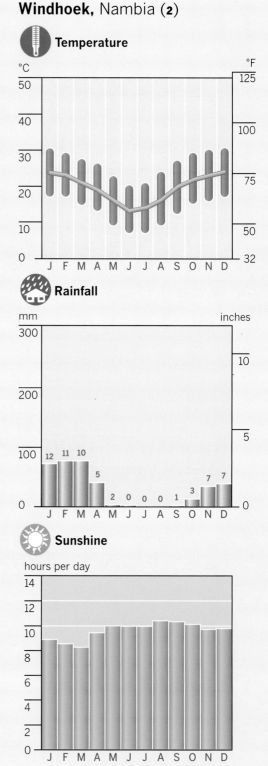

Alice Springs • Christchurch

Australia, New Zealand, Pacific 1

Average recorded monthly features

- **a** Temperature
- **b** Maximum temperature
- **c** Minimum temperature
- **d** Precipitation
- **e** Days with rain
- **f** Daily hours of sunshine

Locator map

Alice Springs • Christchurch

- Alice Springs is at the center of Australia, where temperatures are high in summer but can fall below freezing in winter, and rainfall is sparse.
- Christchurch, in South Island, New Zealand, has a cool, maritime climate.

Elevation

- Alice Springs: 1,901 feet (579 m)
- Christchurch: 32 feet (10 m)

Latitude

- Alice Springs: 23°38' S
- Christchurch: 36°47' S

Köppen climate

- Alice Springs: BWh (low latitude desert, hot in summer, sometimes cold in winter, dry).
- Christchurch: Cfb (maritime west coast, warm summer, mild winter, no dry season).

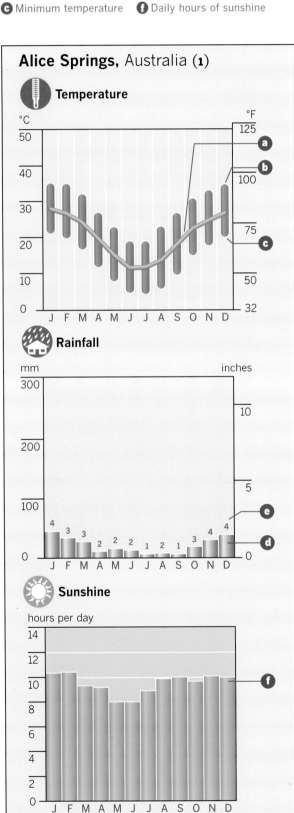

Alice Springs, Australia (1)

Temperature

Rainfall

Sunshine

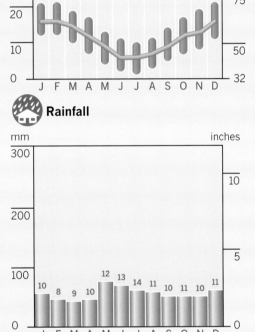

Christchurch, New Zealand (2)

Temperature

Rainfall

Sunshine

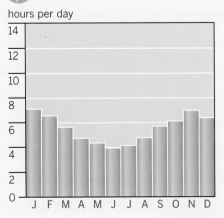

© Diagram Visual Information Ltd.

Darwin • Honolulu

- Darwin, on the northern coast of Australia, has a tropical maritime climate with a summer rainy season.
- Honolulu, Hawaii, is situated on a sheltered southwestern coast, giving it a drier climate than its latitude and maritime location would suggest, with a winter rainy season.

Elevation
- Darwin: 97 feet (30 m)
- Honolulu: 38 feet (12 m)

Latitude
- Darwin: 12°28' S
- Honolulu: 21°19' N

Köppen climate
- Darwin: Aw (tropical savanna, hot all year, dry in winter).
- Honolulu: Am (tropical monsoon, hot all year, winter rainy season).

Darwin • Honolulu
Australia, New Zealand, Pacific 2

Average recorded monthly features
- **a** Temperature
- **b** Maximum temperature
- **c** Minimum temperature
- **d** Precipitation
- **e** Days with rain
- **f** Daily hours of sunshine

Locator map

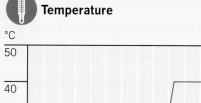

Darwin, Australia (1)

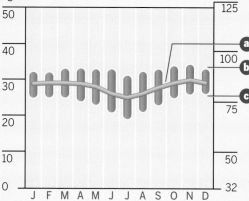

Temperature

Honolulu, Hawaii, USA (2)

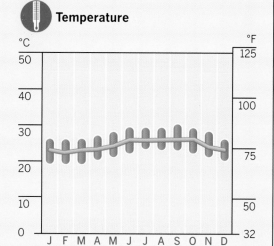

Temperature

Rainfall

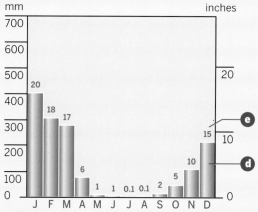

Darwin rainfall (mm): J 20, F 18, M 17, A 6, M 1, J 1, J 0.1, A 0.1, S 2, O 5, N 10, D 15

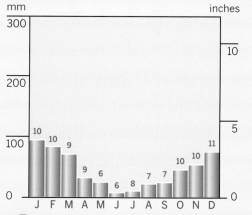

Honolulu rainfall (mm): J 10, F 10, M 9, A 9, M 6, J 6, J 8, A 7, S 7, O 10, N 10, D 11

Sunshine

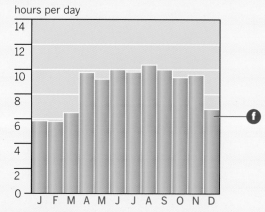

hours per day

Sunshine

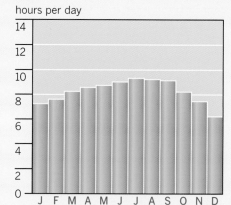

hours per day

Melbourne • Perth

Australia, New Zealand, Pacific 3

Average recorded monthly features

- ⓐ Temperature
- ⓑ Maximum temperature
- ⓒ Minimum temperature
- ⓓ Precipitation
- ⓔ Days with rain
- ⓕ Daily hours of sunshine

Locator map

Melbourne • Perth
- Melbourne, Victoria, in the south-east of Australia, has a warm climate with occasional winter frosts, but the skies are often cloudy.
- Perth, Western Australia, has warm summers, and mild winters with fairly high rainfall.

Elevation
- Melbourne: 115 feet (35 m)
- Perth: 197 feet (60 m)

Latitude
- Melbourne: 37°49' S
- Perth: 31°57' S

Köppen climate
- Melbourne: Cfb (maritime west coast, warm summer, mild winter, no dry season).
- Perth: Csb (Mediterranean, hot, dry summer, mild winter).

Melbourne, Australia (1)

Temperature

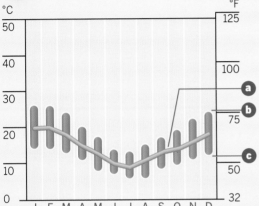

Rainfall

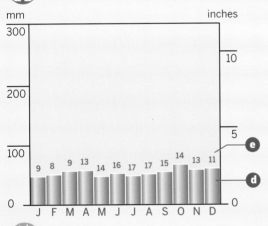

Sunshine

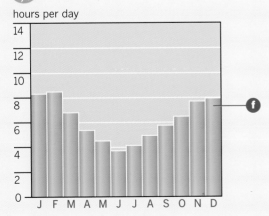

Perth, Australia (2)

Temperature

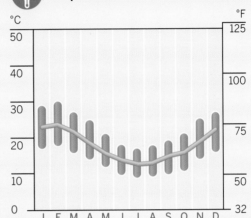

Rainfall

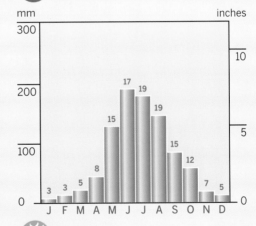

Sunshine

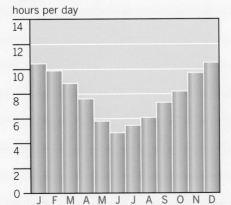

© Diagram Visual Information Ltd.

Sydney

● Sydney, New South Wales, lies on the coast where the proximity of the ocean moderates temperatures to produce an equable climate with moderate rainfall.

Elevation

● Sydney:
138 feet (42 m)

Latitude

● Sydney: 33°52' S

Köppen climate

● Sydney: Cfb (maritime west coast, warm summer, mild winter, no dry season).

Sydney

Australia, New Zealand, Pacific 4

Average recorded monthly features

a Temperature
b Maximum temperature
c Minimum temperature
d Precipitation
e Days with rain
f Daily hours of sunshine

Locator map

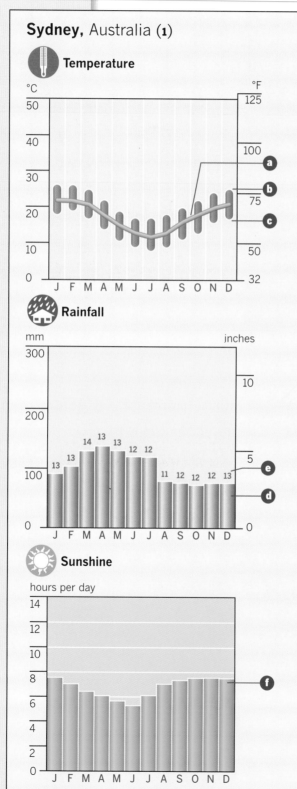

Key to U.S. climate data

pages 154 to 188

Locator map

City, State
A general description of the city, its location, and general climate.

Daily mean temperature
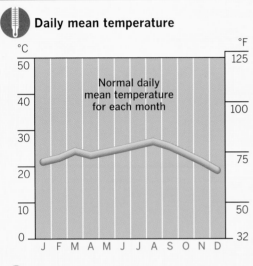

°C / °F

Normal daily mean temperature for each month

J F M A M J J A S O N D

Highest and lowest temperatures
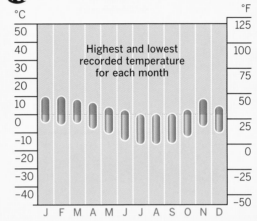

°C / °F

Highest and lowest recorded temperature for each month

J F M A M J J A S O N D

Wind speed (average and maximum)
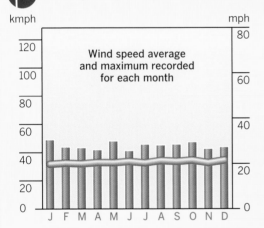

kmph / mph

Wind speed average and maximum recorded for each month

J F M A M J J A S O N D

Sunshine
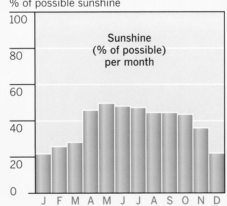

% of possible sunshine

Sunshine (% of possible) per month

J F M A M J J A S O N D

Normal precipitation
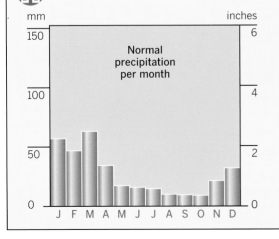

mm / inches

Normal precipitation per month

J F M A M J J A S O N D

Average number of days with some rain
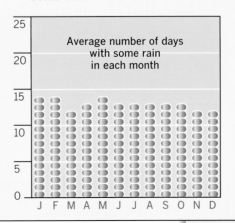

Average number of days with some rain in each month

J F M A M J J A S O N D

Elevation
- The city's average height above sea level in feet and meters.

Latitude
- The city's location in degrees and minutes north or south.

Köppen climate
- The Köppen climate code and description for the city's location.

Location
- Climatically relevant factors of the city's location.

Seasons
- General seasonal trends in the city's climate and any notable seasonal variations.

Albuquerque, New Mexico

Situated in the continental interior on the Rio Grande, with mountains to the west, north, and east. It has a healthy, bracing climate.

Albuquerque

New Mexico

Monthly recorded features

a Daily mean temperature
b Maximum wind speed
c Average wind speed
d Precipitation

e Highest temperature
f Lowest temperature
g Percentage of possible sunshine
h Days with some rain

Locator map

Elevation
● 5,311 feet (1,619 m)

Latitude
● 35°03' N

Köppen climate
● BSk (midlatitude steppe, dry, cool).

Location
● Continental interior, beside a large river.
● Surrounded by mountains.

Seasons
● The continental climate with high elevation produces cold winters and cool summers.
● The weather is almost always sunny.
● Rainfall is low and spread fairly evenly throughout the year.
● Winds are generally light.

Daily mean temperature

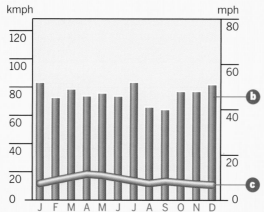

Highest and lowest temperatures

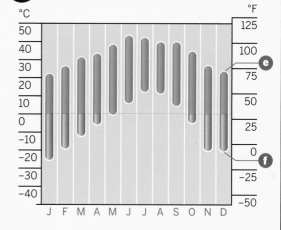

Wind speed (average and maximum)

Sunshine

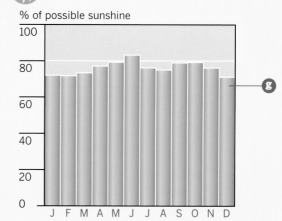

Normal precipitation

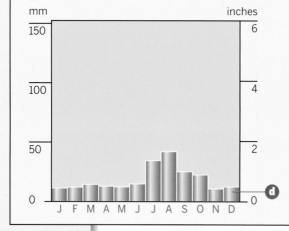

Average number of days with some rain

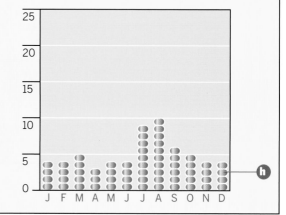

Anchorage

Alaska

Monthly recorded features

- **a** Daily mean temperature
- **b** Maximum wind speed
- **c** Average wind speed
- **d** Precipitation
- **e** Highest temperature
- **f** Lowest temperature
- **g** Percentage of possible sunshine
- **h** Days with some rain

Locator map

Anchorage, Alaska

Situated on a deep, sheltered bay, winters in Anchorage are milder than they are farther inland, but the city receives little benefit from the warm surface waters of the Pacific.

Elevation
- 132 feet (40 m)

Latitude
- 61°14' N

Köppen climate
- Cfb (maritime west coast, mild winters, warm summers, moist all year).

Location
- The city is situated beside Cook Inlet, a deep, sheltered bay on the western coast of Alaska.
- Its sheltered location moderates wind speeds.

Seasons
- Winters are cool, but warmer than they are farther inland. Extreme cold is uncommon.
- Rainfall is moderate and spread fairly evenly throughout the year, with the fall being the rainiest season.
- Winds are light, although there are sometimes storms.

Daily mean temperature

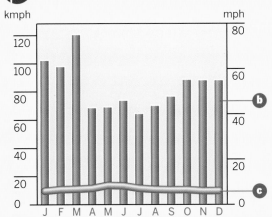

Highest and lowest temperatures

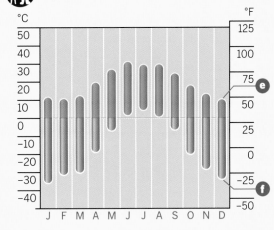

Wind speed (average and maximum)

Sunshine

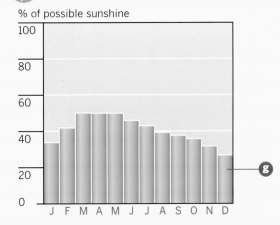

% of possible sunshine

Normal precipitation

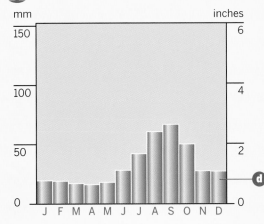

Average number of days with some rain

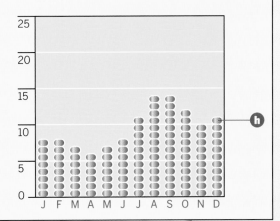

© Diagram Visual Information Ltd.

Atlanta, Georgia

Situated in the foothills of the Blue Ridge Mountains, Atlanta is about 300 miles (483 km) from the ocean with the mountains to its north. It has cool nights despite its low latitude.

Elevation

- 1,054 feet (321 m)

Latitude

- 33°45' N

Köppen climate

- Cfa (humid subtropical, mild winters, hot summers, moist all year).

Location

- The city lies on a watershed in the foothills. It is close enough to the ocean to have a rainy climate, but its high elevation moderates its temperatures.

Seasons

- Summers are warm, although at times conditions can be hot and uncomfortably humid.
- Winters are mild. Frosts occur occasionally in January and February, but they are very uncommon.
- Rainfall is high in every month of the year.
- Winds are usually light. The city is far enough inland to escape hurricanes from the Caribbean.

Atlanta

Georgia

Monthly recorded features

- **a** Daily mean temperature
- **b** Maximum wind speed
- **c** Average wind speed
- **d** Precipitation
- **e** Highest temperature
- **f** Lowest temperature
- **g** Percentage of possible sunshine
- **h** Days with some rain

Locator map

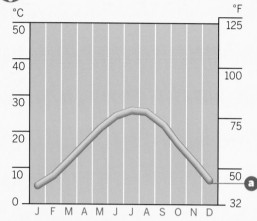

Daily mean temperature

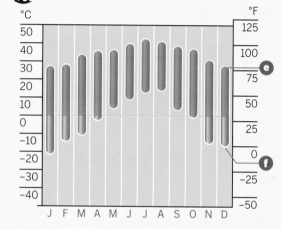

Highest and lowest temperatures

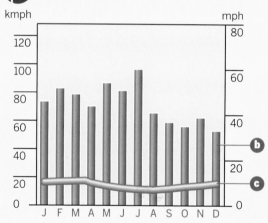

Wind speed (average and maximum)

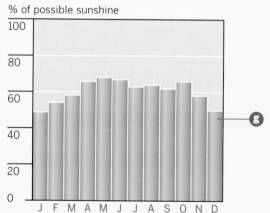

Sunshine

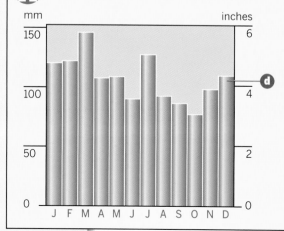

Normal precipitation

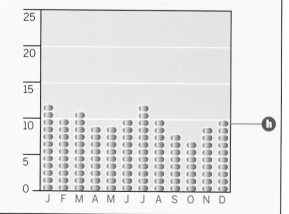

Average number of days with some rain

Atlantic City

New Jersey

Monthly recorded features

- **a** Daily mean temperature
- **b** Maximum wind speed
- **c** Average wind speed
- **d** Precipitation
- **e** Highest temperature
- **f** Lowest temperature
- **g** Percentage of possible sunshine
- **h** Days with some rain

Locator map

Atlantic City, New Jersey

Situated on an island off the east coast, Atlantic City has a climate strongly influenced by the ocean. Its mild temperatures make it a popular holiday resort.

Elevation
- 68 feet (21 m)

Latitude
- 39°24' N

Köppen climate
- Dfb (humid continental, severe winter, no dry season, warm summer).

Location
- Atlantic City is situated on a low-lying east coast island.
- Its climate is maritime, in contrast to the more continental conditions found inland.

Seasons
- Summers are warm, sometimes hot between May and September.
- Winters are mild, temperatures seldom falling below freezing.
- Rainfall is high, and distributed evenly throughout the year.
- Winds are mainly light, but can reach gale force in any month.

Daily mean temperature

°C / °F

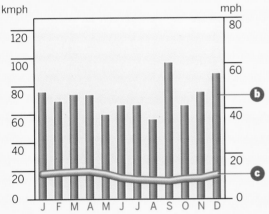

Highest and lowest temperatures

°C / °F

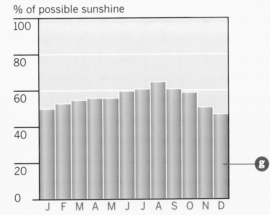

Wind speed (average and maximum)

kmph / mph

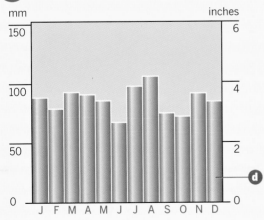

Sunshine

% of possible sunshine

Normal precipitation

mm / inches

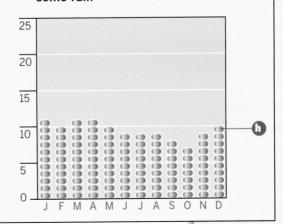

Average number of days with some rain

© Diagram Visual Information Ltd.

Billings, Montana

A city on the western side of the prairie and in the foothills of the Rocky Mountains, Billings has a continental climate moderated by the city's high elevation.

Elevation
- 3,119 feet (951 m)

Latitude
- 45°58' N

Köppen climate
- BSk (midlatitude steppe, semiarid and cool).

Location
- Beside the Yellowstone River, with mountains to the west and the plains to the east. Air approaching from the west loses much of its moisture as it crosses the Rocky Mountains.

Seasons
- Summers are warm, sometimes hot.
- Winters are cool, with average temperatures below freezing from December to the end of February, occasionally falling to below –4°F (–20°C).
- Rainfall is low, with spring and early summer the wettest times of the year.
- Winds are generally light, but severe gales can occur in any month.

Billings
Montana

Monthly recorded features
- **a** Daily mean temperature
- **b** Maximum wind speed
- **c** Average wind speed
- **d** Precipitation
- **e** Highest temperature
- **f** Lowest temperature
- **g** Percentage of possible sunshine
- **h** Days with some rain

Locator map

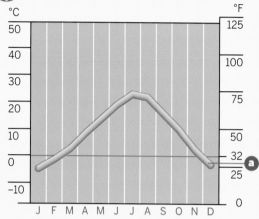

Daily mean temperature

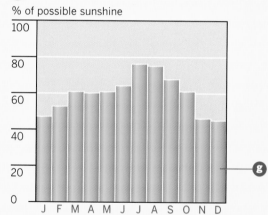

Highest and lowest temperatures

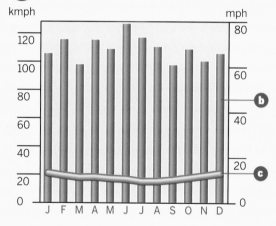

Wind speed (average and maximum)

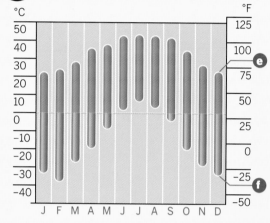

Sunshine

% of possible sunshine

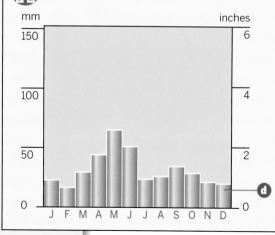

Normal precipitation

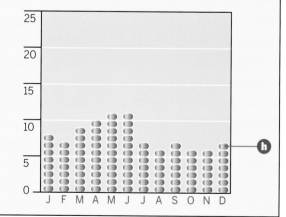

Average number of days with some rain

Boise

Idaho

Monthly recorded features

- **a** Daily mean temperature
- **b** Maximum wind speed
- **c** Average wind speed
- **d** Precipitation
- **e** Highest temperature
- **f** Lowest temperature
- **g** Percentage of possible sunshine
- **h** Days with some rain

Locator map

Boise, Idaho

Far inland and on the western side of the Rocky Mountains, Boise lies in a valley, sheltered by a high ridge on the northern and eastern sides that produces a mild climate.

Elevation
- 2,844 feet (867 m)

Latitude
- 43°34' N

Köppen climate
- H (highland, cold due to elevation).

Location
- Situated in the forested valley of the Snake River and sheltered on two sides by a high ridge, Boise has a milder climate than its elevation would suggest.

Seasons
- Summers are hot by day but cool at night.
- Winters are mild, with average temperatures falling only briefly below freezing, although winter nights can be very cold.
- The climate is dry and very little snow falls in winter.
- Winds are mainly gentle, though gales can occur in any month.

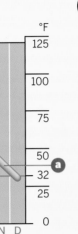

Daily mean temperature

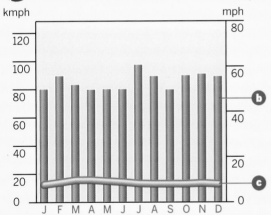

Highest and lowest temperatures

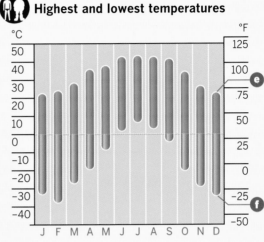

Wind speed (average and maximum)

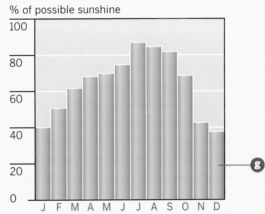

Sunshine

% of possible sunshine

Normal precipitation

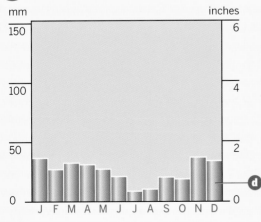

Average number of days with some rain

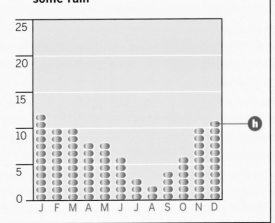

Boston, Massachusetts

Situated on the Atlantic coast with hills to the west, Boston's climate is strongly influenced by the ocean, making it mild and wet.

Boston
Massachusetts

Monthly recorded features

- **a** Daily mean temperature
- **b** Maximum wind speed
- **c** Average wind speed
- **d** Precipitation
- **e** Highest temperature
- **f** Lowest temperature
- **g** Percentage of possible sunshine
- **h** Days with some rain

Locator map

Elevation
- 124 feet (38 m)

Latitude
- 42°22' N

Köppen climate
- Dfb (humid continental, moist throughout the year, cold winters, short cool summers).

Location
- On the coast, at the head of Massachusetts Bay, but to the east of the Great Lakes, which exposes the city to lake-effect snow caused by the passage of moist warm air from the lakes across cold ground to the east.

Seasons
- Summers mild; sometimes hot and humid.
- Winters mild, but temperatures low enough to keep snow lying for several weeks.
- Precipitation high and distributed evenly throughout the year, with much snow in winter.
- Winds generally light, but gales are possible in every month.

© Diagram Visual Information Ltd.

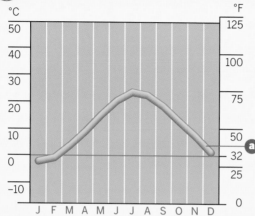

Daily mean temperature

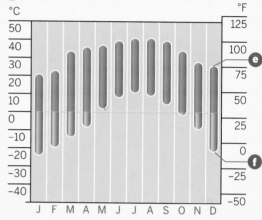

Highest and lowest temperatures

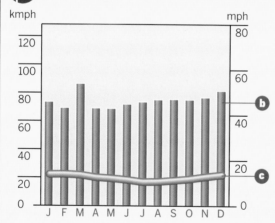

Wind speed (average and maximum)

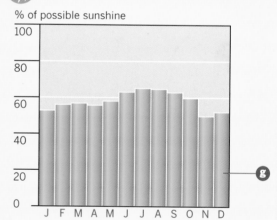

Sunshine

% of possible sunshine

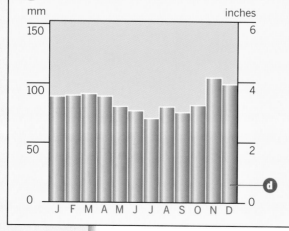

Normal precipitation

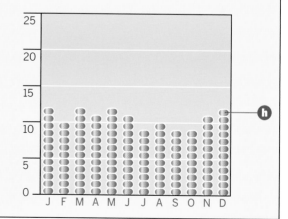

Average number of days with some rain

Charlotte

North Carolina

Monthly recorded features

- **a** Daily mean temperature
- **b** Maximum wind speed
- **c** Average wind speed
- **d** Precipitation
- **e** Highest temperature
- **f** Lowest temperature
- **g** Percentage of possible sunshine
- **h** Days with some rain

Locator map

Charlotte, North Carolina

Lying between the Appalachian Mountains to the west and the low-lying coastal plain to the east, Charlotte has a mild, wet climate.

Elevation

- 774 feet (236 m)

Latitude

- 35°14' N

Köppen climate

- Cfa (humid subtropical, mild winters, hot summers, moist throughout the year).

Location

- Raised above the coastal plain, its elevation gives Charlotte cooler summers than its subtropical latitude would suggest, but it lies on the edge of the region affected by hurricanes from the Caribbean.

Seasons

- Summers mild; sometimes hot and humid by day.
- Winters mild, with average temperatures above freezing, although there can be frosts at night.
- Rainfall is high and distributed evenly throughout the year, with no dry season.
- Winds are generally light, but gales associated with squalls are possible, especially in late summer, and there is a slight risk of hurricanes.

Daily mean temperature

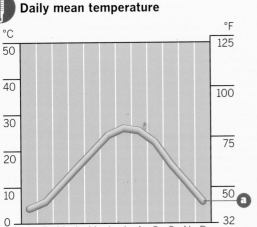

Highest and lowest temperatures

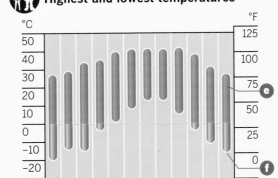

Wind speed (average and maximum)

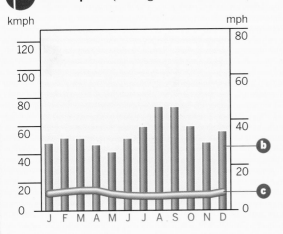

Sunshine

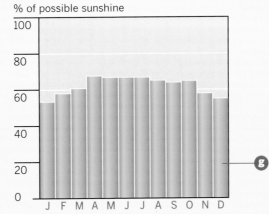

% of possible sunshine

Normal precipitation

Average number of days with some rain

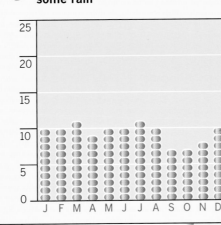

Chicago, Illinois

Situated at the southwestern corner of Lake Michigan, Chicago's climate is strongly influenced by the lake. The weather is highly changeable and large temperature fluctuations are common.

Elevation
- 823 feet (251 m)

Latitude
- 41°53' N

Köppen climate
- Dfa (humid continental, long hot summers, very cold winters, moist throughout the year).

Location
- At the mouth of the Chicago River and the southwestern corner of Lake Michigan, the extremes of the continental climate are moderated by mild, moist air that crosses the lake.

Seasons
- Summers are warm, with hot days but cool nights.
- Winters are cold, with average daytime temperatures at about freezing, but night temperatures can plunge to below –13°F (–25°C).
- Winds are generally moderate and severe gales are uncommon.

Chicago
Illinois

Monthly recorded features
- **a** Daily mean temperature
- **b** Maximum wind speed
- **c** Average wind speed
- **d** Precipitation
- **e** Highest temperature
- **f** Lowest temperature
- **g** Percentage of possible sunshine
- **h** Days with some rain

Locator map

Daily mean temperature
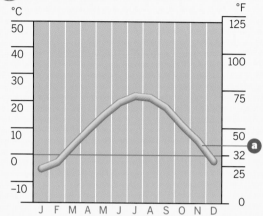

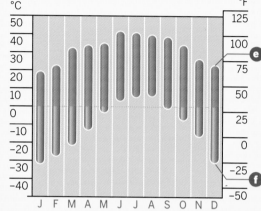
Highest and lowest temperatures

Wind speed (average and maximum)
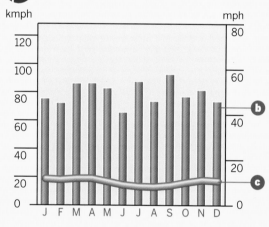

Sunshine
% of possible sunshine
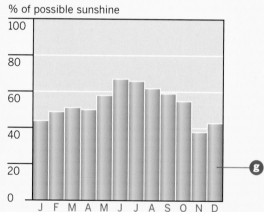

Normal precipitation
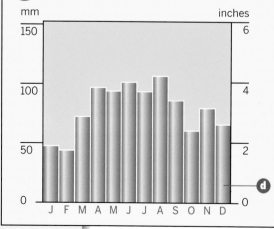

Average number of days with some rain
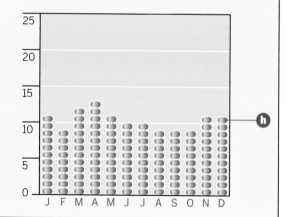

Cleveland

Ohio

Monthly recorded features

- **a** Daily mean temperature
- **b** Maximum wind speed
- **c** Average wind speed
- **d** Precipitation
- **e** Highest temperature
- **f** Lowest temperature
- **g** Percentage of possible sunshine
- **h** Days with some rain

Locator map

Cleveland, Ohio

Situated on the shore of Lake Erie on the eastern edge of the prairie, Cleveland has a cool, wet climate. Blizzards are common in winter.

Elevation
- 767 feet (234 m)

Latitude
- 41°25' N

Köppen climate
- Dfa (humid continental, very cold winters, long hot summers, moist throughout the year).

Location
- At the mouth of the Cuyahoga River, on the southeastern shore of Lake Erie, the proximity of the lake reduces summer temperatures, but in winter cold air often spills southward from Canada, bringing bitter weather and blizzards.

Seasons
- Summers mild, often hot by day but with cool nights.
- Winters cool, with average temperatures below freezing from December to the end of February.
- Precipitation moderate, heavier in winter than in summer. Winter precipitation falls mainly as snow.
- Winds moderate, severe gales uncommon.

Daily mean temperature

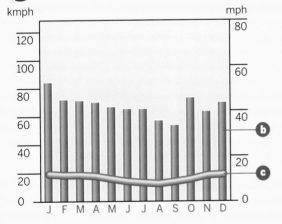

Highest and lowest temperatures

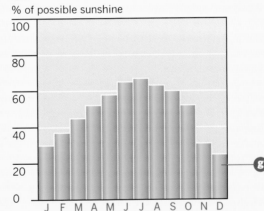

Wind speed (average and maximum)

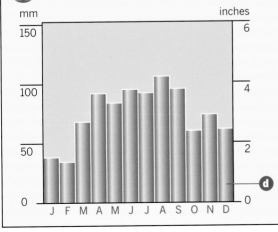

Sunshine

% of possible sunshine

Normal precipitation

Average number of days with some rain

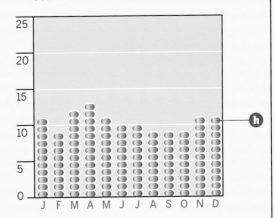

U.S. CLIMATE DATA

Columbus, Ohio

Situated on a flat plain, Columbus has a continental climate, with a wide temperature range, but moderate rainfall and heavy snow in winter.

Elevation
- 724 feet (221 m)

Latitude
- 39°58' N

Köppen climate
- Dfa (humid continental, very cold winters, long hot summers, moist throughout the year).

Location
- On the eastern bank of the Scioto River on the fairly flat Ohio Plain, Columbus lies on the eastern side of the prairie where it experiences a continental climate, with extremes of temperature.

Seasons
- Summers are warm, occasionally hot by day, but much cooler at night, when temperatures have been known to fall close to freezing in July.
- Winters cold, with average temperatures below freezing in January and February.
- Precipitation is moderate and distributed fairly evenly through the year, but with somewhat drier weather in fall.
- Winds are moderate and strong gales uncommon.

Columbus
Ohio

Monthly recorded features
- **a** Daily mean temperature
- **b** Maximum wind speed
- **c** Average wind speed
- **d** Precipitation
- **e** Highest temperature
- **f** Lowest temperature
- **g** Percentage of possible sunshine
- **h** Days with some rain

Locator map

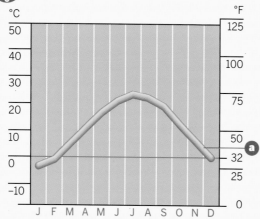

Daily mean temperature

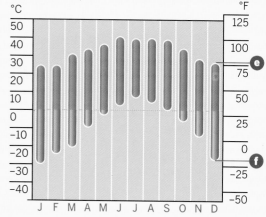

Highest and lowest temperatures

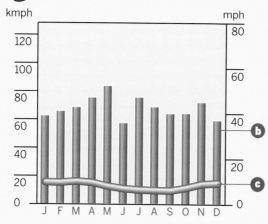

Wind speed (average and maximum)

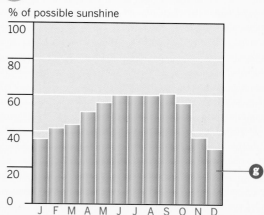

Sunshine

% of possible sunshine

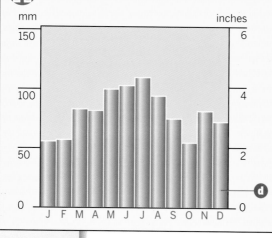

Normal precipitation

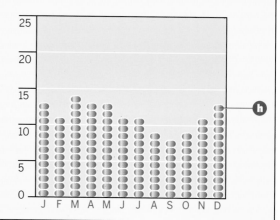

Average number of days with some rain

Dallas

Texas

Monthly recorded features

- **a** Daily mean temperature
- **b** Maximum wind speed
- **c** Average wind speed
- **d** Precipitation
- **e** Highest temperature
- **f** Lowest temperature
- **g** Percentage of possible sunshine
- **h** Days with some rain

Locator map

Dallas, Texas

Situated amid the rolling hills of the Texas prairie, Dallas has a climate with long hot summers and mild winters.

Elevation
- 512 feet (156 m)

Latitude
- 32°46' N

Köppen climate
- Cfa (humid subtropical, hot summers, mild winters, moist throughout the year).

Location
- Beside the Trinity River, in a region of prairie grassland and low hills, Dallas has a subtropical climate with no summer dry season.

Seasons
- Summers are long and hot. Average daytime temperatures reach 75°F (24°C) in April and do not fall below 68°F (20°C) until late October.
- Winters are mild, with average temperatures never falling below freezing, although freezing temperatures have been recorded between October and April.
- Rainfall is moderate and distributed fairly evenly through the year, but with wetter weather in spring and fall.
- Winds are generally light, but squalls can bring gales at any time of year, occasionally of hurricane force.

Daily mean temperature

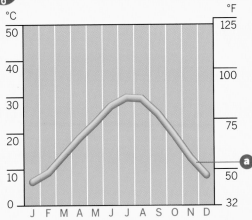

Highest and lowest temperatures

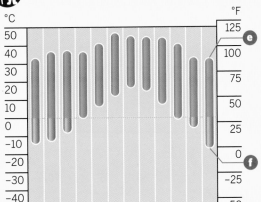

Wind speed (average and maximum)

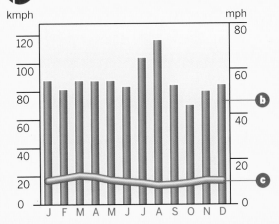

Sunshine

% of possible sunshine

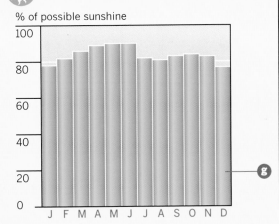

Normal precipitation

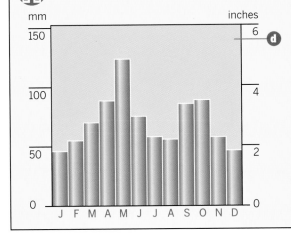

Average number of days with some rain

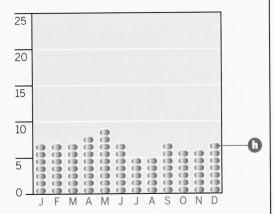

Denver, Colorado

Standing on the western edge of the Great Plains, high above sea level, Denver has a dry, sunny climate.

Denver
Colorado

Monthly recorded features

a Daily mean temperature **e** Highest temperature
b Maximum wind speed **f** Lowest temperature
c Average wind speed **g** Percentage of possible sunshine
d Precipitation **h** Days with some rain

Locator map

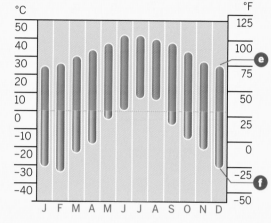

Elevation
● 5,285 feet (1,611 m)

Latitude
● 39°50' N

Köppen climate
● Bsk (midlatitude steppe, cool or cold and semi-arid).

Location
● On the western edge of the central prairie, in the foothills of the Rocky Mountains, Denver has a dry, continental climate, but its elevation reduces summer temperatures, making the climate very pleasant.

Seasons
● Summers are warm, with high daytime temperatures but much lower temperatures at night.
● Winters are mild, with average temperatures remaining above freezing most of the time, although frosty nights can occur between November and early April.
● Precipitation is light, especially in winter, so the weather is usually sunny.
● Winds are generally moderate, but gales can occur in any month.

Daily mean temperature

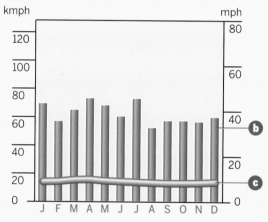

Wind speed (average and maximum)

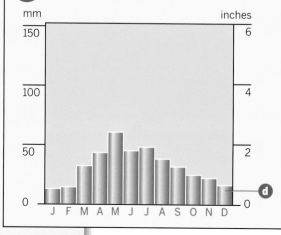

Normal precipitation

Highest and lowest temperatures

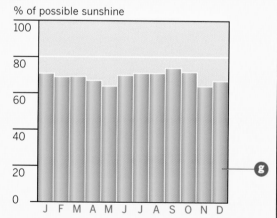

Sunshine

% of possible sunshine

Average number of days with some rain

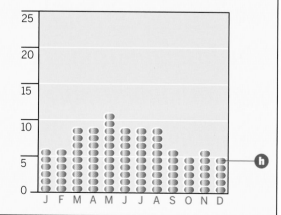

Detroit

Michigan

Monthly recorded features

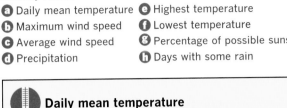

- **a** Daily mean temperature
- **b** Maximum wind speed
- **c** Average wind speed
- **d** Precipitation
- **e** Highest temperature
- **f** Lowest temperature
- **g** Percentage of possible sunshine
- **h** Days with some rain

Locator map

Detroit, Michigan

Situated on the western side of the Detroit River, which links Lakes Erie with Lake Huron, Detroit has a continental climate modified by the lakes that surround it.

Elevation

- 619 feet (189 m)

Latitude

- 42°24' N

Köppen climate

- Dfb (humid continental, very cold winters, short warm summers, moist throughout the year).

Location

- The city lies on a plain with low hills to the west, but is surrounded by lakes that give it a moister climate than it would have if it lay farther to the south.

Seasons

- Summers are warm, and sometimes hot and humid by day.
- Winters are cold, with night temperatures below freezing from December to the end of March, occasionally plunging below −4°F (−20°C) in each of those months.
- Precipitation is moderate and distributed fairly evenly, but with wetter weather in summer.
- Winds are generally light and severe gales uncommon.

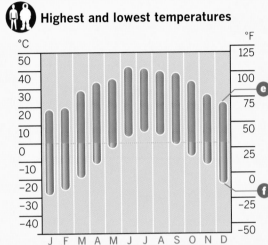

Daily mean temperature

Highest and lowest temperatures

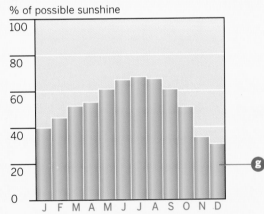

Wind speed (average and maximum)

Sunshine

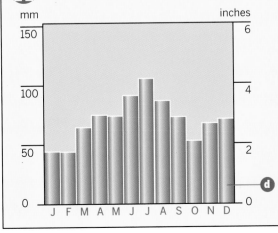

Normal precipitation

Average number of days with some rain

Honolulu, Hawaii

Situated on the south coast of Oahu Island, extending inland across a plain with a mountain range behind, Honolulu has a tropical oceanic climate with a low rainfall.

Elevation

- 38 feet (12 m)

Latitude

- 21°19' N

Köppen climate

- Af (tropical rain forest, hot and rainy throughout the year).

Location

- Its position on the southern coast of Oahu, with mountains inland, shelters Honolulu from the moist northeasterly trade winds. Consequently Honolulu has a much drier climate than towns on the northern coast.

Seasons

- There is little difference between summer and winter temperatures. Average daytime temperatures range from 75°F (24°C) in winter to 82°F (28°C) in summer.
- Rainfall is light, falling mainly in winter.
- Winds are moderate and severe gales uncommon.

Honolulu

Hawaii

Monthly recorded features

- **a** Daily mean temperature
- **b** Maximum wind speed
- **c** Average wind speed
- **d** Precipitation
- **e** Highest temperature
- **f** Lowest temperature
- **g** Percentage of possible sunshine
- **h** Days with some rain

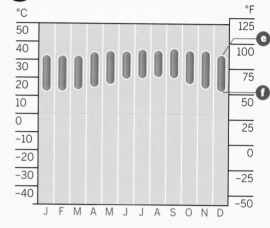

Locator map

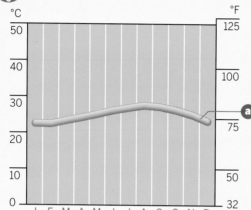

Daily mean temperature

Highest and lowest temperatures

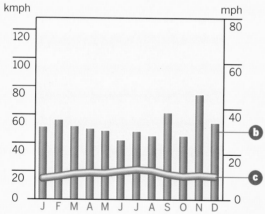

Wind speed (average and maximum)

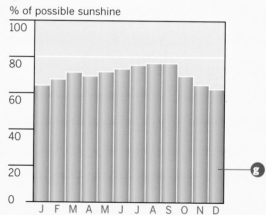

Sunshine

% of possible sunshine

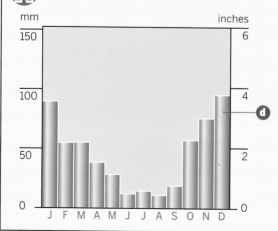

Normal precipitation

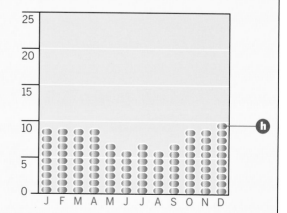

Average number of days with some rain

Houston

Texas

Monthly recorded features

- **a** Daily mean temperature
- **b** Maximum wind speed
- **c** Average wind speed
- **d** Precipitation
- **e** Highest temperature
- **f** Lowest temperature
- **g** Percentage of possible sunshine
- **h** Days with some rain

Locator map

Houston, Texas

Situated almost at sea level near Galveston Bay on the Gulf of Mexico, Houston has a hot, wet climate. It lies in the track of hurricanes crossing the Caribbean.

Elevation
- 41 feet (13 m)

Latitude
- 29°46' N

Köppen climate
- Cfa (humid subtropical, hot summers, mild winters, moist throughout the year).

Location
- Houston is situated about 50 miles (80 km) from the coast on a low-lying plain, where much of its weather is delivered by moist tropical air moving northwards.

Seasons
- Summers are hot, with average daytime temperatures higher than 77°F (25°C) from April until the end of October, and conditions are often uncomfortably humid.
- Winters are mild, with average temperatures never falling below freezing.
- Rainfall is high and distributed fairly evenly throughout the year, but with the wettest weather in spring and fall.
- Winds are generally moderate, but strong gales can occur in any month and Houston lies in the path of hurricanes.

Daily mean temperature

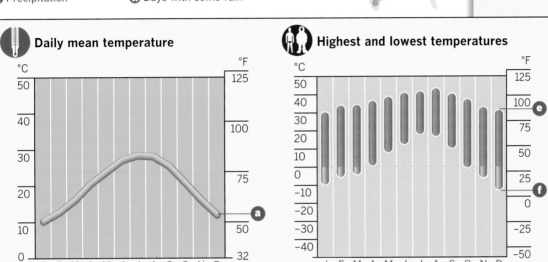

Highest and lowest temperatures

Wind speed (average and maximum)

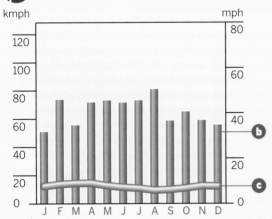

Sunshine

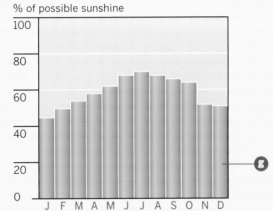

Normal precipitation

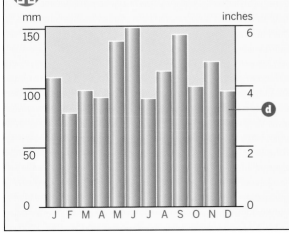

Average number of days with some rain

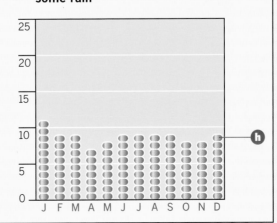

© Diagram Visual Information Ltd.

Indianapolis, Indiana

Situated on a level plain surrounded by low hills on the eastern side of the prairie, Indianapolis has a continental climate, with hot summers and cold winters.

Elevation

- 718 feet (216 m)

Latitude

- 39°46' N

Köppen climate

- Dfa (humid continental, long hot summers, very cold winters, moist throughout the year).

Location

- Its location on the eastern edge of the prairie exposes Indianapolis to dry air approaching from the west, but moderated by moisture from Lake Michigan to the north.

Seasons

- Summers are hot, especially from July to September.
- Winters are cold, with average night temperatures below freezing from December to the end of March.
- Precipitation is moderate and distributed fairly evenly throughout the year, falling as snow in winter.
- Winds are moderate and severe gales are uncommon.

Indianapolis

Indiana

Locator map

Monthly recorded features

- **a** Daily mean temperature
- **b** Maximum wind speed
- **c** Average wind speed
- **d** Precipitation
- **e** Highest temperature
- **f** Lowest temperature
- **g** Percentage of possible sunshine
- **h** Days with some rain

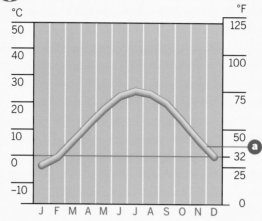

Daily mean temperature

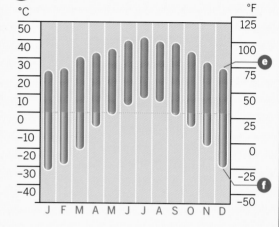

Highest and lowest temperatures

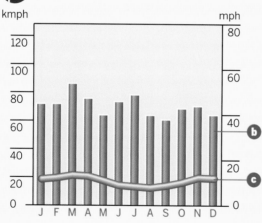

Wind speed (average and maximum)

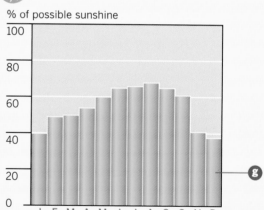

Sunshine

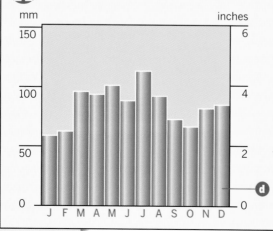

Normal precipitation

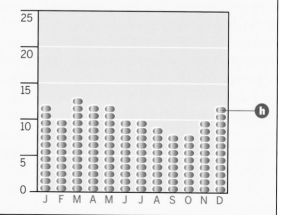

Average number of days with some rain

Las Vegas

Nevada

Monthly recorded features

a Daily mean temperature
b Maximum wind speed
c Average wind speed
d Precipitation
e Highest temperature
f Lowest temperature
g Percentage of possible sunshine
h Days with some rain

Locator map

Las Vegas, Nevada

Las Vegas lies in the rain shadow of the Sierra Nevada Mountains, not far from Death Valley and, beyond that, the edge of the Mojave Desert. It has a warm, dry, sunny climate.

Elevation
● 2,006 feet (612 m)

Latitude
● 36°10' N

Köppen climate
● BWk (midlatitude desert, warm and dry throughout the year).

Location
● In the rain shadow of the mountains, but high above sea level. Its elevation makes the Las Vegas climate cooler than it would be were the city closer to sea level. The dry air makes the heat tolerable.

Seasons
● Summers are hot: day temperatures exceed 104°F (40°C) but fall sharply at night.
● Winter days are warm, with temperatures occasionally exceeding 86°F (30°C) in December and February, but nights are cold, with temperatures often below freezing.
● Rainfall is low, with no month having rain on more than three days on average.
● Winds are generally light and severe gales are rare.

Daily mean temperature

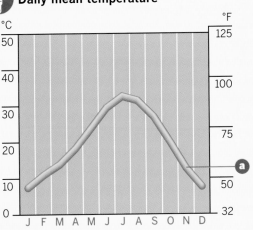

Highest and lowest temperatures

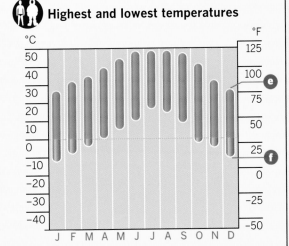

Wind speed (average and maximum)

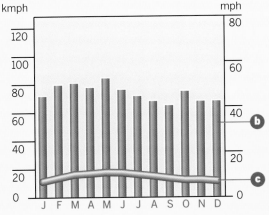

Sunshine

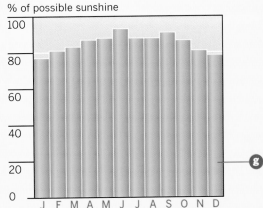

Normal precipitation

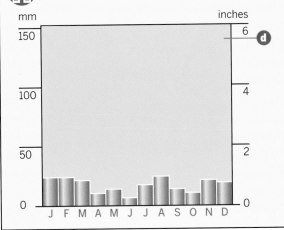

Average number of days with some rain

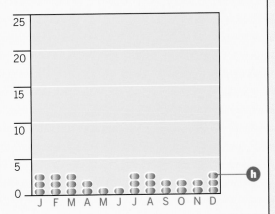

Los Angeles, California

Los Angeles sits in a basin surrounded by mountains on three sides, with the Pacific Ocean to the west. Its climate is dominated by a semi-permanent region of high pressure over the ocean.

Elevation
- 312 feet (95 m)

Latitude
- 34°03' N

Köppen climate
- Csa (Mediterranean, mild winters, hot, dry summers).

Location
- On the coast with mountains behind, and close to the semipermanent subtropical anticyclone over the North Pacific, which brings calm, warm, sunny weather throughout the year.

Seasons
- Summers are warm, but not oppressively hot by day. Temperatures fall to around a comfortable 59°F (15°C) at night.
- Winters are very mild, although frosts can occur at night between December and the end of March.
- Winter rainfall is moderate, but summers are dry. July and August often pass with no rain at all.
- Light winds frequently allow air to stagnate beneath a temperature inversion, leading to the accumulation of pollutants and the development of smog.

Los Angeles
California

Monthly recorded features
- **a** Daily mean temperature
- **b** Maximum wind speed
- **c** Average wind speed
- **d** Precipitation
- **e** Highest temperature
- **f** Lowest temperature
- **g** Percentage of possible sunshine
- **h** Days with some rain

Locator map

Daily mean temperature

Highest and lowest temperatures

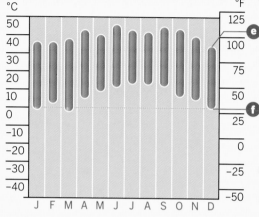

Wind speed (average and maximum)

Sunshine

Normal precipitation

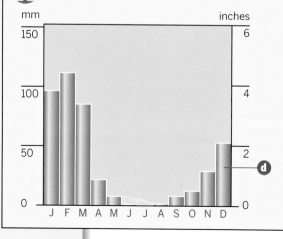

Average number of days with some rain

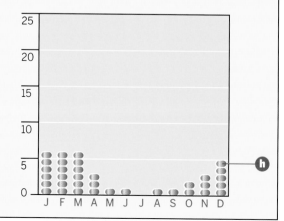
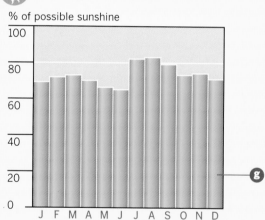
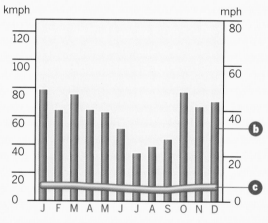

Miami

Florida

Monthly recorded features

- **a** Daily mean temperature
- **b** Maximum wind speed
- **c** Average wind speed
- **d** Precipitation
- **e** Highest temperature
- **f** Lowest temperature
- **g** Percentage of possible sunshine
- **h** Days with some rain

Locator map

U.S. CLIMATE DATA

Miami, Florida

Situated on the southeastern coast with the Everglades to the west, Miami has a climate similar to that of the tropical savannas, but it lies in the path of Atlantic hurricanes.

Elevation
- 25 feet (8 m)

Latitude
- 25°48' N

Köppen climate
- Aw (tropical savanna, hot wet summers, warm dry winters).

Location
- On the Atlantic coast adjacent to the level, low-lying plain of the Everglades.

Seasons
- Summers are hot, but without heat waves, because temperatures are moderated by air crossing the ocean.
- Winters are warm and dominated by the southeasterly trade winds that cross the warm Florida Current (part of the Gulf Stream system).
- Rainfall is moderate but seasonal, falling mainly in summer.
- Winds are generally light, but Miami lies in the path of hurricanes.

Daily mean temperature

Highest and lowest temperatures

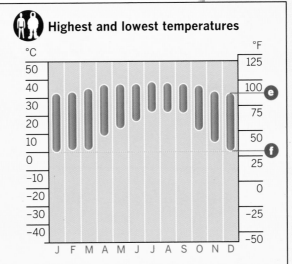

Wind speed (average and maximum)

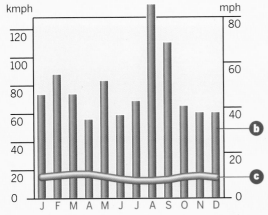

Sunshine

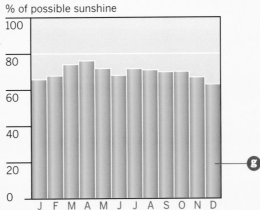

Normal precipitation

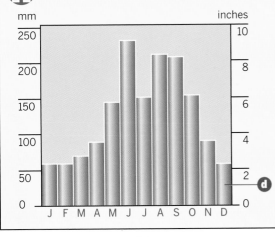

Average number of days with some rain

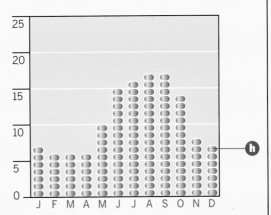

Milwaukee, Wisconsin

Situated on the western shore of Lake Michigan with gentle hills behind, Milwaukee has a continental climate, with warm summers, cold winters, and moderate precipitation.

Elevation
- 650 feet (198 m)

Latitude
- 43°01' N

Köppen climate
- Dfb (humid continental, short, warm summer, cold winter, moist throughout the year).

Location
- On the shore of Lake Michigan, on the eastern prairie.

Seasons
- Summers are warm, but seldom hot.
- Winters last from late October until May, and are cold, with average temperatures below freezing for several months.
- Precipitation is moderate, with summers slightly wetter than winters, and winter precipitation falling as snow.
- Winds are moderate, but winter gales can drive blizzards.

© Diagram Visual Information Ltd.

Milwaukee
Wisconsin

Monthly recorded features

- **a** Daily mean temperature
- **b** Maximum wind speed
- **c** Average wind speed
- **d** Precipitation
- **e** Highest temperature
- **f** Lowest temperature
- **g** Percentage of possible sunshine
- **h** Days with some rain

Locator map

Daily mean temperature

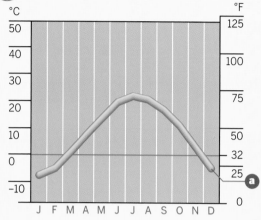

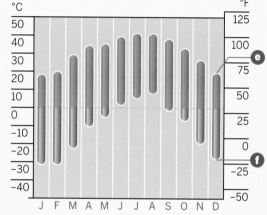

Highest and lowest temperatures

Wind speed (average and maximum)

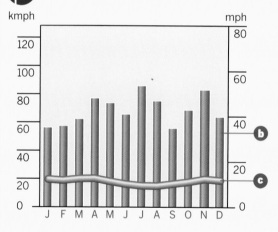

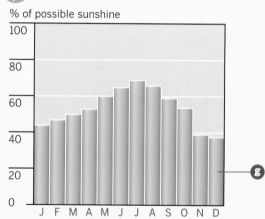

Sunshine

% of possible sunshine

Normal precipitation

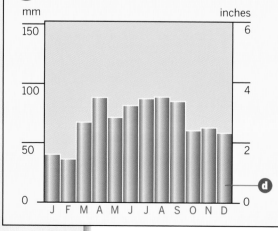

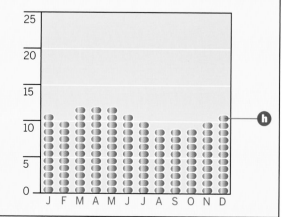

Average number of days with some rain

New Orleans

Louisiana

Monthly recorded features

- **a** Daily mean temperature
- **b** Maximum wind speed
- **c** Average wind speed
- **d** Precipitation
- **e** Highest temperature
- **f** Lowest temperature
- **g** Percentage of possible sunshine
- **h** Days with some rain

Locator map

New Orleans, Louisiana

Set at sea level in a bend on the eastern bank of the Mississippi River, New Orleans has an equable climate, with warm summers and mild winters.

Elevation
- 8 feet (2 m)

Latitude
- 29°57' N

Köppen climate
- Cfa (Humid subtropical, warm summers, mild winters, moist throughout the year).

Location
- Situated at sea level in a large river delta, the New Orleans climate is strongly affected by the proximity of water, making it humid but without extremes of temperature.

Seasons
- Summers are warm, with cool breezes from the Gulf of Mexico preventing temperatures from rising to extremes, although the warm nights can be oppressively humid.
- Winters are mild and the lower humidity makes them pleasant.
- Rainfall is moderate and spread fairly evenly throughout the year, with summer the wettest season.
- Winds are generally light, but the city is sometimes affected by Atlantic hurricanes.

Daily mean temperature

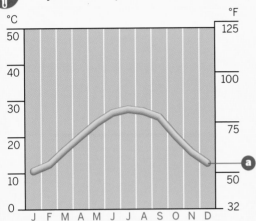

Highest and lowest temperatures

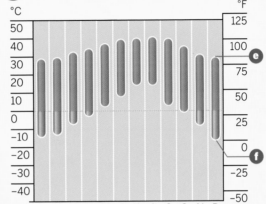

Wind speed (average and maximum)

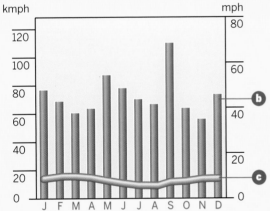

Sunshine

% of possible sunshine

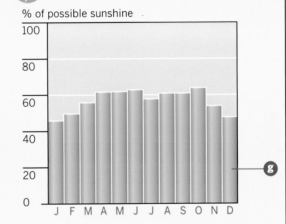

Normal precipitation

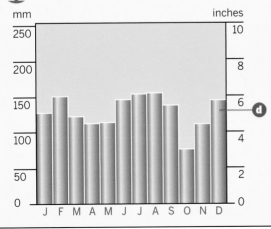

Average number of days with some rain

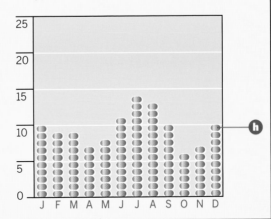

New York City, New York

Its location on the Atlantic coast gives New York City a more maritime climate than is found farther inland, with high precipitation and moderate temperatures.

Elevation
- 131 feet (40 m)

Latitude
- 40°43' N

Köppen climate
- Dfb (humid continental, severe winter, no dry season, warm summer).

Location
- On the eastern coast, where the climate is moderated by air moving inland from over the ocean, but depressions off Cape Hatteras occasionally bring severe spring and fall storms called "nor-easters," with freezing temperatures and heavy snowfalls.

Seasons
- Summers are warm. Temperatures exceeding 95°F (35°C) can occur between May and September.
- Winters are mild, with a likelihood of frost at night from December to early April, but the city is prone to severe winter storms with blizzards.
- Precipitation, falling as snow in winter, is high and distributed evenly throughout the year.
- Winds are moderate, but storms can bring gales at any time of year.

New York City
New York

Monthly recorded features

- **a** Daily mean temperature
- **b** Maximum wind speed
- **c** Average wind speed
- **d** Precipitation
- **e** Highest temperature
- **f** Lowest temperature
- **g** Percentage of possible sunshine
- **h** Days with some rain

Locator map

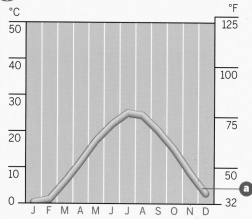

Daily mean temperature

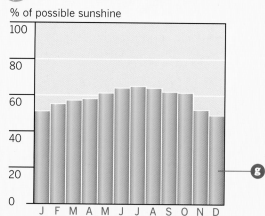

Highest and lowest temperatures

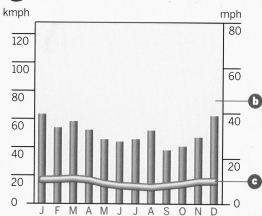

Wind speed (average and maximum)

Sunshine

% of possible sunshine

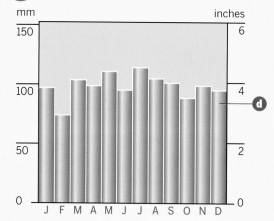

Normal precipitation

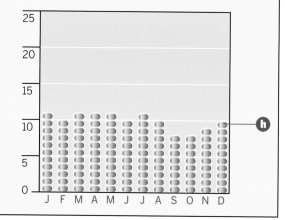

Average number of days with some rain

Oklahoma City
Oklahoma

U.S. CLIMATE DATA

Monthly recorded features

- **a** Daily mean temperature
- **b** Maximum wind speed
- **c** Average wind speed
- **d** Precipitation
- **e** Highest temperature
- **f** Lowest temperature
- **g** Percentage of possible sunshine
- **h** Days with some rain

Locator map

Oklahoma City, Oklahoma

Situated on the Great Plains, Oklahoma City has a continental climate, with dry cold winters and hot wet summers. It also lies inside the region where tornadoes are most frequent.

Elevation
- 1,254 feet (382 m)

Latitude
- 35°29' N

Köppen climate
- Cfa (humid subtropical, hot summers, mild winters, moist throughout the year).

Location
- On the Great Plains, where cold dry air moving southeastwards, hot dry air moving northwards, and warm moist air moving northwestwards from the Gulf of Mexico meet, producing fierce storms, often with tornadoes.

Seasons
- Summers hot by day and warm and humid by night.
- Winters generally mild, with frosts at night from December to February, but cold waves from the north can bring much lower temperatures and blizzards.
- Rainfall moderate, with more falling in summer than in winter.
- Winds are moderate, but severe storms and tornadoes bring much stronger winds.

Daily mean temperature

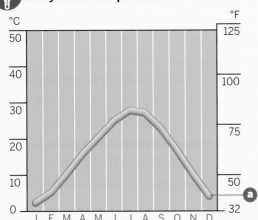

Highest and lowest temperatures

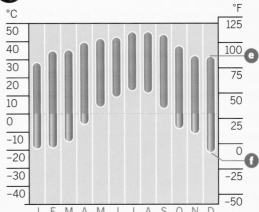

Wind speed (average and maximum)

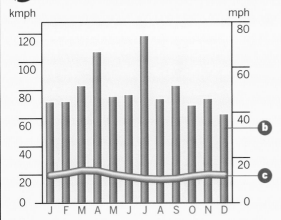

Sunshine

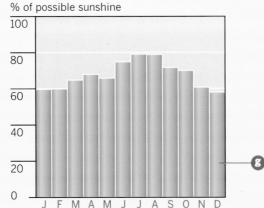

Normal precipitation

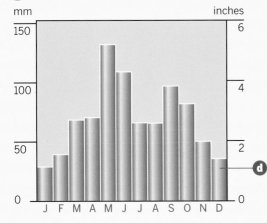

Average number of days with some rain

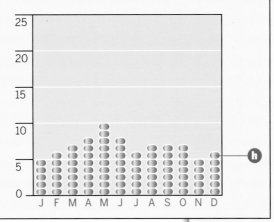

Phoenix, Arizona

Situated in the dry valley of the Salt River, Phoenix is one of the sunniest cities in the United States and its dry climate is believed to be very healthy.

Phoenix
Arizona

Monthly recorded features
- **a** Daily mean temperature
- **b** Maximum wind speed
- **c** Average wind speed
- **d** Precipitation
- **e** Highest temperature
- **f** Lowest temperature
- **g** Percentage of possible sunshine
- **h** Days with some rain

Locator map

Elevation
- 1,083 feet (330 m)

Latitude
- 36°10' N

Köppen climate
- BWk (midlatitude desert, hot summers and mild winters).

Location
- Sited in a saucer-shaped valley with mountains on three sides and in the rain shadow of the Coast Ranges running along the Pacific coast, Phoenix has a dry climate with extremes of temperature.

Seasons
- Summers are hot, with daytime temperatures sometimes exceeding 104°F (40°C), but also falling close to freezing at night. The high temperatures are made tolerable by the low humidity.
- Winters are mild with average temperatures not falling below freezing, although frosts occur occasionally between November and March.
- Rainfall is very low, especially in early summer.
- Winds are generally light. The dry climate and sheltered location make storms uncommon.

Daily mean temperature

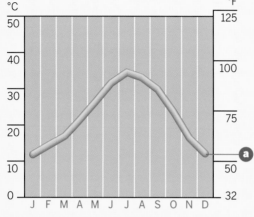

Highest and lowest temperatures

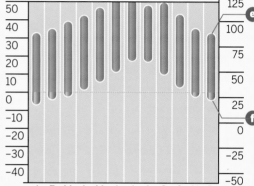

Wind speed (average and maximum)

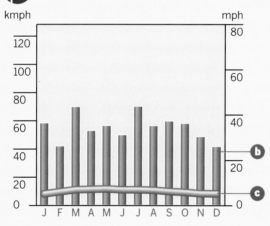

Sunshine

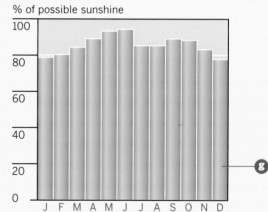

Normal precipitation

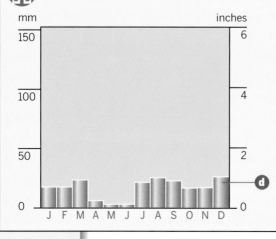

Average number of days with some rain

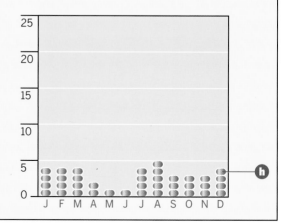

Portland

Oregon

Monthly recorded features

- **a** Daily mean temperature
- **b** Maximum wind speed
- **c** Average wind speed
- **d** Precipitation
- **e** Highest temperature
- **f** Lowest temperature
- **g** Percentage of possible sunshine
- **h** Days with some rain

Locator map

Portland, Oregon

Situated on two peninsulas overlooking Casco Bay on the Pacific coast, Portland has a cool, maritime climate, with high rainfall and cold winters.

Daily mean temperature

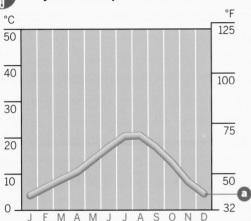

Highest and lowest temperatures

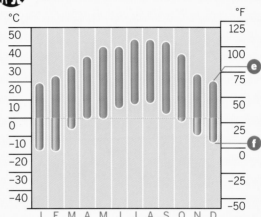

Wind speed (average and maximum)

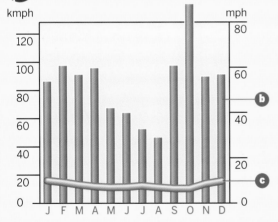

Sunshine

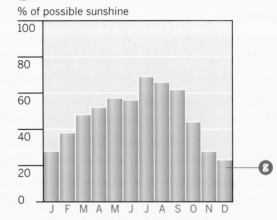

% of possible sunshine

Normal precipitation

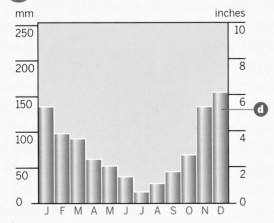

Average number of days with some rain

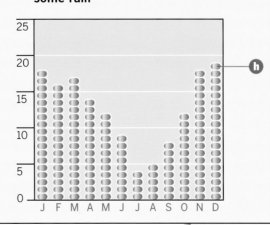

Elevation

- 103 feet (31 m)

Latitude

- 43°39' N

Köppen climate

- Dfb (humid continental, short, warm summers, very cold winters, moist throughout the year).

Location

- On the coast, with a low plain behind and a range of mountains farther inland, Portland has a climate dominated by its proximity to the ocean.

Seasons

- Summers are warm, with average daytime temperatures reaching only 75°F (24°C) in July, and usually last only from June to September.
- Winters are cold, with daytime temperatures hovering around freezing from December to March.
- Precipitation is high, falling as snow in winter, and distributed evenly through the year, although winters are somewhat wetter than summers.
- Winds are generally light and severe gales are uncommon.

© Diagram Visual Information Ltd.

Rapid City
South Dakota

Rapid City, South Dakota

Situated beside Rapid Creek, high above sea level at the eastern edge of the Black Hills, Rapid City has a cool climate with cold, dry winters.

Monthly recorded features

- **a** Daily mean temperature
- **b** Maximum wind speed
- **c** Average wind speed
- **d** Precipitation
- **e** Highest temperature
- **f** Lowest temperature
- **g** Percentage of possible sunshine
- **h** Days with some rain

Locator map

Elevation
- 3,448 feet (1,051 m)

Latitude
- 44°06' N

Köppen climate
- Dfb (humid continental, short, warm summer, very cold winter, moist throughout the year).

Location
- On the western prairie, Rapid City has a continental climate, with cold winters and cool summers.

Seasons
- Summers are warm, but the average July temperature is only about 73°F (23°C) and never reaches 86°F (30°C).
- Winters are cold, with average temperatures below freezing from December through February, although they rarely fall below 10°F (−12°C).
- Precipitation is moderate, falling as snow in winter, but distributed unevenly, with summers much wetter than winters.
- Winds are generally light, but gales can occur at any time of year.

© Diagram Visual Information Ltd.

Daily mean temperature

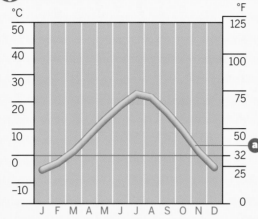

Highest and lowest temperatures

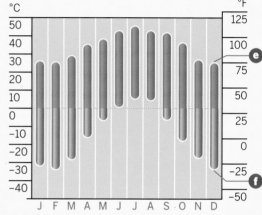

Wind speed (average and maximum)

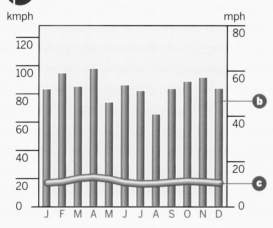

Sunshine

% of possible sunshine

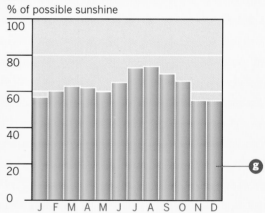

Normal precipitation

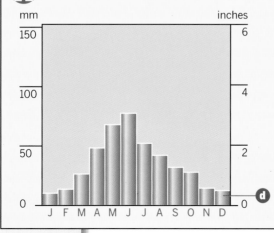

Average number of days with some rain

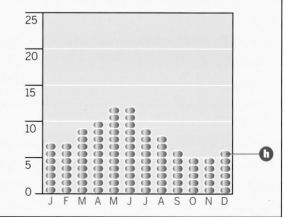

Salt Lake City

Utah

Monthly recorded features

- **a** Daily mean temperature
- **b** Maximum wind speed
- **c** Average wind speed
- **d** Precipitation
- **e** Highest temperature
- **f** Lowest temperature
- **g** Percentage of possible sunshine
- **h** Days with some rain

Locator map

Daily mean temperature

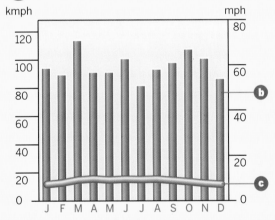

Highest and lowest temperatures

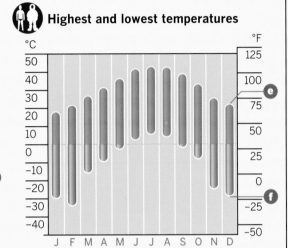

Wind speed (average and maximum)

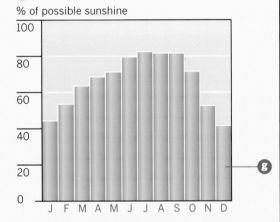

Sunshine

% of possible sunshine

Normal precipitation

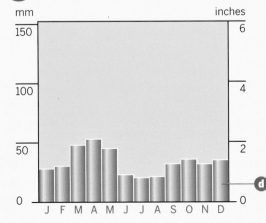

Average number of days with some rain

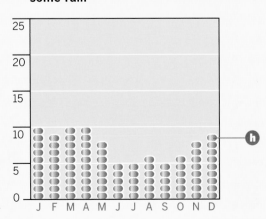

181

U.S. CLIMATE DATA

Salt Lake City, Utah

Situated in the most southerly of the valleys that comprise the valley of the Great Salt Lake, Salt Lake City is surrounded by high mountains. It has warm summers and cold winters.

Elevation

- 4,360 feet (1,330 m)

Latitude

- 40°46' N

Köppen climate

- BSk (midlatitude steppe, dry and cool, with cold winters).

Location

- Sited in a valley to the east of the Great Salt Lake Desert, with the Wasatch Mountains to the east and the Great Salt Lake to the west, Salt Lake City has a dry climate with extremes of temperature.

Seasons

- Summers lasting five months are warm, with temperatures occasionally reaching 104°F (40°C), but nights are cool and the dry air makes the high temperatures pleasant.
- Winters, also lasting about five months, are cold, with freezing temperatures at night and occasional cold spells when temperatures can sink below −4°F (−20°C).
- Precipitation is light and distributed evenly throughout the year, although spring is somewhat wetter than other seasons.

© Diagram Visual Information Ltd.

San Diego, California

The city is situated on the Pacific coast, a few miles from the Mexican border, on a narrow coastal plain with the mountains of the Coast Ranges behind.

San Diego
California

Monthly recorded features
- **a** Daily mean temperature
- **b** Maximum wind speed
- **c** Average wind speed
- **d** Precipitation
- **e** Highest temperature
- **f** Lowest temperature
- **g** Percentage of possible sunshine
- **h** Days with some rain

Locator map

Elevation
- 19 feet (6 m)

Latitude
- 32°44' N

Köppen climate
- Csb (Mediterranean, short, warm, dry summers, mild winters).

Location
- San Diego lies on the narrow coastal plain bordering the Pacific. Air approaching the city from the ocean is chilled as it crosses the cold California Current, preventing temperatures from rising too high in summer. The proximity of the ocean also prevents temperatures from falling very low in winter.

Seasons
- Summers are warm, but seldom hot, and the dry air makes conditions pleasant.
- Winters are only slightly cooler than summers and temperatures rarely fall below freezing.
- Rainfall is light and falls mainly in winter and spring. Almost no rain falls between July and September.
- Winds are light and gales uncommon.

 Daily mean temperature

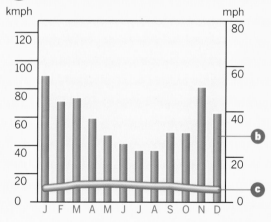

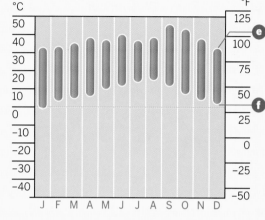 **Highest and lowest temperatures**

 Wind speed (average and maximum)

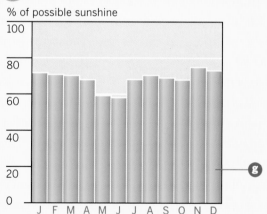 **Sunshine**

% of possible sunshine

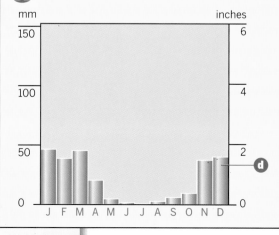 **Normal precipitation**

 Average number of days with some rain

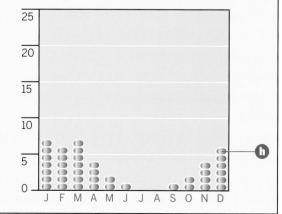

San Francisco

California

Monthly recorded features

- **a** Daily mean temperature
- **b** Maximum wind speed
- **c** Average wind speed
- **d** Precipitation
- **e** Highest temperature
- **f** Lowest temperature
- **g** Percentage of possible sunshine
- **h** Days with some rain

Locator map

San Francisco, California

Situated on one of the two peninsulas that partially enclose San Francisco Bay, the city has a mild, equable climate with refreshing sea breezes in summer, but also with frequent fogs.

Elevation
- 52 feet (16 m)

Latitude
- 37°47' N

Köppen climate
- Csb (Mediterranean, short, warm, dry summer, mild, wet winter).

Location
- The city is sited at the outermost point of a bulge in the coast, bringing it closer to the cold California Current than most other Californian coastal cities. Warm, moist air approaching from the Pacific crosses the current, causing its moisture to condense and form advection fogs that roll inland.

Seasons
- Summers are milder than they would otherwise be because of the breezes and frequent fogs rolling in from the sea.
- Winters are only a few degrees cooler than the summers and temperatures usually remain above freezing.
- Rainfall is light and falls mainly in winter. Almost no rain falls between June and September.
- Winds are moderate, often with fresh breezes or even gales.

Daily mean temperature

°C | °F

Highest and lowest temperatures

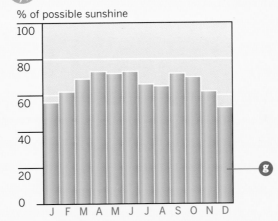

°C | °F

Wind speed (average and maximum)

kmph | mph

Sunshine

% of possible sunshine

Normal precipitation

mm | inches

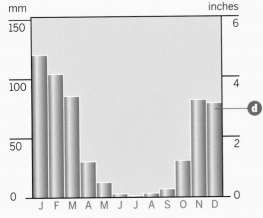

Average number of days with some rain

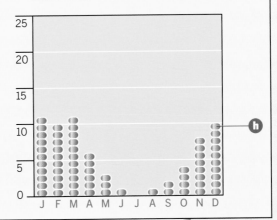

Seattle, Washington

Situated on the eastern shore of Puget Sound, with mountains to the east and west, Seattle is sheltered from both the intense cold of the continental winter and ocean storms.

Elevation
- 125 feet (38 m)

Latitude
- 47°36' N

Köppen climate
- Cfb (maritime west coast, warm summers, mild winters, moist throughout the year).

Location
- Sited on land between Lake Washington to the east and Puget Sound to the west, and sheltered by high mountains, the climate of Seattle is less extreme than its latitude would suggest.

Seasons
- Summers are warm but rarely hot, though temperatures can occasionally rise above 95°F (35°C) by day. Nights are cool.
- Winters are mild, with average temperatures remaining above freezing, although frosts sometimes occur at night any time between October and April.
- Rainfall is moderate, with most falling in winter. Snow is rare.
- Winds are light, and although gales do occur they are uncommon.

© Diagram Visual Information Ltd.

Seattle
Washington

Monthly recorded features
- **a** Daily mean temperature
- **b** Maximum wind speed
- **c** Average wind speed
- **d** Precipitation
- **e** Highest temperature
- **f** Lowest temperature
- **g** Percentage of possible sunshine
- **h** Days with some rain

Locator map

 Daily mean temperature

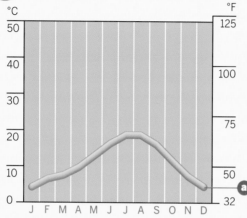

Highest and lowest temperatures

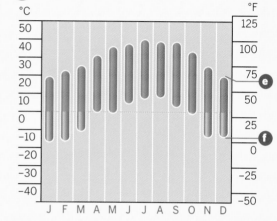

Wind speed (average and maximum)

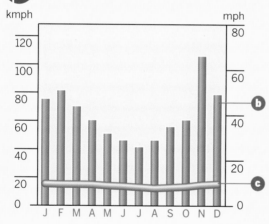

Sunshine

% of possible sunshine

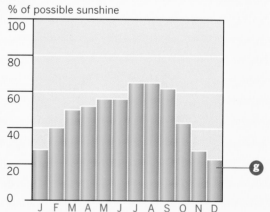

Normal precipitation

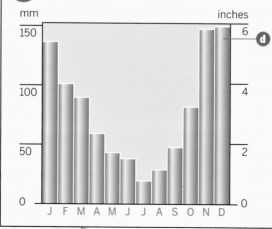

Average number of days with some rain

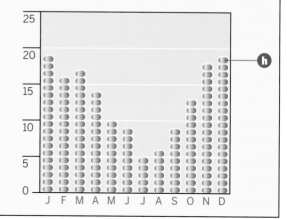

St. Louis
Missouri

Monthly recorded features

- **a** Daily mean temperature
- **b** Maximum wind speed
- **c** Average wind speed
- **d** Precipitation
- **e** Highest temperature
- **f** Lowest temperature
- **g** Percentage of possible sunshine
- **h** Days with some rain

Locator map

St. Louis, Missouri
Situated on the banks of the Mississippi River, St. Louis stands on a plain, where summers are hot, winters mild, and droughts fairly common.

Elevation
- 568 feet (173 m)

Latitude
- 38°28' N

Köppen climate
- Dfa (humid continental, long, hot summers, cold winters, moist throughout the year).

Location
- On the central lowlands of North America, St. Louis has a humid continental climate, with no dry season.

Seasons
- Summers are hot, with average daytime temperatures exceeding 86°F (30°C) in July and August, though nights can be cold, with temperatures occasionally close to freezing in May and September.
- Winters are moderate, with daytime temperatures generally remaining above freezing, but between December and February night temperatures can fall below −13°F (−25°C).
- Rainfall is moderate and spread fairly evenly throughout the year.

Daily mean temperature
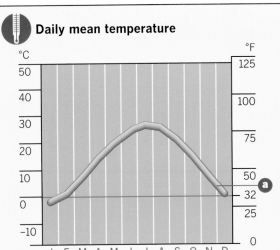

Highest and lowest temperatures
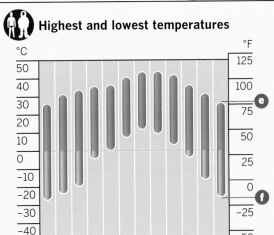

Wind speed (average and maximum)
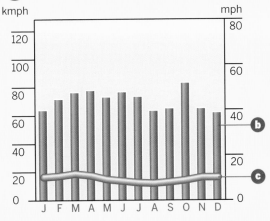

Sunshine
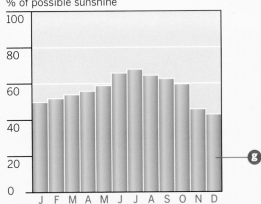

Normal precipitation
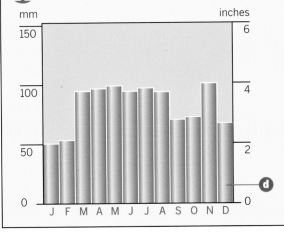

Average number of days with some rain
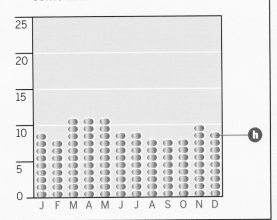

St. Paul, Minnesota

Standing beside the Mississippi River, St. Paul is built on a series of terraces rising from the river valley to a plain surrounded by higher ground on all sides. The climate is continental.

Elevation
● 721 feet (220 m)

Latitude
● 44°34' N

Köppen climate
● Dfb (humid continental, short, warm summers, cold winters, moist throughout the year).

Location
● On the eastern prairie, to the west of the Great Lakes, St. Paul is fully exposed to the continental climate.

Seasons
● Summers are warm, sometimes hot, with temperatures known to exceed 104°F (40°C) between May and July, but at night temperatures can fall close to freezing and 34°F (1°C) has been recorded in June.
● Winters are cold, with average daytime temperatures below freezing from December to February and temperatures below −22°F (−30°C) recorded between December and March.
● Precipitation is moderate, with more falling in summer than in winter. In winter it falls as snow.
● Winds are moderate, but severe storms with strong gales are fairly common.

St. Paul
Minnesota

Monthly recorded features
- **a** Daily mean temperature
- **b** Maximum wind speed
- **c** Average wind speed
- **d** Precipitation
- **e** Highest temperature
- **f** Lowest temperature
- **g** Percentage of possible sunshine
- **h** Days with some rain

Locator map

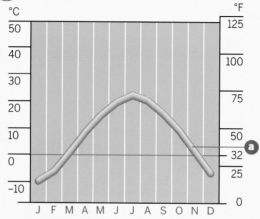

Daily mean temperature

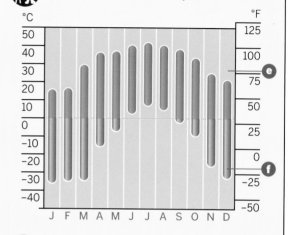

Highest and lowest temperatures

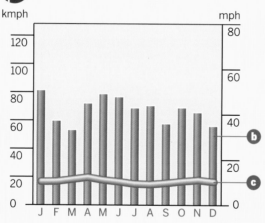

Wind speed (average and maximum)

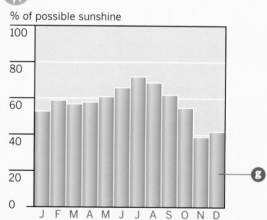

Sunshine

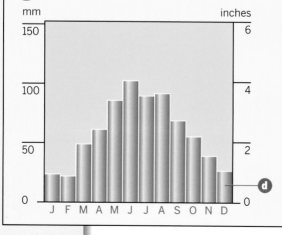

Normal precipitation

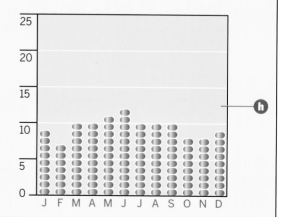

Average number of days with some rain

Tampa

Florida

Monthly recorded features

- **a** Daily mean temperature
- **b** Maximum wind speed
- **c** Average wind speed
- **d** Precipitation
- **e** Highest temperature
- **f** Lowest temperature
- **g** Percentage of possible sunshine
- **h** Days with some rain

Locator map

Tampa, Florida

Situated beside the mouth of the Hillsborough River where it enters Tampa Bay on the western coast of Florida, Tampa has a humid subtropical climate.

Elevation
- 16 feet (5 m)

Latitude
- 27°34' N

Köppen climate
- Cfa (humid subtropical, hot summers, mild winters, moist throughout the year).

Location
- Near the western coast of Florida, on a low-lying plain facing the Gulf of Mexico, but with land between the city and the sea, Tampa lies in the subtropics.

Seasons
- Summers are warm, with temperatures falling only a little at night.
- Winters are mild, with temperatures never falling to freezing.
- Rainfall is heavy, with much more falling between June and September than at any other time.
- Winds are generally light and severe gales uncommon.

Daily mean temperature

Highest and lowest temperatures

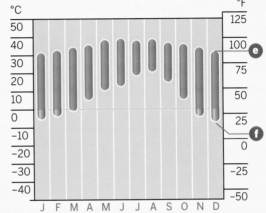

Wind speed (average and maximum)

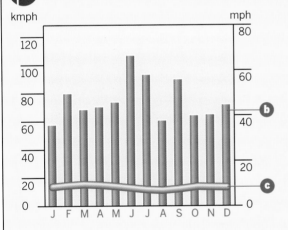

Sunshine

% of possible sunshine

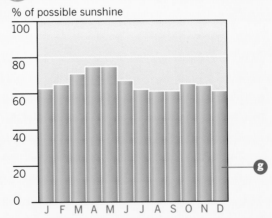

Normal precipitation

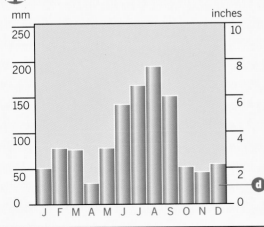

Average number of days with some rain

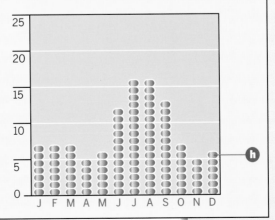

U.S. CLIMATE DATA

Washington, D.C.

Situated on the banks of the Potomac River on the coastal plain, Washington has hot summers, often oppressively humid, and mild winters with moderate snowfall.

Elevation
- 72 feet (22 m)

Latitude
- 38°54' N

Köppen climate
- Dfb (humid continental, severe winter, no dry season, warm summer).

Location
- Standing on the inland side of the coastal plain with the Appalachian Mountains behind, the climate of Washington is influenced by air moving eastward from the mountains and by the ocean.

Seasons
- Summers are hot, with temperatures sometimes exceeding 104°F (40°C) between July and September.
- Winters are fairly mild, with average temperatures remaining above freezing by day, but frosts are likely at night from December to February and temperatures of –13°F (–25°C) have been recorded.
- Precipitation is moderate and distributed evenly throughout the year.
- Winds are moderate, but gales can occur in any month.

© Diagram Visual Information Ltd.

Washington
D.C.

Monthly recorded features
- **a** Daily mean temperature
- **b** Maximum wind speed
- **c** Average wind speed
- **d** Precipitation
- **e** Highest temperature
- **f** Lowest temperature
- **g** Percentage of possible sunshine
- **h** Days with some rain

Locator map

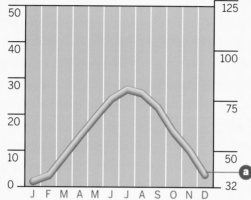
Daily mean temperature

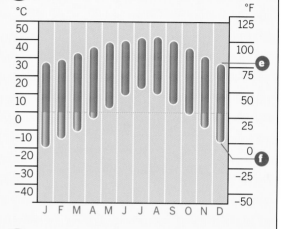
Highest and lowest temperatures

Wind speed (average and maximum)
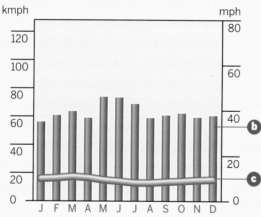

Sunshine
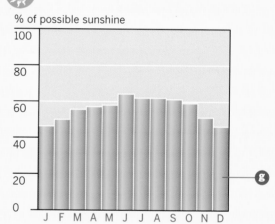
% of possible sunshine

Normal precipitation
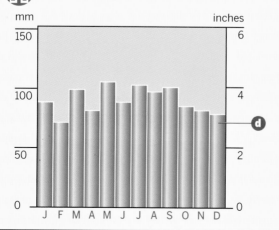

Average number of days with some rain
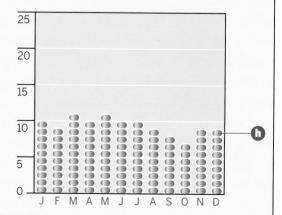

The greenhouse effect

Solar radiation trapped by greenhouse gases: present day

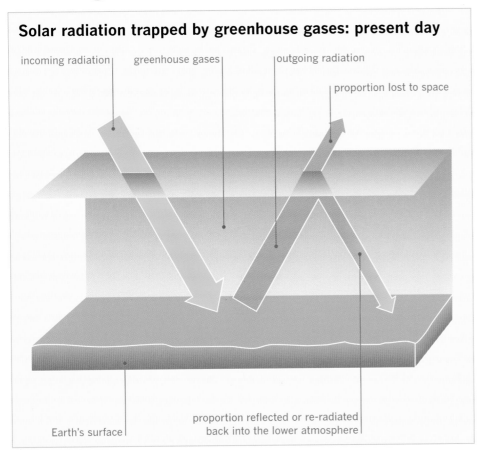

incoming radiation   greenhouse gases   outgoing radiation

proportion lost to space

Earth's surface

proportion reflected or re-radiated
back into the lower atmosphere

Solar radiation: 2030 (projected)

This is the likely situation if greenhouse gas emissions are not reduced.

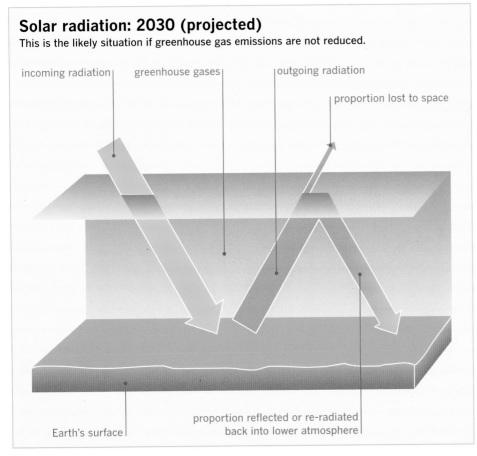

incoming radiation   greenhouse gases   outgoing radiation

proportion lost to space

Earth's surface

proportion reflected or re-radiated
back into lower atmosphere

Key words

atmosphere	greenhouse gas
fossil fuel	longwave
global warming	solar radiation
greenhouse	
effect	

Greenhouse gases

- The *greenhouse effect* refers to the naturally occurring process by which some gases in the atmosphere absorb longwave radiation emitted from Earth's surface and, in turn, radiate that heat in all directions, warming the atmosphere and the surface.

- It is estimated that, without the greenhouse effect, the average temperature of Earth would be about −0.4°F (−18°C) rather than the actual average of 59°F (15°C).

- The gases that produce the greenhouse effect are known as *greenhouse gases*. The most significant of these are carbon dioxide, water vapor, and methane.

- Since about 1750, human activity has been increasing the concentrations of greenhouse gases in the atmosphere and adding new greenhouse gases. This may be causing the greenhouse effect to intensify, which would result in a rise in average global temperatures known as *global warming*.

- Carbon dioxide concentrations in the atmosphere are thought to have increased by almost 30 percent in the last 250 years. This is a result of the massive increase in the burning of fossil fuels and the conversion of large areas of land from prairie and forest to agriculture.

- Methane concentrations in the atmosphere are thought to have increased by almost 145 percent in the last 250 years. This is a result of a massive increase in rice cultivation and the numbers of domestic grazing animals.

- Nitrous oxide concentrations in the atmosphere are thought to have increased by almost 11 percent in the last 250 years.

© Diagram Visual Information Ltd.

Key words

atmosphere	ice age
global warming	
greenhouse	
effect	
greenhouse gas	

Global warming

- *Global warming* refers to a rise in average global temperatures.
- Global warming is known to have occurred in many periods of Earth's history.
- For example, there was a very rapid and large increase in average global temperatures about 55 million years ago known as the "Paleocene-Eocene Thermal Maximum." Analysis of marine sediments indicates that ocean surface temperatures rose by between 14.5°F and 18°F (8°C–10°C) over the course of a few thousand years.
- Most scientists agree that average global temperatures have risen by between 0.7°F and 1.4°F (0.4°C–0.8°C) since the end of the 19th century.
- Some scientists believe that this rise in temperature is within the normal range of average global temperature variation since the end of the last ice age. Others think that the increase may be due to factors that are not related to human activities.
- Some scientists believe that this increase is due to an enhancement of the greenhouse effect caused by an increase in the concentration of greenhouse gases in the atmosphere, and that this increase is a result of human activity.
- Those scientists who believe that abnormal global warming is taking place—and that it is a result of human activity—predict that the phenomenon will become more pronounced if nothing is done to curb emissions of greenhouse gases.
- Predictions of how far average global temperatures may rise vary between about 2.5°F and 10.4°F (1.4°C–5.8°C) by the year 2100.
- Temperature rises, if they do occur, are unlikely to be evenly distributed across the globe.

Global warming

Possible distribution of global warming by 2100

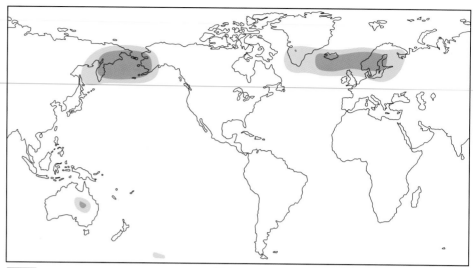

☐ 14.4°F to 18°F (8°C–10°C)	▨ more than 18°F (10°C)

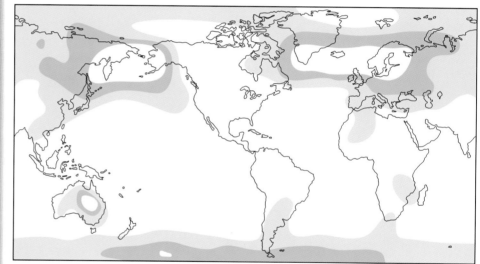

☐ 7.2°F to 10.8°F (4°C–6°C)	▨ 10.8°F to 14.4°F (6°C–8°C)

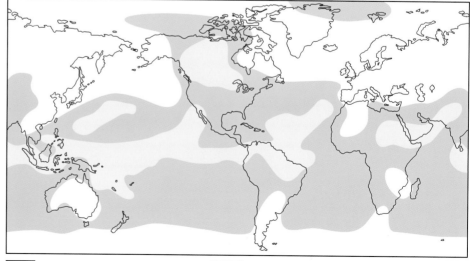

☐ less than 3.6°F (2°C)	▨ 3.6°F to 7.2°F (2°C–4°C)

Areas at risk from sea-level rise

1 Long Beach, CA
2 Columbia River delta
3 Gulf and Atlantic coasts of Mexico and the United States
4 Orinoco delta
5 Amazon delta
6 River Plate estuary
7 Southern and eastern England
8 Southern Baltic coast
9 Northern Germany, Netherlands, Belgium, and France
10 Loire estuary, France
11 Vendée, France
12 Lisbon region, Portugal
13 Guadalquivir estuary, Spain
14 Ebro delta, Spain
15 Rhône delta, France
16 Northern Adriatic coast
17 Danube delta, Romania
18 Sea of Azov
19 Southeastern Turkey
20 Tigris-Euphrates delta
21 Tunisian coast
22 Nile delta

23 West African coast
24 Zambesi delta
25 Indus delta
26 East coast of India
27 Ganges delta
28 Irrawaddy delta
29 Bangkok
30 Mekong delta
31 Eastern Sumatra
32 Northern Java
33 Sepik delta
34 Adelaide
35 Corner Inlet
36 Northern Taiwan
37 Red River delta, Vietnam
38 Hwang-Ho delta
39 Tokyo Bay
40 Niigata, Japan

Key words

global warming
sea level
sea-level rise

Sea-level rise

- *Sea-level rise* refers to an increase in average global sea level.
- Measurements indicate that average sea level has been rising by about 0.04 to 0.08 inches per year (1–2 mm per year) since the beginning of the twentieth century.
- Some scientists believe that this rise is a result of global warming.
- Warmer average global temperatures are thought to cause sea levels to rise because they cause the water in the oceans to expand thermally and cause more glacial ice to melt, increasing the overall volume of water in the oceans.

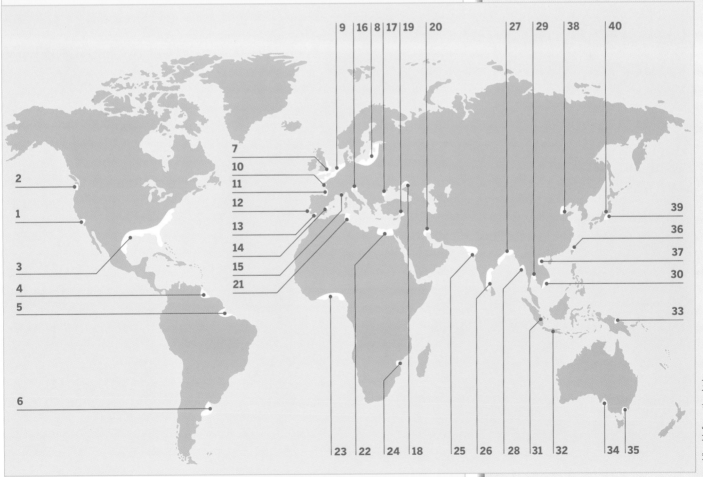

Florida's future

© Diagram Visual Information Ltd.

Key words

sea level

Effect of sea level rise on Florida panhandle

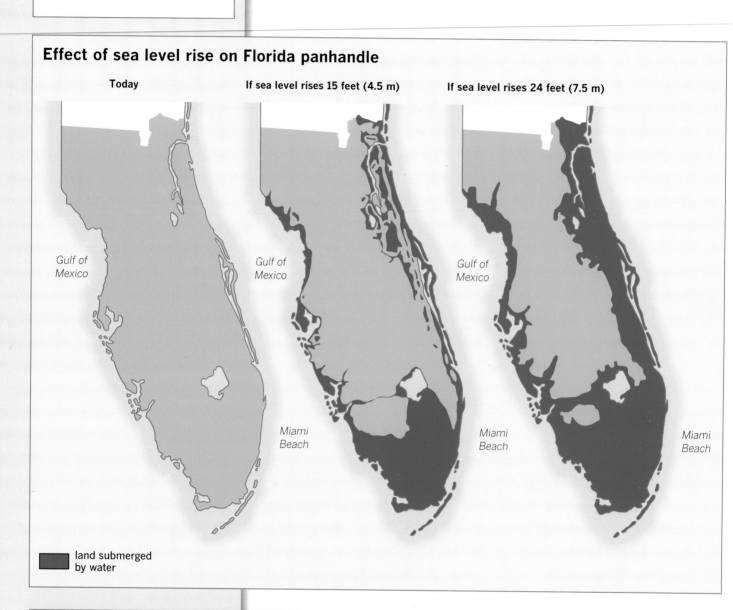

Today

If sea level rises 15 feet (4.5 m)

If sea level rises 24 feet (7.5 m)

Gulf of Mexico

Miami Beach

land submerged by water

The threat to coastal cities

● Many of the world's major cities are located on coasts, very close to sea level, and the whole of the eastern seaboard of the United States is low-lying. During the 20th century sea level rose by about 3 inches (76 mm). Scientists estimate that by 2100 rising global temperatures may produce a sea-level rise of 4.3–30 inches (11–77 cm). The most likely change will be toward the lower end of this range, bringing a rise of less than 10 inches (25 cm).

● Most of the rise is caused by the expansion of seawater as it grows warmer. If temperatures continue rising, however,

it is possible that several centuries from now the polar ice sheets may begin to melt. Between them, the Greenland and Antarctic ice sheets hold about 6.85 million cubic miles (28.56 million km³) of water. If some of this ice were to melt, it would cause much greater rises in sea level (and if all of it were to melt the sea level would rise by about 230 feet, 70 m).

● The diagrams show what would happen to the map of Florida if the sea level were to rise by 15 feet (4.5 m) or 24 feet (7.5 m). Fortunately, a sea-level rise of this magnitude is highly unlikely.

Acid rain

Air pollution

- *Acid rain* refers to any form of precipitation with a *pH* value lower than 5.6.
- A pH value or "potential of hydrogen" value is a measure of the acidity or alkalinity of a substance. A pH of 7 indicates that a substance is neutral. A pH of less than 7 indicates acidity, and a pH of more than 7 indicates alkalinity.
- Distilled water has a pH value of 7. Under normal atmospheric conditions some carbon dioxide in the atmosphere is dissolved by precipitation to form weak carbonic acid resulting in precipitation with a pH value of about 5.6.
- High concentrations of sulfur or nitrogen oxides in the atmosphere may combine with precipitation to form sulfuric or nitric acids resulting in precipitation with a pH value of less than 4.5.

- Sulfur and nitrogen oxides are emitted into the atmosphere in large quantities by volcanoes and by some biological processes. Both of these are sources of acid rain.
- The release of sulfur and nitrogen oxides during industrial processes, such as the burning of sulfur-rich coal, has greatly increased the incidences of acid rain over the last 250 years.
- Industrial pollution often produces acid rain hundreds of miles away from the site of its release as well as locally.
- Acid rain has been shown to have a direct effect on biospheres. Almost no fish can survive in lakes with pH values below 4.5. Acid rain also harms trees by breaking down the waxy surface layers of leaves, causing nutrients to be lost.

Key words

acid rain
atmosphere
biosphere
precipitation

The pH of water

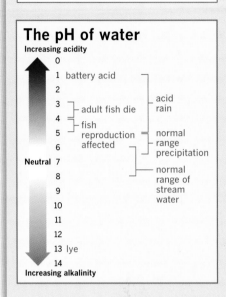

Increasing acidity

0
1 battery acid
2
3 — adult fish die
4 — fish reproduction affected
5
6
Neutral 7
8
9
10
11
12
13 lye
14

Increasing alkalinity

acid rain

normal range precipitation

normal range of stream water

Regions with rain pH of 6.0 or less

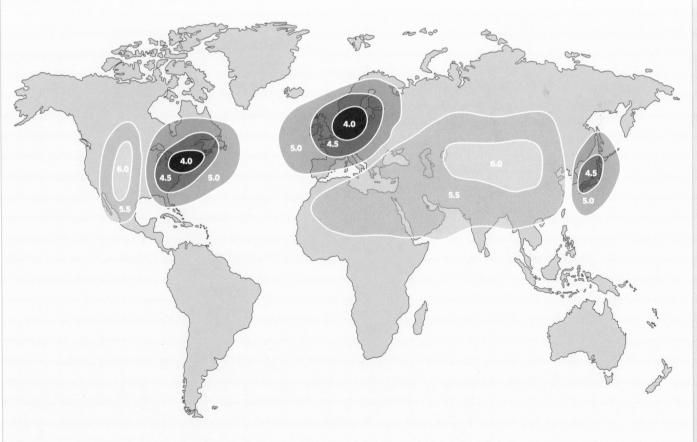

Key words	
acid rain	greenhouse
air quality	effect
chlorofluoro-	greenhouse gas
carbons (CFCs)	ozone
global warming	sulfurous smog

Air pollution

- The worst pollutant gases implicated in *air quality* problems arising from human activity are carbon dioxide, sulfur dioxide, nitrogen oxides, and methane.
- Carbon dioxide (CO_2) is produced by human activities such as the burning of fossil fuels. It is a greenhouse gas. The amount of CO_2 in the atmosphere has been increasing since the nineteenth century, raising global temperatures as a result.
- Sulfur dioxide (SO_2) is a by-product of power stations and industry. It is also a human irritant in the form of sulfurous smog, and causes acid rain, which destroys plant life.
- Nitrogen oxides (NO_x) are also by-products of human industry that produce ozone (a pollutant when in the wrong place), smog, and acid rain.
- Methane (CH_4) is a natural product of plant decay, but atmospheric levels have risen dramatically in the last century as a result of intensive farming. It is also a greenhouse gas and contributes to global warming.
- Chlorofluorocarbons (CFCs) cause the breakdown of stratospheric ozone. They were in widespread use in refrigeration and aerosols until about 1990, but have now been largely replaced by less damaging chemicals.

Causes of air pollution

Major gases

CO_2 carbon dioxide
SO_2 sulfur dioxide
NO_x nitrogen oxides
CH_4 methane

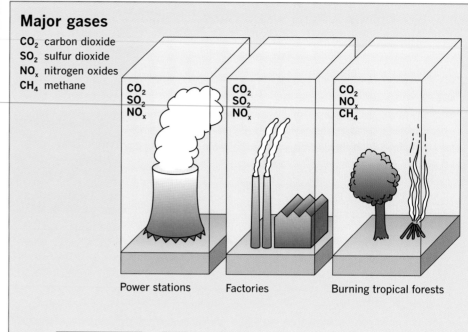

Power stations   Factories   Burning tropical forests

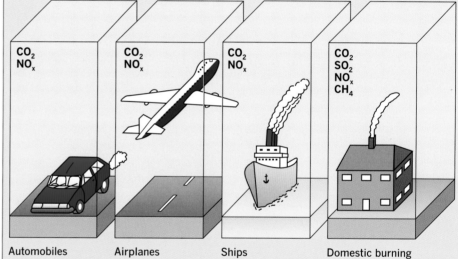

Automobiles   Airplanes   Ships   Domestic burning

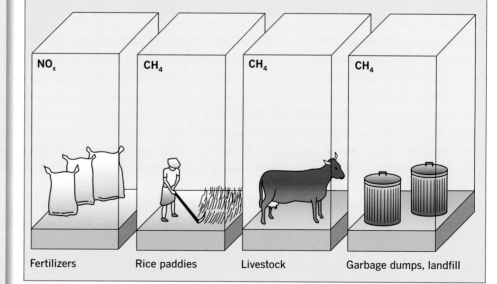

Fertilizers   Rice paddies   Livestock   Garbage dumps, landfill

The ozone layer

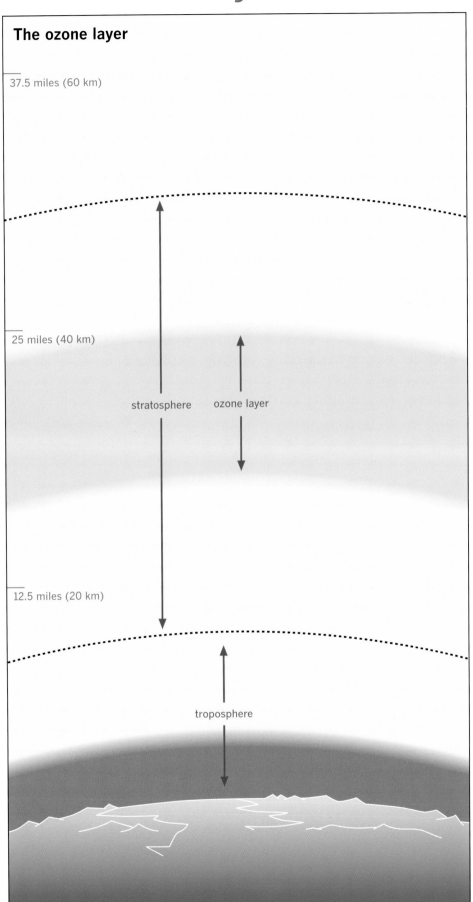

The ozone layer

37.5 miles (60 km)

25 miles (40 km)

stratosphere ozone layer

12.5 miles (20 km)

troposphere

Key words

atmosphere	solar radiation
ozone	stratosphere
ozone layer	troposphere
ozone-oxygen	
cycle	

Ozone layer

- *Ozone* is a naturally-occuring tri-atomic molecule of oxygen (O_3). It is less common than the typical bi-atomic form (O_2) found in air.
- The *ozone layer* is a layer of Earth's atmosphere where concentrations of ozone are at their greatest. It is found within the stratosphere at altitudes of between 10 and 25 miles (16–40 km).
- Ozone is formed in Earth's atmosphere when ultraviolet radiation from the Sun strikes bi-atomic oxygen molecules (O_2), causing them to split into two single oxygen atoms. Some of these single atoms of oxygen combine with other O_2 molecules to form ozone molecules (O_3).
- These O_3 molecules are also split by ultraviolet radiation into O_2 molecules and single oxygen atoms. A cycle of ozone creation and destruction known as the *ozone-oxygen cycle* keeps quantities of stratospheric ozone stable.
- The ozone-oxygen cycle absorbs about 90 percent of the ultraviolet radiation that arrives at Earth's atmosphere. It is for this reason that the ozone layer is referred to as an *ultraviolet shield*.

Ozone variation

- The amount of ozone present in a region of the stratosphere depends primarily on the amount of solar radiation it receives. The more solar radiation there is, the more ozone molecules are destroyed as they absorb ultraviolet radiation.
- In the tropics there is little variation in solar radiation over the year, so there is little variation in stratospheric ozone. Over the poles there is a large variation in solar radiation over the year and therefore great variation in stratospheric ozone.

© Diagram Visual Information Ltd.

Key words

chlorofluoro-carbon (CFC)	*ozone hole*
dobson unit	*ozone–oxygen*
latitude	*cycle*
ozone	*stratosphere*

The ozone "hole"

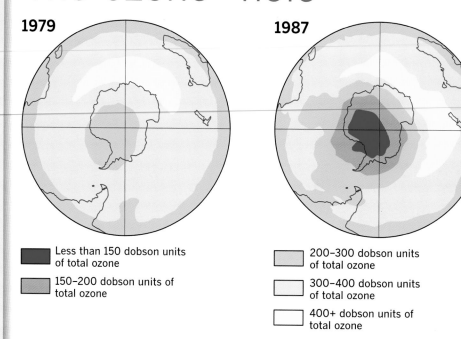

1979   1987

Less than 150 dobson units of total ozone

150–200 dobson units of total ozone

200–300 dobson units of total ozone

300–400 dobson units of total ozone

400+ dobson units of total ozone

Ozone depletion

- Between 1979 and 1990 scientists detected a five percent reduction in levels of stratospheric ozone.

- In particular it was found that levels of stratospheric ozone were dropping by up to 70 percent over Antarctica and 30 percent over the Arctic during the spring. These extreme geographical and seasonal variations became known as "holes" in the ozone layer.

- The depletion of ozone was found to be occurring because of the presence of *chlorofluorocarbons (CFCs)* in the atmosphere. CFCs are human-made chemicals that were in widespread use for much of the twentieth century.

- CFCs break down and produce chlorine radicals such as chlorine monoxide when exposed to ultraviolet light. These chlorine radicals break down ozone molecules, so disrupting the balance of the ozone–oxygen cycle.

- Concentrations of chlorine monoxide were found to be highest at latitudes where ozone depletion was most extreme.

Concentrations of chlorine radicals and ozone

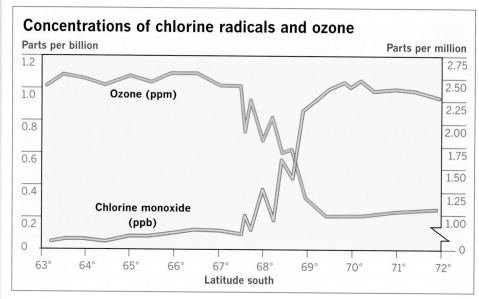

Sources of CFCs

Percentage of ozone loss caused by products containing various CFCs

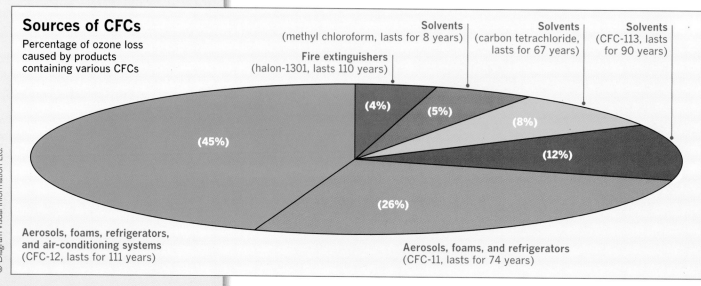

Fire extinguishers (halon-1301, lasts 110 years)

Solvents (methyl chloroform, lasts for 8 years)

Solvents (carbon tetrachloride, lasts for 67 years)

Solvents (CFC-113, lasts for 90 years)

Aerosols, foams, refrigerators, and air-conditioning systems (CFC-12, lasts for 111 years)

Aerosols, foams, and refrigerators (CFC-11, lasts for 74 years)

Responses to ozone depletion

Key words

*chlorofluoro-
    carbon (CFC)*
ozone
ozone hole

Ozone depletion potential

Compound	Lifetime (years)	Ozone depletion potential
CFC-11	75	1.0
CFC-12	111	1.0
CFC-113	90	0.8
CFC-114	185	1.0
CFC-115	380	0.6
HCFC-22	20	0.05
Methyl chloroform	6.5	0.10
Carbon tetrachloride	50	1.06
Halon-1211	25	3.0
Halon-1301	110	10.0
Halon-2402	not known	6.0

Montreal Protocol

- The *Montreal Protocol on Substances that Deplete the Ozone Layer* is an international treaty that requires its signatories to eliminate the production of substances that are thought to be responsible for the depletion of the ozone layer.
- The treaty came into force in 1989 and has since been revised five times, the latest revision being the result of a conference in Beijing in 1999.
- The substances considered to be the most detrimental to the ozone layer are listed under Group 1 Annex A. These are CFC-11, CFC-12, CFC-113, CFC-114, and CFC-115. The treaty called for production of these substances to cease completely.
- Timetables were also given for the phasing out of other substances such as halon-1211, halon-1301, halon-2402, carbon tetrachloride, and methyl chloroform.
- One hundred and eighty-three nations, including the United States, are currently signatories to the Montreal Protocol and its revisions.

Impact

- Although the Montreal Protocol has been very successful at reducing the production of substances harmful to the ozone layer, much of the material produced before the introduction of the treaty remains in the atmosphere.
- The largest ozone hole over Antarctica ever recorded occurred in September 2000, despite the fact that CFC production had already been reduced by more than 98 percent by that date.

CFC production

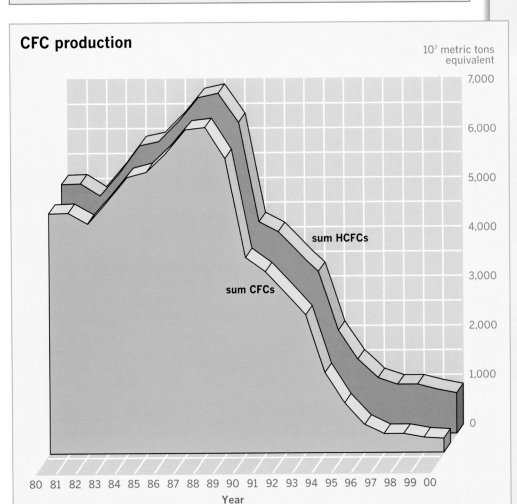

10^3 metric tons equivalent

sum HCFCs

sum CFCs

7,000 — 6,000 — 5,000 — 4,000 — 3,000 — 2,000 — 1,000 — 0

80 81 82 83 84 85 86 87 88 89 90 91 92 93 94 95 96 97 98 99 00

Year

Key words

22° halo An optical phenomenon that projects a halo of light around the Sun with a perimeter at a distance of 20 degrees of arc from the Sun itself. It is caused by internal reflections of sunlight in ice crystals suspended in the atmosphere.

absolute humidity The mass of water vapor present in a given volume of air. It is usually expressed in grams per cubic meter.

acid rain Rain that is more acidic than normal as a result of air pollution. It can be defined as rain with a pH value of less than 5.6.

advection fog Fog that is formed when warm moist air is carried across a colder surface. "Advection" refers to the transport of heat due to the movement of air or water.

air mass A large body of air that has approximately constant temperature and humidity throughout. Air masses are typically large enough to cover the majority of a continent or a substantial part of an ocean. The interaction of air masses with differing characteristics is one of the main causes of weather.

air quality Refers to the extent to which the air across a given area is polluted. Air quality is said to be high when there is little pollution present.

albedo The ratio of the amount of light arriving at a body and the amount of light reflected by it. It is a measure of the reflectivity of an object. Albedo is usually expressed as a percentage—a body that reflects no light is said to have an albedo of 0 percent and a body that reflects all light is said to have an albedo of 100 percent. Earth has an average albedo of 37 to 39 percent.

altocumulus A variety of middle-altitude cloud composed of long thin elements and arranged in lines or waves.

altostratus A variety of middle-altitude cloud that has the appearance of a thin veil or uniform sheet. They are commonly pale gray or blue in color.

anemometer An instrument used to measure wind speed.

aneroid barometer A barometer that measures the effect of atmospheric pressure on a flexible, partially evacuated chamber. An increase in atmospheric pressure causes the chamber to compress. A decrease in atmospheric pressure causes the chamber to expand.

annual temperature range The difference between the average temperature on the coldest night and the average temperature on the warmest day of the year for a given location.

anticyclone A region in which atmospheric pressure is higher than in the surrounding area. Air flows outward from an anticyclone.

anticyclonic wind A flow of air caused by the presence of an anticyclone. It flows outward from an anticyclone in a clockwise direction in the Northern Hemisphere and anticlockwise in the Southern Hemisphere.

antisolar point The point in the sky that is directly opposite the Sun from the point of view of an observer. When the Sun is above the horizon, the antisolar point is always below the opposite horizon.

anvil A term used to describe the characteristic shape of the upper portion of a mature cumulonimbus cloud. Also known as a thunderhead.

arc An optical phenomenon caused by ice particles suspended in the atmosphere reflecting and refracting sunlight.

atmosphere The envelope of gases gravitationally bound to Earth.

atmospheric pressure The pressure exerted by the weight of the atmosphere across a given area. At any given location atmospheric pressure varies depending on atmospheric conditions but standard atmospheric pressure is defined as 101.325 kilopascals (1013.25 millibars).

aurora Optical phenomena caused by the interaction of the solar wind with oxygen and nitrogen atoms in the upper atmosphere. They are most often visible above latitudes 66.5°, but are sometimes visible at latitudes as low as 40°.

aurora australis Auroras that are visible south of the equator. They are also known as the "southern lights."

aurora borealis Auroras that are visible north of the equator. They are also known as the "northern lights."

barometer An instrument used to measure atmospheric pressure.

Beaufort wind scale A system for classifying winds according to their speeds and effects.

biogeochemical cycle The interaction of biological, geological, and chemical processes.

biosphere The entire volume of Earth's land, air, and ocean that supports or is capable of supporting life.

blizzard A snow storm with winds of at least 35 miles per hour (56 kmph) and sufficient snow in the air to reduce visibility to less than 0.25 miles (400 m).

Campbell-Stokes recorder An instrument used to measure the duration and intensity of sunshine.

carbon cycle The continuous circulation of carbon through the biosphere, hydrosphere, lithosphere, and atmosphere.

chlorofluorocarbons (CFCs) A group of artificial compounds used in industry that interfere with the ozone–oxygen cycle in the upper atmosphere, resulting in lower concentrations of stratospheric ozone.

circumzenithal arc A circular optical phenomenon that appears more than 58° of arc above the Sun when it is below 32° declination. It is caused by the refraction of sunlight by ice crystals suspended in the atmosphere.

cirrocumulus A form of high-altitude cloud composed of ice crystals that has the appearance of groups of small circular patches.

cirrostratus A form of high-altitude cloud composed of ice crystals that has the appearance of a thin white veil. It is often associated with halos and other optical phenomena.

cirrus A form of high-altitude cloud composed of ice crystals that has the appearance of narrow bands, diffuse filaments, or white patches.

climate The typical weather at a location over the course of many years.

cloud base The lowest part of a cloud or the altitude above sea level of the lowest part of a band of cloud.

cloud condensation nucleus (CCN) A microscopic solid particle in the atmosphere onto which water vapor easily condenses. Cloud condensation nuclei allow the condensation of the water droplets that make up clouds.

cold occlusion An occluded front in which the advancing cold air mass is cooler than the retreating cold air mass.

condensation level The altitude at which a parcel of air reaches its dew point temperature.

condensation nucleus A microscopic solid particle in the atmosphere onto which water vapor easily condenses. Condensation nuclei allow the condensation of the water droplets that make up fog.

continental antarctic Refers to an air mass that originates over a continental Antarctic source region.

continental arctic Refers to an air mass that originates over a continental Arctic source region.

continental polar Refers to an air mass that originates over a continental Antarctic or Arctic source region.

continental tropical Refers to an air mass that originates over a continental tropical source region.

convection cloud A cloud that develops as the result of the transport of warm moist air by convection. "Convection" is the transport of heat through vertical motion in a fluid.

convective rain Rain that develops as the result of the transport of warm moist air by convection.

convergence The coming together of airflows at a common low-pressure center that results in a column of rising air above the low-level convergence, which eventually reaches an altitude at which it diverges.

Coriolis effect The tendency for ocean currents and winds to be deflected by Earth's rotation. Deflection is to the right in the Northern Hemisphere and to the left in the Southern Hemisphere.

cumulonimbus A form of cloud that may extend from low to high altitudes. It usually has a flat top and a rounded cloud base. The base is commonly dark gray while the body of the cloud is bright white. Cumulonimbus clouds are associated with thunderstorms, tropical cyclones, and tornadoes.

cumulus A form of billowing or pillowlike cloud that forms as a result of convection.

cup anemometer An anemometer with three or four rigid cups attached to a central axis. Airflow pushes the cups and causes the axis to rotate.

cyclogenesis The life cycle of a midlatitude cyclone.

cyclone An area in which atmospheric pressure is lower than the surrounding area. Air flows inward toward a cyclone.

cyclonic rain Rain associated with a cyclone.

cyclonic wind A flow of air caused by the presence of a cyclone. It flows inward toward a cyclone in a clockwise direction in the Northern Hemisphere and counterclockwise in the Southern Hemisphere.

deposition nucleus A microscopic particle in the atmosphere onto which water vapor freezes to form a six-sided ice crystal that can become the core of a snow flake.

dew point The temperature at which a parcel of air becomes saturated if it is cooled and there is no change in the amount of water vapor it contains or in atmospheric pressure.

divergence A high-pressure center from which airflows move apart.

dobson unit A unit of measurement used to describe the concentration of a gas in the atmosphere. It refers to the depth of the layer around Earth that the gas would form if it were brought to sea level and subjected to standard sea-level atmospheric pressure.

downdraft A current of air inside a cumulonimbus cloud moving vertically toward Earth's surface. Downdrafts usually travel at no more than about 10 miles per hour (16 kmph), but may be stronger in large storms.

dry bulb thermometer A thermometer with a dry bulb exposed to the air.

dry season A period of the year in which a region consistently receives less rainfall than at other times.

environmental lapse rate The rate at which temperature decreases with increasing altitude. It is highly variable from place to place, depending on atmospheric conditions.

equator An imaginary line around Earth's diameter exactly halfway between the North and South poles.

equatorial Refers to the region within a few degrees of latitude above or below the equator.

equinox One of the two occasions each year on which the Sun crosses the plane of the equator. In the Northern Hemisphere the vernal, or spring, equinox occurs on or about March 21st and the autumnal equinox on or about September 22nd. These dates are transposed for the Southern Hemisphere.

evaporation The change in state from a liquid to a gaseous phase.

evaporation fog Fog that forms as the result of the evaporation of water that is warmer than the surrounding air.

evapotranspiration Refers to the combined processes by which water is transferred to the atmosphere from the surfaces of bodies of water or ice, from Earth's surface, and from the surfaces of respiring plants.

eye The roughly circular area of relatively still air at the center of a tropical cyclone.

Ferrel cell An element of the three-cell model of global atmospheric circulation found between the tropical Hadley cell and the polar cell in each hemisphere. In the Ferrel cell air rises at the polar front and subsides in the tropics.

first atmosphere The predominantly helium-hydrogen atmosphere that surrounded Earth shortly after the planet was formed.

flood The accumulation of water over areas not usually submerged.

fog A cloud with a cloud base at or close to Earth's surface. A meteorologist's definition also includes the requirement that it restricts visibility to less than 0.6 miles (1 km).

fossil fuel A naturally occurring carbon or hydrocarbon fuel such as coal or oil formed from the decomposition of living organisms.

freezing fog Fog that forms when air temperatures are below freezing. Water droplets in freezing fog freeze onto exposed surfaces to create rime ice.

front A boundary between air masses with differing characteristics.

frontal cloud Cloud that forms in association with a front where a warm air mass is being lifted above a cold air mass.

frontal fog Fog that forms in association with a front where a warm air mass is lifted above a cold air mass .

frontal lifting The ascent of a warm air mass as it is propelled above a cold air mass along a warm front or as a cold air mass undercuts it along a cold front.

frontal weather All forms of weather occurring because of the presence of a front.

frost point A dew point temperature below 32°F (0°C).

Fujita-Pearson scale A six-point scale used to classify the intensity of hurricanes according to the amount and type of damage they are capable of causing.

geomagnetic South Pole Another name for the magnetic South Pole.

geostationary orbit An Earth orbit that travels in the same direction as Earth's rotation and that takes twenty four hours to complete, the result of which is that the orbiting spacecraft constantly remains above the same spot on Earth's surface.

glaciation A period of an ice age in which ice caps and glaciers are generally expanding and advancing.

global warming A rise in average global temperature.

greenhouse effect A warming of the atmosphere that results from the absorption of heat by certain gases.

greenhouse gas A gas that contributes to the greenhouse effect.

ground fog Fog that obscures less than 60 percent of the sky and does not extend to the base of any cloud that may lie above it.

groundwater Water in the saturation zone below ground level.

gyre A circular rotation of water in an ocean that results from prevailing winds and the Coriolis effect.

Hadley cell A part of the global pattern of atmospheric circulation in which warm air rises at the equator, moves toward north or south at high altitude, and then descends near the tropics.

halo An optical phenomenon resembling a circle of white light surrounding the Sun or Moon and caused by the refraction of light through ice particles suspended in the atmosphere.

humidity A reference to the amount of water vapor present in the air.

hurricane A severe tropical cyclone occurring over the North Atlantic, the Caribbean, the Gulf of Mexico, or the eastern North Pacific.

hydrologic cycle Another term for the water cycle.

hydrosphere All the water present around, on the surface of, and beneath the surface of Earth.

hygrograph An instrument that measures and records humidity.

ice age A cold period in geologic time in which glaciers and ice sheets are expanding.

ice fog A form of fog composed of particles of ice suspended in the air.

inferior mirage A mirage in which the image appears lower than the object it is a projection of.

infiltration The movement of water from above to below ground level.

insolation The amount of solar radiation reaching Earth's surface.

interglacial A warm period between two glaciations. Glaciers and ice caps either remain static or retreat and shrink during interglacials.

ionosphere The region of the atmosphere containing the highest concentrations of ions and electrons. The ionosphere extends from an altitude of about 45 miles (70 km) upwards to the top of the atmosphere.

jet stream A narrow band of strong wind in the upper troposphere or lower stratosphere. A jet stream is typically thousands of miles long and hundreds of miles wide, but only a few miles deep.

Köppen classification A method of classifying climate types based on mean annual temperature and rainfall and taking account of life zones.

land breeze A light wind blowing from the land to the sea driven by a pressure gradient that results when the land is warmer than the adjacent sea surface.

langley A unit of solar radiation equal to one calorie per square centimeter per minute.

latent heat The energy absorbed or released when a substance changes phase.

latent heat of evaporation The energy released or absorbed when a substance changes phase from gas to liquid or liquid to gas.

latent heat of melting The energy released or absorbed when a substance changes phase from liquid to solid or solid to liquid.

latitude An angular measure of distance north or south of the equator.

leader stroke An element of lightning that travels from a cloud to the ground.

leeward In the opposite direction to a wind or facing away from a wind.

life zone Refers to areas at particular elevations in which certain kinds of organisms (particularly plant types) dominate because they are best adapted to the conditions there.

lightning A short-lived, high current electrical discharge in the atmosphere.

lithosphere The rock and nonbiological sediment on Earth taken as a whole, as distinct from the atmosphere (gases) and the hydrosphere (water). It also refers to the hard outermost layer of Earth composed of the crust and mantle.

longitude An angular measure of distance east or west of the prime meridian.

longwave Electromagnetic energy with a wavelength of four microns or greater.

lower tangent arc An optical phenomenon that produces a U-shaped line of light below the Sun. It is caused by internal reflections in ice crystals suspended in the atmosphere.

magnetopause The boundary between the magnetosphere and interplanetary space.

magnetosphere The region in which Earth's magnetic field dominates.

maritime polar (mP) Refers to an air mass that originates over an ocean in polar regions.

maritime tropical (mT) Refers to an air mass that originates over an ocean in tropical regions.

maximum thermometer A thermometer that registers and records the maximum temperature in a given time period.

mercury barometer A barometer in which atmospheric pressure is measured according to the height of a column of mercury it supports.

mesopause The boundary between the mesosphere and the ionosphere.

mesosphere A region of the atmosphere above the stratosphere and below the ionosphere. It extends from an altitude of about 20 miles (32 km) upwards to an altitude of about 50 miles (80 km). Air temperature decreases with altitude throughout the mesosphere.

midlatitude Refers to one of the two regions (one in the Northern and one in the Southern Hemisphere) that lie between the subpolar and subtropical regions.

midlatitude cyclone A cyclone that develops in a midlatitude region.

millibar A unit of atmospheric pressure (one thousandth of a bar) equivalent to 100 pascals. A bar is equivalent to 29.531 inches (750.1 mm) of mercury at 32°F (0°C) at a latitude of 45°.

minimum thermometer A thermometer that registers and records the minimum temperature in a given time period.

mirage An optical illusion in which light is refracted by layers of air with different temperatures.

mist Very thin fog. A strict meteorological definition includes the requirement that it does not restrict visibility to less than 0.62 miles (1 km).

monsoon A seasonal shift in the prevailing wind direction caused by the greater seasonal variation in temperature over landmasses than over adjacent oceans. Monsoons also correspond to large seasonal variations in the quantity of rainfall.

mountain breeze A local wind that occurs when air at high altitude cools at night and flows down the slope of a mountain.

nimbostratus A variety of middle- to low-altitude cloud that often produces heavy precipitation. It generally appears as a formless, dark gray layer.

occluded front A frontal system that develops when a cold front overtakes a warm front. It is the final stage in the life cycle of a midlatitude cyclone.

KEY WORDS

ocean basin A low-lying region of Earth's crust that forms the floor of an ocean.

ocean current A steady flow of ocean water in one direction that is not due to tides.

okta A measure of the amount of sky covered by cloud. One okta is equivalent to 12.5 percent, or one eighth, of the total visible sky.

orographic cloud Cloud that forms when air is forced to rise by the topography of Earth's surface.

orographic lifting Lifting that occurs as a result of the topography of Earth's surface.

orographic rain Rain that occurs as a result of the formation of orographic cloud.

ozone A naturally occurring tri-atomic molecule of oxygen (O_3) that is less common than the typical bi-atomic form (O_2).

ozone hole A region where there is an extreme seasonal depletion in the concentration of ozone in the ozone layer.

ozone layer The layer of Earth's atmosphere where concentrations of ozone are at their greatest. It is found within the stratosphere and extends from an altitude of about 10–25 miles (16–40 km).

ozone–oxygen cycle A process in which ozone molecules are destroyed when they absorb ultraviolet radiation and their constituent parts are later reformed into new ozone molecules.

parhelic circle A form of halo at the altitude of the Sun and parallel to the horizon.

parhelion Another name for a sun dog. An optical phenomenon in which a bright spot of light is formed at an angle of 22° to the Sun. They often form in pairs (plural: *parhelia*), one on either side of the Sun, and are caused by internal reflections in ice crystals suspended in the atmosphere.

photochemical smog A form of smog with a high concentration of ozone resulting from chemical reactions between nitrogen oxides and hydrocarbons in the presence of sunlight.

photosynthesis The process by which plants use light energy to convert water and carbon dioxide into food.

pilot balloon An untethered balloon that is observed as it rises into the atmosphere in order to determine wind speeds and directions at various altitudes.

planetary wave Another term for a Rossby wave.

polar Relating to the region within or close to either of the polar circles.

polar cell One of the three principal heat convection cells in the atmosphere above the Northern and Southern hemispheres.

polar circle A collective term for the Arctic and Antarctic circles—lines of latitude at 66.5° N and 66.5° S respectively.

polar front The region where warm air heading toward the poles meets cooler air traveling toward the equator. It is a permanent feature of the world's weather and occurs at latitudes of about 60° N and 60° S.

polar jet stream A jet stream at the polar front.

pole The northernmost point (North Pole) or southernmost point (South Pole) on Earth. A geographical pole is one of two points on Earth where its axis of rotation intersects its surface. A magnetic pole is one of two points on Earth where the geomagnetic field points vertically.

positive streamer Channels that extend upwards from the ground or from tall objects on the ground when stepped leaders approach them. When a positive streamer meets a stepped leader the bright return stroke of a lightning strike occurs.

precipitation The transfer of water, in any form, from the atmosphere to the land or the ocean.

precipitation fog Fog that forms as a result of precipitation that evaporates as it falls to the ground or shortly after reaching the ground.

prevailing wind The direction from which the wind most often blows for any given location.

primary rainbow The brightest and usually the only visible arc in a rainbow.

radiation fog Fog that forms as a result of heat being radiated from the surface of Earth into the atmosphere.

radiosonde A package of instruments that measure, record, and transmit various atmospheric conditions such as temperature and pressure.

radiosonde balloon A balloon designed to carry a radiosonde into the atmosphere.

rainbow An optical phenomenon caused by the reflection and refraction of sunlight by droplets of water suspended in the atmosphere.

rain day A day on which rain occurs. Rain days are significant because they indicate the seasonal distribution of rain and the kind of weather that produces it. For example, it may be usual for a location in an arid region to receive all of its average monthly rainfall during heavy downpours on one or two days rather than spread evenly across several days, as would be expected in a temperate region.

rainfall gauge An instrument that measures the quantity of rainfall over a given period.

rainshadow A region of drastically reduced rainfall on the lee side of a raised topographical feature, such as a mountain range, compared to the windward side.

relative humidity The ratio of water vapor in a given volume of gas and the maximum amount of water vapor that volume of gas at the same temperature could contain before reaching saturation point.

return stroke The flow of current through an ionized channel from ground to cloud that produces the bright flash and shock waves of sound that are associated with a lightning strike.

Rossby wave A large-scale wave occurring in the oceans or atmosphere, driven by variation in the Coriolis effect at different latitudes. Also known as a planetary wave it typically propagates at rates of only a few inches per second, has wavelengths of hundreds of miles, and wave heights of a few inches.

runoff Precipitation that flows off the land and into rivers and streams.

Saffir-Simpson scale A scale used to categorize tropical cyclones according to their sustained wind speeds and the amount of damage they are likely to cause.

saturation point The maximum concentration of water vapor that a given volume of air can contain at a given temperature.

scattering The processes by which light is diffused or deflected by collisions with particles suspended in the atmosphere.

sea breeze A wind blowing from the sea to the land driven by a pressure gradient that results when the sea surface is warmer than adjacent land.

sea level The average level of the surface of the sea.

sea-level rise A rise in average global sea level.

season A division of a year according to recurrent climatic patterns. The existence of seasons is due to the fact that Earth is tilted on its axis of rotation.

secondary rainbow A dimmer arc of less vibrant colors sometimes visible outside of a primary rainbow.

second atmosphere Earth's atmosphere at a time when the concentration of carbon dioxide was much higher than it is today. The high level of carbon dioxide is thought to have been due to volcanic activity.

shortwave Refers to electromagnetic energy with a wavelength of less than four microns.

smog A combination of smoke and fog. Also used to refer to any kind of air pollution.

snow line The altitude above which almost no vegetation is able to survive. The altitude of the snow line varies with latitude. It is generally at a lower altitude as latitude increases.

solar radiation The electromagnetic radiation emitted by the Sun.

solar wind The outward flow of charged particles from the Sun.

solstice One of two occasions in a year on which the Sun reaches its furthest point north or south of the plane of the equator. In the Northern Hemisphere the summer solstice occurs on or about June 21st and the winter solstice on or about December 22nd. These dates are transposed for the Southern Hemisphere.

source region A large area of Earth with more or less uniform surface conditions over which a volume of air with equally uniform characteristics known as an air mass can form. Source regions are described according to their latitude and whether they are on land or at sea. For example, a "continental tropical" source region would be located on land in the tropics.

squall A sudden and intense wind storm of short duration that may accompany an advancing cold front.

station model A set of symbols on a weather chart that indicate all the available information for a particular weather station.

steam fog Fog that forms when air moves across the surface of a cooler body of water.

stepped leader A negatively charged, branching channel that propagates toward the ground from the base of a cloud and initiates a lightning strike.

storm surge A rise in sea level caused by high winds. Storm surges are usually associated with tropical cyclones.

stratocumulus A form of low-level cloud usually forming lines of groups of individual rounded masses.

stratopause The boundary between the stratosphere and the mesosphere.

stratosphere A region of the atmosphere above the troposphere and below the mesosphere. It extends from an altitude of about 8 miles (14 km) upwards to an altitude of about 20 miles (32 km). Air temperature generally increases with altitude throughout this region.

stratus A form of low-level cloud forming a thin layer with a flat and uniform base.

sublimation A change in state from solid to vapor or vapor to solid without passing through an intermediate liquid phase.

subpolar Near but outside a polar circle.

subtropical Near but outside a tropical region.

subtropical jet stream A jet stream at a latitude of between 20° and 40°.

sulfurous smog A form of smog with a high concentration of sulfur oxides that result from the burning of coal and other fossil fuels.

sun dog Another name for a *parhelion*.

sunshine recorder An instrument that measures and records the duration (or the duration and intensity) of sunlight over a given period.

superior mirage A mirage in which the image appears above the object it is a projection of.

KEY WORDS

synoptic chart A map or chart that gives meteorological data for an extended area at a given time.

temperate Refers to the regions or the climate typical of the regions between the tropics and the polar circles in both the Northern and Southern hemispheres.

thermograph An instrument that measures and records temperature.

thermometer An instrument that measures temperature.

thermosphere The outermost region of the atmosphere extending from the top of the mesosphere to space. It stretches from an altitude of about 50 miles (80 km) to the extremely diffuse edge of the atmosphere at about 1,000 miles (1,600 km). Temperature increases with altitude throughout the region.

third atmosphere The atmosphere characteristic of Earth today. It has a much lower carbon dioxide content than the atmosphere of billions of years ago and also has significant amounts of oxygen.

three-cell model A model of atmospheric circulation that postulates the existence of three large-scale heat convection cells in both the Northern and Southern hemispheres. These cells are known as the Hadley Cell, the Ferrel Cell, and the Polar Cell.

thunder The sound produced by shock waves created when air is rapidly heated by lightning.

thunderhead A term for the uppermost part of a cumulonimbus cloud. Also known as the anvil.

thunderstorm A storm in which thunder and lightning accompanies often very heavy precipitation.

tornado A rapidly rotating column of air in contact with the ground.

tornado outbreak The occurrence of six or more tornadoes during a twenty-four hour period.

total solar irradiance (TSI) The amount of solar radiation arriving at the top of Earth's atmosphere when Earth is at its mean distance from the Sun. It is estimated to equal 1,368 watts per square meter.

tropical Relating to the region south of the Tropic of Cancer and north of the Tropic of Capricorn.

tropical cyclone An intense cyclonic storm that develops over a tropical ocean, known as hurricanes in the Atlantic and typhoons in parts of the Pacific.

Tropic of Cancer A line of latitude at 23.5° N.

Tropic of Capricorn A line of latitude at 23.5° S.

tropics A collective term for the Tropic of Cancer and the Tropic of Capricorn or for the area that lies between them.

tropopause The boundary between the troposphere and the stratosphere.

troposphere The region of the atmosphere closest to Earth's surface. It extends from ground level to an altitude of about 8 miles (14 km). Almost all weather phenomena occur in the troposphere.

turbulence cloud Cloud that forms as a result of air turbulence caused by winds passing over a topographically uneven surface.

typhoon A severe tropical cyclone occurring over the western Pacific Ocean.

updraft A rising current of air.

upper atmosphere The entire atmosphere above the troposphere.

upper tangent arc An optical phenomenon that produces a wing-shaped line of light above the Sun. It is caused by internal reflections in ice crystals suspended in the atmosphere.

upslope fog Fog produced when air is forced up topographical slopes.

UV radiation Ultraviolet radiation is a form of electromagnetic radiation with wavelengths of between 10 and 380 nanometers.

valley breeze A wind caused by air at the bottom of a valley being heated and rising up the sides of the valley.

Van Allen belt A belt of charged particles trapped by Earth's magnetic field.

warm occlusion An occluded front in which the advancing cold air mass is warmer than the retreating cold air mass.

warm sector In a mature midlatitude cyclone, the volume of warm air behind an advancing warm front and in front of the more rapidly advancing cold front that will eventually occlude it.

water cycle The constant circulation of water on Earth between the atmosphere, the oceans, and the land.

water table The level below the surface of the land at which the soil or rock is saturated with water.

weather satellite A satellite able to measure, record, and transmit meteorological data.

wet bulb thermometer A thermometer used to relate air temperature to humidity. The bulb of the thermometer is kept in contact with a wet muslin sheath.

wildfire An unmanaged and unplanned fire.

wind chill The cooling effect of wind in addition to the effect of low temperature.

windward In the direction of the wind or facing an oncoming wind.

Internet resources

There is a lot of useful information on the internet. Information on a particular topic may be available through a search engine such as Google (http://www.google.com). Some of the Web sites that are found in this way may be very useful, others not. Below is a selection of Web sites related to the material covered by this book.

The publisher takes no responsibility for the information contained within these Web sites. All the sites were accessible in March 2006.

American Meteorological Society
Promotes the development and dissemination of information and education on the atmospheric and related oceanic and hydrologic sciences.
http://www.ametsoc.org

Bad Meteorology
Refutes widely-held but mistaken beliefs about the weather, including the idea that raindrops are shaped like teardrops.
http://www.ems.psu.edu/~fraser/BadMeteorology.html

BBC Weather
Current global weather forecasts, with information and factsheets on weather and climate.
http://www.bbc.co.uk/weather

Climate Diagnostics Center
A government agency that analyzes, interprets, and forecasts climate variations.
http://www.cdc.noaa.gov

Disaster Research Center
Includes online publications, data, bibliographies, and other information relevant to the sociology of disasters such as the impact of severe weather incidents on human societies.
http://www.udel.edu/DRC

Encyclopedia of the Atmospheric Environment
Provides simple explanations for atmospheric terminology, and includes thousands of hyperlinks to more detailed and academic material.
http://www.ace.mmu.ac.uk/eae/english.html

Global Hydrology and Climate Center
Provides integrated scientific understanding of Earth's systems to enable better decisions improving the global quality of life.
http://www.ghcc.msfc.nasa.gov

Global Warming International Center
Disseminates information on global warming science and policy, serving governments, nongovernmental organizations, and industries.
http://www.globalwarming.net

Greenpeace
A leading campaign for the conservation of the planet's resources. One of its priorities is the prevention of human-induced climate change.
http://www.greenpeace.org

International Research Institute for Climate Prediction
Aims to enhance the knowledge, anticipation, and management of the impacts of seasonal climate fluctuations, to improve human welfare and the environment.
http://iri.ldeo.columbia.edu

National Center for Atmospheric Research
The NCAR exists to increase understanding of Earth's changing systems for the benefit of society.
http://www.ucar.edu

National Climatic Data Center
The world's largest archive of weather data.
http://www.ncdc.noaa.gov/oa/ncdc.html

National Hurricane Center/Tropical Prediction Center
Includes explanations of hurricane formation as well as detailed records of past hurricanes.
http://www.nhc.noaa.gov

National Oceanic and Atmospheric Administration
Information and advice on meteorological and marine matters from the government.
http://www.noaa.gov

National Severe Storms Laboratory
One of NOAA's internationally known research laboratories, NSSL leads the way in investigations of all aspects of severe weather.
http://www.nssl.noaa.gov

INTERNET RESOURCES

National Weather Center
A confederation of organizations working to understand events occurring in Earth's atmosphere.
http://nwc.ou.edu

National Weather Service
Weather forecasting from the National Oceanic and Atmospheric Administration.
http://weather.gov

National Weather Service Space Environment Center
Continually monitoring Earth's space environment, this agency is the government's official source of space weather alerts and warnings.
http://www.sec.noaa.gov

NOAA Education Resources
Brings together the many educational resources provided by the National Oceanic and Atmospheric Administration.
http://www.education.noaa.gov

Ocean Surface Topography from Space
A dazzling introduction to the use of satellites TOPEX/Poseidon and Jason-1 in the study of oceanic behavior, with real-time data and educational resources online.
http://topex-www.jpl.nasa.gov

Open Directory Project: Meteorology
A comprehensive listing of internet resources for meteorology.
http://dmoz.org/Science/Earth_Sciences/Meteorology

Open Directory Project: Paleoclimatology
A comprehensive listing of internet resources for the study of long-term climate change and its historic impact on Earth.
http://dmoz.org/Science/Earth_Sciences/ Paleogeography_and_Paleoclimatology

Severe Weather Information Center
A severe weather warning website from the World Meteorological Organization.
http://severe.worldweather.org

Storm Prediction Center
Specific storm information with real-time data from NOAA.
http://www.spc.noaa.gov

United Nations Environment Programme
The UNEP's stated mission is to encourage care for the environment by inspiring people to improve their quality of life without compromising that of future generations. Some content is relevant to the study of weather and the human impact on climate change.
http://www.unep.org

United States Climate Change Science Program
Integrates federal research on climate and global change.
http://www.climatescience.gov

United States Historical Climatology Network
A high quality dataset of daily and monthly records of basic meteorological variables from over 1,000 observing stations across the 48 contiguous states.
http://cdiac.ornl.gov/epubs/ndp/ushcn/newushcn.html

Weatherbase
An easily queryable database of world climate statistics.
http://www.weatherbase.com

World Carbon Dioxide Information Analysis Center
The primary global-change data and information analysis center of the Department of Energy. CDIAC responds to data and information requests from users concerned with global climate change.
http://cdiac.ornl.gov

WorldClimate.com
An alternative queryable database of global climate statistics.
http://www.worldclimate.com

World Meteorological Organization
The UN's voice on the state and behavior of Earth's atmosphere, its interaction with the oceans, the climate it produces, and the resulting distribution of water resources. WMO plays a unique and powerful role in contributing to the welfare of humanity, organizing against natural disasters, safeguarding the environment, and enhancing the economic and social well-being of all sectors of society in areas such as food security, water resources, and transport.
http://www.wmo.int

Index

Index of subject headings.

DATE DUE
